The Having of Negroes Is Become a Burden

UNIVERSITY PRESS OF FLORIDA

Florida A&M University, Tallahassee
Florida Atlantic University, Boca Raton
Florida Gulf Coast University, Ft. Myers
Florida International University, Miami
Florida State University, Tallahassee
New College of Florida, Sarasota
University of Central Florida, Orlando
University of Florida, Gainesville
University of North Florida, Jacksonville
University of South Florida, Tampa
University of West Florida, Pensacola

The Having of Negroes Is Become a Burden

The Quaker Struggle to Free Slaves
in Revolutionary North Carolina

Michael J. Crawford

University Press of Florida
Gainesville · Tallahassee · Tampa · Boca Raton
Pensacola · Orlando · Miami · Jacksonville · Ft. Myers · Sarasota

Copyright 2010 by Michael J. Crawford
Printed in the United States of America on acid-free paper
All rights reserved

First cloth printing, 2010
First paperback printing, 2014

Library of Congress Cataloging-in-Publication Data
The having of Negroes is become a burden : the Quaker struggle to free slaves in revolutionary North Carolina / [edited by] Michael J. Crawford.
p. cm.
Includes bibliographical references and index.
ISBN 978-0-8130-3470-6 (cloth: alk. paper)
ISBN 978-0-8130-6030-9 (pbk.)
1. Slavery—North Carolina—History—18th century—Sources.
2. Antislavery movements—North Carolina—History—18th century—Sources. 3. Quaker abolitionists—North Carolina—History—18th century—Sources. 4. Quakers—North Carolina—History—18th century—Sources. 5. Slavery and the church—Society of Friends—History—18th century—Sources. 6. North Carolina—Social conditions—18th century—Sources. I. Crawford, Michael J.
E445.N8H38 2010
975.6'03—dc22   2009051032

The University Press of Florida is the scholarly publishing agency for the State University System of Florida, comprising Florida A&M University, Florida Atlantic University, Florida Gulf Coast University, Florida International University, Florida State University, New College of Florida, University of Central Florida, University of Florida, University of North Florida, University of South Florida, and University of West Florida.

University Press of Florida
15 Northwest 15th Street
Gainesville, FL 32611-2079
http://www.upf.com

For Elva

Although they were generally in the practice of keeping slaves, yet they had begun to see the error of it, and were desirous to be relieved of the burden, but saw no way to effect it, to the satisfaction of themselves and their slaves, because of the cruel laws in force in these colonies; by which, if a man set his slaves free, they would be liable to be seized and sold to the highest bidder; which appears grievous, both to themselves and their owners.

David Ferris, *Resistance and Obedience to God*

Contents

Preface and Acknowledgments ... xi
Chronology of Principal Events ... xv
Introduction ... 1

Part I. An Individual: George Walton Confronts Slavery ... 27

1. 1772–1773: George Walton's Accounts of Two Dreams ... 29
2. 1774: George Walton's Letters on Slavery, with an Account of a Dream ... 37
3. 1775–1777: George Walton's Journal from 2d, 6th Month, 1775, to 12th, 10th Month, 1777 ... 49

Part II. The Community: The Society of Friends in North Carolina Chooses Manumission ... 69

1. 1767: Thomas Nicholson Urges Gradual Emancipation ... 73
2. 1768–1773: Evolution of the North Carolina Yearly Meeting's Policy on Slave Trading ... 76
3. 1772–1773: Advice from London ... 80
4. 1774–1775: Evolution of the North Carolina Yearly Meeting's Policy on Slave Ownership ... 82
5. Circa 1775: Thomas Nicholson Urges Immediate Emancipation ... 84
6. 1776: Thomas Newby's Manumission Paper ... 87
7. 1777: Thomas Newby's Petition to Free His Slave Hannah ... 89
8. 1776–1789: The Progress of Manumission ... 91
9. 1777–1797: List of Emancipated Blacks Who Were Re-Enslaved ... 100

Part III. The State: North Carolina Thwarts Quaker Manumission ... 107

1. 1777: An Act to Prevent Domestic Insurrections ... 111
2. 1777: The Trial of Several Negroes Manumitted by Friends ... 113
3. 1777–1778: Accounts of Sales of Blacks Emancipated by Friends ... 117

4. 1777: Friends' Reasons for Releasing Their Negroes
     from a State of Slavery   120
  5. 1778: The Superior Court Annuls Re-Enslavements   122
  6. 1779: New State Legislation Annuls the
     Superior Court's Judgment   126
  7. 1779: Memorial from Friends Who Manumitted Slaves
     to the North Carolina General Assembly   128
  8. 1779: Thomas Nicholson Upbraids an Informer   131
  9. 1788: Memorial from the North Carolina Yearly Meeting
     to the North Carolina General Assembly   133
 10. 1788: An Act to Amend an Act Entitled "An Act to
     Prevent Domestic Insurrections"   135
 11. 1797: A Bill to Thwart Quaker Manumissions   137

**Part IV. The Nation: African-American Freedom and
the Manumission Debate in Congress**   139

  1. 1797: Petition of Freemen   143
  2. 1797: Congress Debates the Freemen's Petition   149
  3. 1797: Pennsylvania Friends' Yearly Meeting Memorial
     to the Congress of the United States   158
  4. 1797–1798: Congress Debates the
     Pennsylvania Friends' Memorial   162
  5. 1798: The Society of Friends Reacts to
     the House's Rejection of Its Memorial   182

Epilogue   183
Notes   193
Bibliography of Works Cited   213
Index   221

Preface and Acknowledgments

Despite the size and continual growth of the body of scholarly literature on antislavery in America, *The Having of Negroes Is Become a Burden* makes new and unusual contributions to that literature. Whereas the bulk of the literature treats the antebellum era, this book deals with the era of the American Revolution. Whereas studies of the rise of antislavery among Quakers in the colonial and revolutionary eras focus on the center of American Quaker culture of Pennsylvania, especially Philadelphia, this book examines an area on the periphery, a region of rural tidewater North Carolina. Whereas the antislavery movement has been best understood as it evolved in the North and in the Upper South, this book explores antislavery in the heart of the slave South. And whereas biographies of Quaker leaders of the antislavery movement examine the prominent and well known—individuals such as Anthony Benezet, Moses Brown, John Pemberton, and John Woolman—the sources reproduced here provide insight into the life, motivation, and influence of an obscure man. The life of George Walton, a hitherto unknown figure, reveals much about what a profound understanding of the evil inherent in slavery meant to people of conscience living in the midst of a society defined by slavery. This book tells how the influence of individuals with awakened consciences developed and spread and eventually touched the conscience of a nation.

George Walton is representative of several of his contemporaries in late colonial tidewater North Carolina who came to the conviction that slaveholding was wrong. Walton came to this understanding at the same time that he joined the Society of Friends, the Quakers. His belief drove him to undertake a campaign to persuade his co-religionists to set their slaves free. Part I of this book documents this process from Walton's personal papers.

The Quaker community of North Carolina soon endorsed the notion that slaveholding was sinful and organized to persuade and help all slaveowning Quakers to free their slaves. Part II of this book documents the new antislavery movement using records of the Society of Friends.

The Quakers met resistance from the government of North Carolina, whose laws restricted manumissions by requiring slaveowners to obtain permission from the county courts. The courts granted such permission only in cases where a slave had earned freedom by some meritorious act or service. Part III describes the confrontation between North Carolina's Quakers and the government authorities about manumission, drawing on Quaker, colony, and state records.

In 1797, the confrontation between the Quakers of North Carolina and the state of North Carolina came to debate on the floor of the U.S. House of Representatives as the result of two petitions, one from four former North Carolina slaves manumitted by their Quaker owners and the other from the Society of Friends in Pennsylvania. The debates in the U.S. Congress underscored the sensitivity of the issue of slavery on the national level and the deep sectional divide that threatened the stability of the union of states under the Constitution of the United States, then still an experiment of fewer than ten years. Part IV of this work contains the texts of the petitions and the record of the debate. This book thus follows the manumission movement from individual to community to state to nation, as the influence of the movement made itself felt in expanding circles.

My work on this book began a decade ago when my wife, Dr. Elva Bogert Crawford, then curator of the National Society Daughters of the American Revolution's Americana Collection of early American manuscripts and imprints, knowing my interest in the religious history of early America, brought to my attention a recent accession, the papers of North Carolina Quaker George Walton, dated from 1772 through 1778. The rich imagery of Walton's dreams immediately arrested my attention, and my examination of the complete set of Walton papers revealed its relationship to an episode important in the history of antislavery in America but little known outside a small circle of specialists. I soon concluded that Walton's writings deserve publication in an edition with informative apparatus that would make them accessible to a wide audience.

The 2005 Seth and Mary Hinshaw Fellowship, awarded by the North Carolina Friends Historical Society, financed essential research at the Friends Historical Collection at Guilford College in Greensboro, North Carolina. That collection's librarian and archivist, Gwen Gosney Erickson, went out of her way to help me find materials in the collection pertinent to my study during my research visit there and continued to do so as I queried her later by post and e-mail. Christopher Densmore, curator of the Friends Historical Library of Swarthmore College, was likewise gracious in assisting my research. J'aime Wells, Executive Secretary and Research Assistant Special Collections, Haverford College Library Information Resources, Haverford, Pennsylvania, provided information found in that institution's Quaker Collection.

I thank the editors of *The Southern Friend* for publishing some of the results of my research (Michael J. Crawford, "'The Small Black Boy at my right hand is Christ': George Walton and Friends' Manumission of Slaves in Revolutionary-Era North Carolina," 28, no. 2 (2006): 3–17) and for allowing me to use portions of that article in modified form in this book.

Christine F. Hughes, a colleague at the Naval History and Heritage Command in Washington, D.C., helped me obtain copies of published materials, and Charles E. Brodine, Jr., another center colleague, gave a thoughtful reading to a draft of the book's manuscript and suggested useful improvements.

The following institutions gave permission to print texts of documents in their possession, for which they have my sincere gratitude: Friends Historical Collection, Hege Library, Guilford College, Greensboro, North Carolina; Friends Historical Library of Swarthmore College, Swarthmore, Pennsylvania; The Historical Society of Pennsylvania, Philadelphia, Pennsylvania; Library of the Religious Society of Friends, Friends House, Yearly Meeting of the Religious Society of Friends in Britain, London, England; and National Society Daughters of the American Revolution, Washington, D.C.

Chronology of Principal Events

1672   Quaker founder George Fox makes a missionary tour of North Carolina.

1680   The Society of Friends holds its first monthly meeting in North Carolina.

1753   Philadelphia Quaker John Woolman receives permission to publish *Some Considerations on the Keeping of Negroes*.

1755   The Philadelphia Yearly Meeting labels participation in the slave trade sinful.

1758   The Philadelphia Yearly Meeting excludes slave traders and slaveowners from society business affairs.

1768   The North Carolina Yearly Meeting condemns slave trading for profit.

1772   The North Carolina Yearly Meeting prohibits the buying and selling of slaves without permission of the local meeting and begins considering how to advise Friends who want to free their slaves.

1773   George Walton, of Perquimans County, North Carolina, is welcomed into the Society of Friends.

1774   The Philadelphia Yearly Meeting disowns slave traders.

         Quaker Thomas Newby, of Perquimans County, North Carolina, requests advice about freeing his slaves; North Carolina Yearly Meeting decides that Friends who want to free slaves must request permission of their monthly meeting.

1775	The North Carolina Yearly Meeting renounces slaveholding.
	George Walton urges Friends to avoid service on night patrols.
	North Carolina revolutionaries establish provisional government.
	Virginia's royal governor, Lord Dunmore, proclaims freedom for slaves who join the king's troops.
1776	The Philadelphia Yearly Meeting disowns slaveowners.
	Thomas Newby manumits ten slaves.
	The Continental Congress adopts the Declaration of Independence, which proclaims that all men are endowed with the inalienable right of liberty.
1777	The North Carolina General Assembly adopts "An Act to Prevent Domestic Insurrections," authorizing re-enslavement of improperly manumitted slaves.
	The Society of Friends recognizes George Walton as a public Friend.
	The North Carolina Yearly Meeting engages lawyers to defend manumitted slaves.
	The Perquimans and Pasquotank county courts in North Carolina order that slaves manumitted by Friends are to be resold into slavery.
1778	The North Carolina superior court reverses the decision of the Perquimans and Pasquotank county courts, finding that the "Act to Prevent Domestic Insurrections" violates protections against ex post facto prosecutions.
1778–1782	George Walton serves on the Standing Committee of the North Carolina Yearly Meeting.
1778–1779	George Walton serves as clerk of the Standing Committee.
1779	The North Carolina General Assembly legalizes seizure and sale of improperly manumitted slaves.
1781	The North Carolina Yearly Meeting authorizes disownment of slaveowners.

1783	The Philadelphia Yearly Meeting petitions the Congress of the Confederation to end importation of slaves.
1788	North Carolina's "Act to Amend an Act Entitled 'An Act to Prevent Domestic Insurrections'" strengthens provisions for re-enslaving improperly manumitted slaves.
1789	The Philadelphia Yearly Meeting petitions the U.S. Congress for an amendment to the U.S. Constitution to immediately abolish importation of slaves.
	The Society of Friends disowns George Walton for habitual inebriation.
	George Walton dies.
1791	Black revolution begins in Haiti.
1793	Eli Whitney designs a simplified cotton gin.
	The U.S. Congress adopts the Fugitive Slave Law.
1795	North Carolina requires freed slaves to post bonds.
1797	The U.S. House of Representatives debates a petition regarding the Fugitive Slave Law from four former slaves freed by North Carolina Quakers.
1797–1798	The U.S. House of Representatives debates the petition of the Philadelphia Yearly Meeting regarding North Carolina's laws affecting manumitted slaves.
ca. 1800	North Carolina Friends begin mass migration to the Old Northwest.
1808	The North Carolina Yearly Meeting appoints trustees to accept slaves as gifts from Friends who want to cease owning slaves.
1824	The North Carolina Yearly Meeting begins effort to liberate slaves it holds in trust and move them to free states and to Haiti and Liberia.

Introduction

During the night of 17 December 1772, George Walton, captain of a merchant ship from Perquimans County, North Carolina, who had only recently joined the Quakers, had a long, complex, and vivid dream. The next day he recorded this dream, along with his interpretation of its meaning. In his dream, Walton saw himself walking up a mountain along a broad but wet and slippery road. He overtook two people, a gentleman and a black boy. Walton took a dislike to the man and attempted to run up the hill, passing between the man and the boy. The man tried to stop Walton by threatening him with a great stick. The boy, who Walton now realized was not the man's servant, gave Walton a stick strengthened against splitting with a binding of rope. With this Walton could fight his way up. Seeing that Walton went boldly on, the man stopped threatening him, and they continued up the mountain. When they reached the top and started down the other side, the man slipped and fell down the mountain and out of sight into a pit. Walton, in contrast, walked down easily on fine grass that kept his feet from slipping.

In interpreting the meaning of this dream, Walton assigned a symbolic significance to every aspect. "The slippery mountain and broad path I had to go up," he wrote, "is the world and the gentleman in the way to hinder my running up is the Devil which is afraid I should make his deceit known to the world that others might come to the blessed truth, therefore he attempted to hinder me. The small black boy at my right hand is Christ, which was represented black, to show how much the Devil is exalted and Christ abased. The stick he gave me was his Holy Spirit bound round with truth so that it could not be shaken by which I must fight against all the slippery paths and wiles of Satan. The being upon the top of the mountain shows my first entering the world after having overcome; and the gentleman's falling down shows that Satan will have no more power over me."[1]

Walton's firsthand recounting of this dream and his own interpretation of it are the first texts reproduced in this collection. This dream serves as a fitting introduction to the Quaker manumission movement in Revolutionary War–era North Carolina. The dream underscores the emotional aspects of the movement and touches on the themes of what motivated antislavery activists, relations between free whites and enslaved blacks, the role of blacks as actors in their own history, conflict between Friends and the world, the functions of leaders and followers in the antislavery movement, and the significance of the Society of Friends in that movement. Shortly after recording this dream, Walton became a local leader of the movement to end Quaker ownership of slaves.

Job Albert was one of the North Carolina slaves set free by their Quaker masters as a result of that movement. Job's former master, Benjamin Albertson, provided him with a house in which to live with his wife, who had been liberated by another Quaker. But men sought to take Job into custody, authorized by state law to re-enslave unlawfully manumitted slaves. Lodging his wife safely at Benjamin Albertson's, Job hid in the fields and watched while armed men hunted him with dogs and rifled his dwelling. His pursuers discovered his hiding place, captured him, bound him with ropes, and marched him four miles to a Hartford, North Carolina, prison. After about four weeks, Job escaped with the help of a fellow prisoner, a white man. In a foreshadowing of the Underground Railroad of a later era, a "humane person" carried Job and his wife "in a covered wagon by night," to Virginia for three dollars. Job worked outside Portsmouth, Virginia, as a sawyer until he and his wife were advised to move northward. They traveled to Philadelphia. There he worked both in vessels and on land in the summer and sawed wood in the winter. Although his mother and sister had also been set free by their North Carolina Quaker owners, both had been re-enslaved.

In 1797, twenty-five years after George Walton dreamed of a black boy whom he identified as symbolizing Christ, Job Albert and three other black male residents of Philadelphia petitioned the U.S. Congress requesting protection from the unjust application of the Fugitive Slave Act, which had been enacted to implement the Constitution's provision requiring the return of persons bound to labor who escaped across state lines. Their petition recounts the story of the manumission movement from the perspective of former slaves who had been freed by their North Carolina Quaker owners and documents how they sought their own freedom. As Job Albert had, Jupiter Nicholson, Jacob Nicholson, and Thomas Pritchet resisted re-enslavement and fled across the North Carolina border. Their petition, a related petition from the Philadelphia Yearly Meeting of the Religious Society of Friends, and the debates that these two petitions engendered in Congress conclude the 25-year span of documents printed in this compilation.[2] The documents contained in this record of the Quaker movement to free their slaves in Revolutionary War–era North Carolina depict with penetrating clarity and emotion a microcosm of the larger struggles over slavery and freedom in the contemporary Atlantic world.

The First Century of the Society of Friends

Its distinctive belief system and its peculiar history fitted the Society of Friends to be among the earliest organized groups to put antislavery sentiments into action by freeing their own slaves. Yet nearly a century passed after its founding before the Society of Friends began to actively oppose slavery.

Quakers shared beliefs with both the mainstream and the left wing of the Protestant Reformation, but their central tenet of the inner light set the Society of Friends apart. The Quakers arose in the religious ferment of mid-seventeenth-century England when a group of religious seekers coalesced around the teaching of radical Protestant preacher George Fox (1620–1691) and under his leadership formed the Society of Friends. With the mainstream of the Reformation, they emphasized salvation by faith rather than works and rejected liturgical ceremony and formal creeds. With the left wing of the Reformation, they embraced plainness of lifestyle, egalitarianism, and the priesthood of all believers, rejecting a paid clergy, superfluous luxuries, and frivolous pastimes. A perfectionist ethic led them, like other radical Christians, to eschew the swearing of oaths and military service.[3]

It was their conviction that every person could experience the light of Christ, "the true Light, which lighteth every man that cometh into the world" (John 1:9), that led Friends into beliefs and practices that distinguished them from their contemporaries. Quaker meetings for worship consisted of the silence of unspoken prayer broken only when an individual felt moved by the Holy Spirit to give voice to the truth revealed to him or her by the inner light. Holding that divine truth can be revealed to anyone, Friends were one of the few groups of their age open to preaching by women. Convinced that everyone had the capacity of responding to the inner light, they rejected predestination with its spiritual aristocracy of the elect. Similarly, their opposition to social distinctions between rich and poor induced them to forego customary acts of deference to social superiors, such as doffing the hat. They further offended their social betters by addressing them with the familiar "thee" rather than the formal "you." To minimize social differences as well as to emphasize purified wills weaned from the attractions of the world, they dressed plainly, without frills or ornamentation.[4]

The principle of the unity of truth limited the atomistic and anarchistic effects of the Friends' belief in individual revelation. The strong sense they felt of the presence of God in communal worship brought Quakers to value the unity of their fellowship. Treasuring the mutual support, love, and harmony of the Christian community, members submitted their spiritual insights to the corporate judgment of the Society of Friends. Monthly, quarterly, and yearly meetings for discipline achieved unity by waiting for consensus, what they referred to as the "sense of the meeting," rather than through the decision of a leadership or majority vote.[5]

In the movement's early years, a perfectionist vision inspired Quakers to witness publicly in confrontational ways to their renunciation of prevailing social mores. With missionary zeal they strove to convert the world to true Christianity. After the restoration of the Stuart monarchy, intense persecution in England drove Friends from activism into a focus on the Quaker community and family life. With the Glorious Revolution and the subsequent Act of Toleration, Quakers came to identify with other nonconformist groups in England and "sought and achieved peace, quiet, order, and prosperity."[6]

The history of the Quakers in British North America followed a trajectory similar to the one it followed in England between the mid-seventeenth and mid-eighteenth centuries. Quakers first appeared in the British North American colonies during the commonwealth period. In New England they suffered persecution, including martyrdom. But after the Restoration they found refuge in colonies south of New England, not just in Pennsylvania, where they enjoyed the patronage of Quaker proprietor William Penn, but elsewhere, including New Jersey and North Carolina. George Fox and other Quakers made missionary tours of North Carolina in 1672, and the Society of Friends held its first monthly meeting there in 1680. By the end of the seventeenth century, the Society of Friends was the largest denomination in North Carolina, and from 1695 to 1696 the colony even had a Quaker governor. In 1704, however, the imposition of oaths excluded Quakers from political office in the colony. About the time that Quakers were excluded from office holding, they accounted for about a tenth of the population, a percentage that they probably never again equaled, although their absolute numbers continued to increase.[7]

In the second half of the eighteenth century, new circumstances moved the Friends to begin to look outward once more and engage more directly with the world by turning their energies to benevolent causes. Antislavery became one of those causes. Still, the movement within the Society of Friends to require members to set their slaves free was a work of time.

Origins of American Quaker Antislavery

Many Quakers in colonial British North America owned slaves. From the beginnings of large-scale Quaker migration to Pennsylvania in the latter half of the seventeenth century, for instance, wealthy Friends moving to America imported slaves from Barbados or Africa or bought slaves on arriving in Pennsylvania. The majority of wealthy Friends in seventeenth-century Philadelphia owned slaves and found that slaveownership enhanced their social prestige. Early in the eighteenth century, slaveownership spread among craftsmen and other middle-class Quakers in Philadelphia as a ready supply lowered the price of human property. Many rural Pennsylvania Friends also owned slaves, employing them as farm laborers.[8]

From early on in colonial Pennsylvania, individual Friends and a few isolated meetings raised their voices against slaveholding, pointing out its inconsistencies with Quaker beliefs. Slaveholding denied the spiritual equality of all persons, and the practice could be sustained only through violence, in contradiction to Quaker pacifism. Ownership of slaves undermined the Quaker commitment to plain living and renunciation of superfluities. In addition, slaveholding shattered the Golden Rule, to do unto others as you would have them do unto you. It broke up families and led men and women into adulterous relationships.[9]

The Friends' yearly meeting in Philadelphia consisted of representatives of monthly meetings in New Jersey, Delaware, and parts of Maryland as well as in Pennsylvania. By the early eighteenth century, some of those monthly meetings began recommending that the yearly meeting renounce the practice of owning slaves among Friends. However, as long as a cadre of influential slaveowning Friends dominated the leadership, the yearly meeting took no action that formally questioned the morality of slavery and the Committee on Publications refused to permit members to publish antislavery tracts.[10]

By 1750, patterns of slaveholding in Pennsylvania had shifted. An increased availability of free labor because of the immigration of large numbers of Germans and Scots-Irish made it practical to turn from slave labor, while the decrease in the size of individual farms due to partible inheritance made it unprofitable for many farmers to employ slave labor. These changes decreased the number of leading Friends economically bound to slavery and helped bring the leadership of the yearly meeting into the hands of those who did not own slaves. In the 1750s a coalition of active reformers and the formerly silenced minority of antislavery delegates attained power and led the yearly meeting to the adoption of stronger antislavery resolutions.[11]

Antislavery and the Eighteenth-Century Quaker Reform Movement

The Society of Friends in Pennsylvania went through a period of great internal soul-searching during the 1750s. The most dramatic and public evidence of the movement occurred during the bloody French and Indian War (1754–1763), when Pennsylvania's legislative assembly gave in to public pressure and approved war measures and, subject to the same influences, office holders undertook to enforce those measures. In order to avoid direct involvement in waging war and thereby avoid violating their pacifism, a majority of Quaker delegates (sixteen of twenty-eight) gave up their seats in the legislature and withdrew from politics during the period 1756–1758.[12] This withdrawal from politics reinforced a movement already under way toward sectarianism within the Society of Friends in Pennsylvania, a movement for reform that emphasized Friends' distinctive identity and separation from the "world," by which Quakers meant the culture of the larger society.[13]

Seventeenth-century Quaker immigrants to Pennsylvania were mainly converts who had personally experienced the illumination of the Inner Light and had voluntarily subjected themselves to persecution by becoming Quakers. In contrast, by the mid-eighteenth century most Pennsylvania Quakers were American born and had been raised within the Society of Friends rather than having been converted by the Inner Light. In Pennsylvania, Quakers enjoyed political freedoms, social prestige, and economic prosperity. Reforming Friends sensed that in these easy circumstances Pennsylvania's Quakers had lost the religious zeal of the colony's founding generation and had slipped into worldliness and spiritual complacency. At the same time, the renewed emphasis on denominational identity among Presbyterians and other evangelical churches resulting from the revival movement known as the Great Awakening made Quakers more aware of their own sectarian identity, while the political crisis brought about by the French and Indian War helped emphasize the differences between Quakers and non-Quakers. Turning inward, the Society of Friends renewed its commitment to fundamental values and tightened enforcement of discipline. It was in this context of internal moral reform that the yearly meeting took official notice of slavery's questionable morality.[14]

The antislavery movement among Pennsylvania's Quakers advanced gradually, though. Beginning at the end of the seventeenth century, the yearly meeting's policy was twofold: exhort Friends who owned slaves to treat their slaves with kindness and discourage Friends from importing or buying imported slaves. In 1730, the policy added cautions against buying slaves but attached no penalty to those who disregarded these cautions. The backwardness of the Philadelphia yearly meeting in condemning slaveholding was attributable in part to its desire to maintain the worldwide unity of Friends. The Pennsylvania Friends were reluctant to condemn practices engaged in widely by Friends in other parts of the British Empire and hesitated to take a step that might politically embarrass Friends contending for civil liberties in Great Britain.[15]

In 1753, a sign of change appeared when the Philadelphia yearly meeting approved publication of John Woolman's antislavery tract, *Some Considerations on the Keeping of Negroes*.[16] The following year, the meeting issued its own antislavery publication, *An Epistle of Caution and Advice, Concerning the Buying and Keeping of Slaves,* suggesting for the first time the incompatibility of not just the slave trade but of slaveholding itself with Christianity.[17] The 1755 yearly meeting gave local meetings the responsibility for bringing Friends who imported or bought slaves to an understanding of the wrongfulness of their actions. The 1758 meeting adopted a new rule of discipline: Any Friend who imported, bought, or sold a slave would be excluded by the monthly meeting from sitting in the society's business meetings, contributing funds, or serving as a representative of the society. Although it did not ban slaveholding or disown slaveowners, the meeting condemned slaveholding as wrong and set a goal of ending the practice among Friends. The rule also had the practical effect of removing slaveholders from deliberations regarding discipline. The yearly meeting adopted no additional significant changes in its policy on slavery until 1774.[18]

During the course of the sixteen years from 1758 to 1774, monthly meetings varied greatly in the rigor with which they implemented the new disciplinary rules and the vigor with which they undertook a program of visitations to convince slaveholding members of the wrongfulness of slavery. That variability illustrates the lack of consensus on slavery among Friends under the discipline of the Philadelphia yearly meeting.[19]

In the meantime, the extent of slaveholding in Pennsylvania (and in Philadelphia in particular) continued its decline. In rural areas, both wheat farming and iron production increased. The seasonal demands for labor in these two sectors reduced the demand for slaves who had to be supported year round and made free laborers, who were readily available among the large numbers of European immigrants, more attractive. In Philadelphia, slaves and indentured servants fell from 40 percent of the workforce in 1750 to about 6 percent in 1783.[20]

It took until 1774 for the moral sentiment against slaveholding to spread sufficiently and the economic argument in favor of slaveholding to decline enough among members of the Society of Friends for the yearly meeting to institute disownment of Friends involved in slave trading. Finally, in 1776, the meeting enacted an uncompromising ban on slaveownership. Thus, nearly a quarter-century passed between the Pennsylvania society's approval of John Woolman's first antislavery tract and the decision to disown any Friend who obstinately continued to own slaves.

Even after the enactment of the 1776 ban on slaveholding, many of Pennsylvania's Quaker slaveholders proved reluctant to relinquish their human property. Committees appointed by the yearly meeting dealt with Friends who did not comply in a process that continued in some cases for several years before final disownment. When slaveowning Friends finally signed manumission papers, frequently those papers included a clause that stated that the individual would serve for a number of years before manumission would take effect.[21]

Propagation of Antislavery among North Carolina's Quakers

Where the Pennsylvania yearly meeting led, Friends' meetings elsewhere in North America followed. The New England Yearly Meeting of the Religious

Society of Friends strengthened its cautions against importing and buying slaves in 1760, prohibited selling slaves in 1770, and adopted disownment for those who persisted in slaveholding in 1773. The New York meeting discouraged the purchase of slaves in 1762, prohibited buying and selling slaves in 1774, excluded slaveholders from business affairs of the Society in 1776, and disowned obstinate slaveowners in 1777. The Maryland meeting cautioned against importing slaves in 1759, forbade the buying and selling of slaves without approval of the local meeting in 1762, disowned those who bought or sold slaves in 1768, set up a system of treating with slaveholding members in 1772, and adopted disownment for slaveholders in 1778. The Virginia meeting opposed engaging in the slave trade as a business as early as 1722, prohibited the buying and selling of slaves in 1768, and adopted disownment of slaveowners in 1784. By the middle of the 1780s, Quakers throughout North America found it difficult to own slaves and remain in good standing with their yearly meetings.[22]

The antislavery movement appeared much later in North Carolina than in Pennsylvania but advanced there much more quickly. In North Carolina, the yearly meeting's position on slavery passed through the same evolution it had gone through in Pennsylvania, beginning with denouncing slave trading in 1768, moving to prohibiting buying and selling slaves without approval of the local meeting in 1772, and advancing to the resolution that all members end involvement in slaveholding in 1775. Although the North Carolina meeting did not authorize disownment of slaveholders until 1781, by 1776 the North Carolina and Pennsylvania meetings held essentially identical positions on the immorality of slavery.

North Carolina Friends found it even more difficult to give up their slaves than did Friends in Pennsylvania. Whereas Pennsylvania was a society with slaves, North Carolina was a slave society.[23] A rough estimate gives North Carolina's population in 1770 as 197,200 whites and 69,600 blacks.[24] Slaves as a proportion of North Carolina's population increased steadily during the twenty years preceding the outbreak of the Revolutionary War, from about 22 percent in 1755 to close to 30 percent in 1775. Distribution of slaves within the colony was uneven; the smallest percentage was in the western counties (8 percent in 1767) and the heaviest concentration (62 percent in 1767) was in the Lower Cape Fear region. In the Albemarle region the percentage of slaves rose from about 25 in 1755 to about 30 in 1767.[25] In Perquimans County, the center of the events recorded in the documents below, almost half (48.4 percent) of the males subject to the poll tax were enslaved in 1772.

More than half (55 percent) of the households of free whites owned slaves. For every household of free whites, there was an average of two slaves of taxable age. Counting only those households where there were slaves, the average number of slaves of taxable age per household was 3.75. Thus, the county's enslaved population was proportionally large and slaveholding was widely distributed among the white population.[26] Moreover, in North Carolina, slaveownership was the means to wealth and prestige.[27] On the eve of the War of Independence, slavery was much more deeply embedded in the economy of North Carolina than in that of Pennsylvania.

The Quakers' Antislavery Motivations

In their investigations of what factors motivated American Quakers to free their slaves, historians have identified two types of reformers among eighteenth-century Friends. These two groups might be designated the benevolent reformers and the moral reformers.[28]

The benevolent reformers sought to improve society through exemplary behavior. This group of Quakers encouraged manumissions by setting the example themselves. They exhibited genuine concern for the condition of the enslaved and sought to redress the injustices done them. Benevolent reformers in the Shrewsbury, New Jersey, quarterly meeting interacted readily with members of other denominations and were tolerant of members who married nonmembers.[29]

The moral reformers sought to maintain the separate identity of Friends. A focus on separation from the world intensified among Pennsylvania Friends through the first half of the eighteenth century as Quakers declined from the dominant element to an ever-smaller minority of the colony's population. By 1750, Quakers comprised only about a quarter of Philadelphia's households.[30] To uphold exclusivity of membership, the moral reformers disowned members who married non-Quakers. They emphasized the practices that made Quakers distinct, disciplining those who took oaths, paid military taxes, engaged in brawls, drank to excess, failed to meet financial obligations, or lived ostentatiously.[31] Many of this group of reformers came to see slaveownership as an evil practice that morally injured the slaveowners, encouraging violence, pride, and luxury. The Chesterfield, New Jersey, monthly meeting offers good examples of moral reformers; members there proved more interested in disciplining slaveowners than they did in ameliorating the condition of the slaves.[32]

In Pennsylvania, a coalition of both types of reformers, benevolent and moral, enacted the antislavery program of the Society of Friends in the third quarter of the eighteenth century. While the philanthropic impulses of the former brought the condition of slaves to the forefront, it was the sectarian impulse to reject worldly values that enabled the Society of Friends at large to renounce slavery. The radical step of condemning a practice so deeply embedded in the prevailing culture necessitated a willingness to appear peculiar and bear ridicule and loss of popular esteem.[33]

Impressionistic data suggests that the movement in North Carolina also involved both types of reformers. George Walton, whose papers are the core of the first part of this book, shared the hallmarks of the benevolent reformer. His writings reveal a genuine compassion for oppressed blacks. In contrast, the few extant writings on slavery by Thomas Nicholson, one of the more influential Friends of Perquimans County and the author of an antislavery tract submitted to the yearly meeting for approval, reflected the thought of the moral reformers. Nicholson urged slaveholders to free their slaves and thereby free themselves from sin, even though their former slaves were likely to be re-enslaved and subject to even crueler bondage.[34] In September 1782 the Symons Creek monthly meeting issued a testimony to Nicholson's memory that was approved by the yearly meeting the following year. The testimony notes that Nicholson

> was deeply distressed toward the latter part of his time . . . on account of his keeping negroes in slavery; but he was favored to extricate himself from this practice by restoring freedom to all that were then in his possession; wherein he witnessed such peace and satisfaction of mind, that, he hath expressed himself to some of his friends to this effect; That he would not again be entangled with slaves for their weight in GOLD.[35]

Nicholson believed that rescuing Friends from sin was a sufficient incentive apart from any desire to rescue the oppressed from slavery, that personal reform was as important as effecting a positive change in the condition of the enslaved.

Just as they had in Pennsylvania, Friends had dominated in North Carolina in the late seventeenth century, both as a proportion of the population and in political power, and, just as in Pennsylvania, North Carolina Friends lost that dominance over the course of the early eighteenth century. As did moral reformers in the middle colonies, meetings in North Carolina sought to maintain the distinctiveness of the Society of Friends to stave off amalgamation with other groups. Like the moral reformist meeting in Chesterfield, New Jersey, the meeting in Perquimans, North Carolina, strictly enforced marriage discipline. Yet unlike the Chesterfield Friends and suggestive of a mixture of motives, the Perquimans meeting was patient with slaveholding Quakers, treating with them through the course of many years without disowning them. Ejecting slaveowners might purify the meeting, but it would not free any slaves.

The Abolition Revolution

When George Walton joined the Quakers and committed himself to the manumission of their slaves, he became a first-generation participant in one of the most remarkable revolutionary freedom movements in the history of mankind, the movement to abolish slavery. By the time of the invention of writing, slavery already existed. While the annals of history include accounts of numerous slave revolts, few of those revolts had as their object the destruction of slavery as a system before the eighteenth century. Several individuals questioned the right of any person to own another before the mid-eighteenth century, but theirs were solo voices, not those of a chorus. From Plato to Locke, political philosophers accepted slavery as a given, an inevitable condition for a substantial portion of the human population.[36]

In 1772, when Walton began his manumission crusade, more than three-quarters of all people on earth were not free, according to one reckoning. These included slaves bound to work for their masters, serfs bound to the land, and peasants bound by debt to work for their landlords. Some form of bondage was the condition of much of the population of Russia, India, China, Africa, and the Americas. When Walton dreamed of Christ as a small black child, legal systems from Patagonia to Labrador promoted the enslavement of black Africans and their descendants and no law restricted the transportation of slaves from Africa to the Americas. In the period 1500 to 1820, when some 2.6 million white Europeans made the transatlantic voyage to the Americas, slave traders carried some 8.7 million black Africans to the New World. Each year from 1791 to 1800, nearly eighty thousand blacks from Africa arrived in shackles on American shores.[37]

Beginning in the mid-eighteenth century, the most remarkable revolution in the story of human freedom took place with astonishing rapidity. By the end of the next century, serfdom and slavery had been ended by law almost everywhere and few could be found to defend their legitimacy. In 1808, both the U.S. Congress and the British Parliament outlawed the international slave trade. The United Kingdom subsequently negotiated treaties with several European nations to end the international slave trade, and in 1819 the United States made it the crime of piracy for its citizens to engage in that trade, a crime that was punishable by death. The Royal Navy's West Africa Squadron diligently patrolled Africa's "Slave Coast" to enforce the prohibition, as did a smaller U.S. Navy force. By 1830, Haiti, Mexico, Central American countries, and several northern states of the United States had abolished slavery and gradual emancipation laws were bringing an end to slavery in Rhode Island, Connecticut, Pennsylvania, New Jersey, and most of South America (with the notable exception of Brazil). The British abolished slavery in their colonies in 1833. An act of 1843 made slavery illegal in India, although the ban had to be reenacted in 1861. Tsar Alexander II signed the Emancipation Manifesto ending Russian serfdom in 1861. The Dutch enacted gradual emancipation for their colonies in 1863. The Thirteenth Amendment to the U.S. Constitution ended slavery in the United States in 1865. Spain adopted gradual emancipation for Cuba's slaves in 1870 and ended slavery in all its colonies in 1886. Brazil finally ended slavery in 1888.[38]

Abolition's trajectory has not been a straight line from slavery to freedom, nor has the legal abolition of slavery always brought about its actual extinction. Portugal abolished slavery in its possessions in 1836 but authorized forced labor in 1899. Forced labor returned to Portuguese Angola in 1911, was abolished there in 1913, and was reestablished in 1926 under António de Oliveira Salazar and maintained until the liberation of that nation in 1974. Although slavery was legally abolished in Libya in 1853, it continued there into the 1890s. Attempts to end slavery in Mauritania in 1905 and 1981 proved ineffective, and in the first decade of the twenty-first century, a U.S. government investigation reported that "there continued to be reports that slavery in the form of forced and involuntary servitude persisted in some isolated areas [of Mauritania], that unofficial, voluntary servitude persisted, and that former slaves continued to work for former masters or others."[39]

In 1772, the existence of slavery was only beginning to shock and appall. This is not to say that antislavery sentiments were new. There is evidence that bondage elicited popular revulsion as early as the Middle Ages, for common folk feared the power of slaveholders when dealing with free persons and town and city charters included provisions that gave freedom to bonded persons who established residence. Medieval monarchs, too, viewed slavery unfavorably, because it removed individuals from their authority.[40] Since 1900, however, the continued existence of slavery has appeared to the vast majority of people to be not merely unpleasant and undesirable but also a gross anomaly and an execrable injustice.

Quaker Antislavery and the Problem of Slavery in the Age of Revolution

To place the Quaker manumission movement in revolutionary-era North Carolina in context, a series of questions must be addressed. What happened in the eighteenth century to begin this remarkable change in sentiment toward a system that had existed in human society since time immemorial? How did the change in sentiment lead some people to take action to end slavery? What was the role of religion in general in this movement? And what role did the Society of Friends in particular play?

A brief summary of the argument David Brion Davis, the dean of antislavery studies, has presented provides a broad-based answer to the first of these questions: What brought about the change in sentiment?

In the sixteenth and seventeenth centuries, perfectionist and millennialist Christian sects denounced slaveholding as incompatible with their goal of a sinless life of mutual love. These groups hardly left an imprint on Western thought, for the repressive response of the social order that they condemned either destroyed them or forced them to retreat into mysticism. An exception was the Society of Friends, which proved adaptable enough to survive and even flourish economically within the prevailing social order. Quakers in America became as involved with slaveholding as any other group, accommodating themselves to the contradictions inherent in treating humans as property. However, the spiritual crisis in the mid-eighteenth century brought the Quaker community to commit itself to ending its complicity in slavery.[41]

Quaker antislavery rhetoric coincided with a torrent of secular antislavery publications. The arguments of the intellectuals who produced those writings reflected what Davis calls "a profound transformation in moral perception, a transformation that led a number of Europeans and Americans to see the full horror of a social evil [chattel slavery] to which mankind had been blind for centuries." He identifies four principal sources of that transformation. First, the social philosophy of the Enlightenment viewed all men as equal and naturally free and questioned the authority of traditional ways. Second, popularization of an ethic of benevolence promoted the ideal of the "man of feeling" who empathized with innocent victims. Third, the evangelical revival with its faith in instantaneous conversion and evident sanctification pictured the slaveowner as a sinner stained with blood and guilt. It also led men to the conclusion that attempts to Christianize the relationship between master and slave were hopeless—the system was invulnerable to reform. Finally, a strain of primitivism in eighteenth-century literature portrayed the African as an innocent child of nature, a figure Europeans could feel sympathy for and identify with. "By the eve of the American Revolution," Davis concludes, the convergence of these cultural and intellectual developments "at once undercut traditional rationalizations for slavery and offered new modes of sensibility for identifying with its victims."[42]

According to Davis, few outside of the Society of Friends paid much attention to the Quaker voices raised against slavery until "the emergence of an enlightened climate of opinion, defining liberty as a natural and fundamental right . . . brought outside sanction to Quaker reformers."[43] Quakers did not need Enlightenment philosophy or sentimental literature to persuade them to oppose slavery. But these sources helped create allies for them in the antislavery cause.

From Sentiment to Activism

As historian Christopher Leslie Brown points out, the growth of antislavery opinion is not a sufficient explanation for the rise of movements to end systems of human bondage. Individuals can believe that something is morally reprehensible without being moved to do something to stop it. Brown isolates two conditions that favored antislavery activism. One was the likelihood that efforts to oppose slavery would have some success: The better the chances for ending the slave trade appeared to be and the better the prospect that others would help, the more individuals were encouraged to take action. The second condition that promoted activism was the likelihood that antislavery efforts would win the reformer the esteem of others and enhance the reformer's self-image.⁴⁴

Social dynamics within and external political challenges to the Society of Friends in Pennsylvania precipitated the antislavery movement within the society in the 1750s. Quaker hostility to slavery derived from the Quaker belief system, but action against slaveholding did not come until a crisis of identity in the 1750s. Renouncing slaveholding became a way of asserting the distinctive identity of the Society of Friends.⁴⁵ In the 1750s, American Friends began to discourage slaveownership by Quakers as a function of self-discipline and moral purification. But not until the emergence of Brown's two critical conditions during the American dispute with Great Britain over political rights did American Quakers expand the movement beyond the bounds of the Society of Friends. When some non-Quakers seized on antislavery as a political tool with which to contend with British authorities, American Quakers saw potential allies in those polemicists as well as a source of outside approval of their principled stand against slavery.

Among the American Quaker reformers, Anthony Benezet and John Woolman were unusual in that they sought to push antislavery activism on the larger society before the Revolution. Benezet and Woolman formed a partnership that employed a new approach to promoting antislavery commitment. Instead of merely condemning, they employed reason to convince. Instead of working singly, they built a community of allies. In Pennsylvania, Benezet sought to restore the Society of Friends' influence by replacing the political leadership that Quakers had lost with moral leadership. Turning his sights outward beginning in 1763, he worked to awaken the British to the evils of the slave trade. His 1766 *A Caution and a Warning to Great Britain and Her Colonies* was reprinted in England in 1767 and 1768 and distributed to all Members of Parliament, among others. In 1762 Woolman published an antislavery tract whose subtitle, *Recommended to the Professors of Christianity of Every Denomination,* indicated that he sought to bring Christians of all stripes into the antislavery movement initiated within the Quaker community.⁴⁶

The debate over political rights that arose in the 1760s between the colonists and the British government created a situation that was more favorable to the antislavery cause. In Brown's words, by invoking purportedly universal principles rather than established law or custom, by describing liberty as a natural right, and by defining their political crusade as a campaign against slavery, North American colonists inadvertently alerted themselves to the dubious justice of holding African men and women, girls and boys, in lifelong bondage. . . . By 1775 . . . the sale, purchase, and ownership of slaves had become for several communities what these practices had been for some time within the Society of Friends: customs that trouble the conscience.[47]

In their resistance to British regulations, Brown argues, some American polemicists came to see antislavery action as a political tool. These Americans believed that if they could abolish slavery, they would demonstrate their moral superiority over the British, on whom they laid the blame for the continuation of the importation of slaves from Africa.[48] With the prospect of greater acceptance, more Friends widened the horizon of their antislavery vision. Taking advantage of the politicization of the antislavery movement, American Quakers expanded their involvement beyond the circle of the Society of Friends, first on the colony and state level. For example, Quakers supported colonial legislatures' petitioning of the king to end the importation of slaves to America and, in 1780, Pennsylvania's law that abolished slavery gradually.

Quakers pressed for national legislation against the slave trade in the postwar period. But in North Carolina, where any hopes for ending slavery were unrealistic, Friends focused on purifying their sect. Before and after the War of Independence, they limited their actions to petitioning for legislation that prohibited slave importations into North Carolina.

For important sectors of the antislavery movement, political action was subordinate to and an instrument employed in the cause of religion. Both Quakers and evangelicals in the Church of England opposed slavery on the basis of a religious conviction that it was morally wrong to hold other humans in bondage, but both groups viewed antislavery activism as a means of enhancing the importance of religion generally in private and public life. Religious motives inspired most of the principal leaders of the English antislavery movement in the 1780s, which included Thomas Clarkson, Hannah More, James Ramsay, Granville Sharp, and William Wilberforce, to name a few. Two developments in England in the late eighteenth century provided an opportunity for the success of an antislavery movement by creating a body of potential allies for Quakers and evangelicals. The first development was the emergence of secular antislavery sentiment whose rise David Brion Davis has dissected. The second was the politicization of slavery as a result of the American Revolution, as Christopher Brown has analyzed. The British contended with Americans for the moral high ground, asserting their moral superiority over the slaveowning American revolutionaries by seeking to transform the British Empire into an empire of liberty.[49]

These same studies of the antislavery movement in England underscore the critical role of Quakers in supporting the transformation of antislavery opinion into a movement to put an end to lifelong human bondage. Davis concludes that the main contribution of British and American Quakers was in initiating and sustaining the first antislavery movements, providing "what no other group seemed capable of: decision, commitment, and most important, organization."[50] In other words, Quakers gave impetus and vigor to the transformation of antislavery sentiment into an antislavery movement.

Following the trend among North American yearly meetings, the London yearly meeting banned Friends from participating in the slave trade in 1761. The London Meeting for Sufferings reprinted one of Benezet's antislavery tracts and distributed copies to all the Members of Parliament.[51] During the War of Independence, England's Quakers remained relatively quiet about slavery and hesitated to agitate the issue. But after the Treaty of Paris, under pressure by American Friends in the moral reform camp, England's Friends not only embraced the movement but from 1783 to 1787 "stood nearly alone in the attempt to organize a political crusade."[52]

Quakers and evangelicals had another set of allies in their struggle against the system of racial slavery, namely blacks themselves. Whether free or unfree, Africans and their descendants living in England and the British colonies seized opportunities to strike blows against slavery. It frequently happened that the antislavery cause advanced because of actions taken by blacks.

Black Resistance to Slavery

In the 1797 "Petition of Freemen," document 1 in Part IV of this volume, we hear directly from slaves who were affected by the revolutionary-era North Carolina Quaker manumissions and through that petition witness firsthand the steps they took to secure their freedom. Yet even the documents produced earlier by Quaker masters and state authorities testify to the active engagement of the slaves in their own fates. George Walton subconsciously recognized the activism of the blacks, as his dreams make clear. In one dream, a black boy gives Walton a strong stick with which he is able to resist Satan. In another dream, a slave recently arrived from Africa reproves Quaker elders for their unfaithfulness to pacifism. The steps state authorities took to prevent insurrection provide evidence that they believed it was likely that slaves would take the initiative if given any encouragement.

The movement of North Carolina Friends to free their slaves called forth a powerful condemnation from North Carolina's government because of white fears of black insurrection. North American slaveowners took the threat of servile insurrection seriously and were well aware that slave communities frequently took advantage of political crises and war to revolt. Recent slave rebellions in several West Indian communities graphically illustrated the strength of black aspirations for freedom and the ease with which those aspirations could be fanned into the flames of rebellion. The 1760s and early 1770s had been pregnant with Caribbean slave revolts: three major rebellions in Jamaica (1760, 1765, and 1766), an extensive plot in Montserrat (1768), and four rebellions in Tobago (1770–1774). Black unrest in Antigua, Barbados, Montserrat, Nevis, and St. Kitts had moved whites in those islands to implement extra precautions.[53]

Like the Quakers, blacks used religious arguments as well as the rhetoric of white revolutionaries about inalienable rights to advocate for emancipation. Black insurrectionists seized on both Christian theology and the Lockean justification for revolution to defend their attempts to end their bondage. Some planters in Jamaica attributed the 1776 insurrection there to the ideology of the American Revolution. Slaves were not passive objects of policy decisions made by their white masters but were participants who took active steps to free themselves. North Carolina's authorities recognized this and opposed anything that stimulated slaves' thoughts of freedom.[54]

Slaves in the British Empire in North America saw in the armed conflict between Great Britain and its rebellious colonies opportunities to gain their freedom. Most American slaves concluded that their best chances for freedom lay with the British side. In 1772, a British court issued the Somerset decision, which was popularly believed to have made slavery illegal in Great Britain, although it was decided on a much narrower principle. Word of the Somerset decision was soon circulating among slaves in America, leading them to conceive of England as the land of liberty.[55]

By 1775, slaves from Georgia to Virginia believed that the British were their allies. In the course of the War of Independence, thousands of slaves fled to the British, crossing the lines into their camps, even risking death by drowning to board their warships. A recent recalculation conservatively estimates that 20,000 slaves ran away to the protection of British forces. This figure does not include slaves who deserted their masters but did not flee to the British. Self-liberated slaves fought to maintain their freedom by aiding the British as guides, pilots, laborers on fortifications, and soldiers. Many took the opportunities presented by the disruptions of war to run off to forests and swamps, where they formed maroon communities. Some slaves were emboldened to organize insurrections. The approach of British forces caused other slaves to simply become less subservient and more assertive. The fact that during the British reconquest of Georgia a third of Georgia's fifteen thousand slaves escaped bondage measures the breadth of the blacks' desire for freedom and the height to which the approach of British forces could raise the hopes of slaves.[56]

The attempts of slaves to emancipate themselves failed to put an end to the slave system in the South during the War of Independence because major obstacles stood in the way. The most significant of those obstacles was the pervasiveness of white power, but almost as significant was the ambiguous policy of the British. British leaders debated and rejected using black emancipation as a means of defeating the rebellion. In 1775, Virginia's royal governor, John Murray, Lord Dunmore, rallied the rebels' slaves to his banner by offering to free those who fought under his command. In 1779, on the eve of his southern campaign, British general William Cornwallis issued a proclamation stating that slaves captured from rebels would be sold, whereas those that voluntarily deserted the rebels and came over to serve the British would be allowed to follow whatever occupations they chose. Neither Dunmore nor Cornwallis intended their proclamation to end slavery as a labor system in America, no more than did Patriots who sought to lure slaves to enlist in the Continental Army. In the restored royal governments of Georgia and South Carolina, the policies of the British military and British civilian authorities were incompatible; rampant plundering in which British commanders treated the slaves they captured as spoils of war undercut the efforts of civilian authorities to create a sense of order and normalcy in economic and social relations. Never committed to emancipation, the British army presented an inconstant face to fugitive slaves, sometimes welcoming them with offers of freedom, sometimes turning them away or even returning them to their owners, and sometimes seizing and selling them back into slavery. During the British invasion of Virginia in 1781, slaves hesitated to rise in armed rebellion because of their uncertainty about what support they could expect from the British.[57]

Just as black assertiveness played a decisive role in antislavery initiatives in England, including the Somerset decision, black activism played a crucial role in the ending of slavery in the northern United States during and after the War of Independence. The Patriots' rhetoric of liberty raised the expectations of the enslaved, prompting them to petition for freedom. Those petitions and legal action by white antislavery promoters both helped persuade courts and legislatures to abolish slavery or (more often) put it on the road to extinction in every state north of Delaware within three decades of the Declaration of Independence.[58] Restiveness in the slave societies of the southern states, from Virginia south, had the opposite effect, leading to the tightening of social controls on those in bondage. North Carolina was alone in restricting the right of owners to free their slaves in 1790.[59] In the aftermath of Gabriel's Rebellion in Virginia in 1800, the Old Dominion amended its liberal manumission law of 1782 and enacted a series of measures to control the privileges and freedom of movement of blacks, both slave and free.[60]

George Walton in Historical Context

The years 1772–1774, during which George Walton dreamed of Christ in the form of a black boy, joined the Society of Friends, and began his campaign to persuade fellow Quakers to free their slaves, were especially significant in the antislavery movement within the British Empire. Consider the following antislavery milestones: The Somerset decision that marked the beginning of the end of chattel slavery within England was handed down in 1772 and in its wake slaves in Massachusetts began filing petitions for freedom; the antislavery crusade of American abolitionist leader John Woolman came to a close in 1772, when he died during a sojourn in England; Moses Brown freed his slaves in 1773, an act "virtually unprecedented in Rhode Island," and proposed that the Rhode Island General Assembly prohibit the importation of slaves to the colony and institute gradual abolition in 1774; and that same year, John Wesley, founder of English Methodism, published his *Thoughts upon Slavery*.⁶¹ The timing of this sequence contributes to an understanding of Walton's religious transformation and the depth of his antislavery commitment. While cultural, social, and intellectual developments were causing many individuals across the British Empire to reconsider their personal involvement with slavery in the third quarter of the eighteenth century, Quakers took the lead in actually doing something to end their connection with the slave system. By the early 1770s, the antislavery movement had reached beyond the borders of the Society of Friends and was attracting outsiders to the movement.

Consider the striking parallels and coincidences in the experiences of George Walton and Moses Brown. Brown, scion of the prosperous Brown merchant family of Providence, Rhode Island, which owned ships involved in the slave trade between Africa and the West Indies, found himself attracted to the Quaker religion and antislavery by 1772. The following year Brown freed the seven slaves he owned. In 1774, Brown applied for and was granted admission to the Society of Friends, just as Walton had applied for and received admission the year before, and, like Walton, immediately entered into a campaign to persuade his fellow Quakers to free their slaves. There are additional parallels between the cases of Brown and Walton. Each man first looked seriously into the Society of Friends as a result of a relationship with a woman. Brown began attending Quaker services after his wife led the way. Walton's application for admission to the Society of Friends followed on his decision to wed a Quaker after the death of his first wife. Just as Brown broke with his brother John, refusing to continue in the African slave trade, Walton questioned the propriety of his continued involvement in trade with the West Indies.⁶²

It is hard to say with any degree of certainty why any particular individual, such as Walton or Brown, embraced antislavery when the majority of others reared in the same cultural milieu and subject to the same social and intellectual influences did not. Consider that the Quaker reform movement of the 1750s attracted many Friends in Pennsylvania and New Jersey but none embraced it as completely and internalized its values as deeply as did John Woolman, who implemented reform ideas in his behavior so radically that observers judged him eccentric and obsessive. Historians have identified causes of the reform movement, but who can explain its most famous eighteenth-century exemplar?⁶³

Fully integrated into the Friends' transatlantic communications network, North Carolina's Quaker community was far from insulated from the reform movement washing over Quakerdom in the middle of the eighteenth century. The various yearly meetings kept in touch through the exchange of annual letters. The direct visits traveling ministers paid were more influential, however. Religious visits by reform-minded public Friends carrying letters of endorsement from their meetings helped spread the impulse for moral transformation, a recommitment to shared values, and antislavery concerns.[64] Quaker preachers frequently crossed the ocean in a two-way exchange between Great Britain and America. Visiting public Friends sometimes traveled the length of Britain's North American colonies, visiting meetinghouses in every region. Visits between meetings in neighboring regions were even more common. George Walton's journal mentions such visits from New Jersey, Pennsylvania, and Virginia Friends and his own visits to meetings in Virginia.[65]

John Woolman visited North Carolina in 1746 and again in 1757; the second visit took place fifteen years before Walton's commitment to Quakerism and antislavery. During that second visit, Woolman was not moved to speak directly about the issue of slaveholding in public meeting. But Woolman debated the morality of slavery with the slaveowning Quakers he lodged with. That tour, which exposed Woolman to the conditions of slaves in a thoroughgoing slave society, had more influence on him than it did on North Carolina Quakers.[66] Even though there is no evidence that Walton was directly influenced by Woolman or read any of his writings, Walton was an heir to Woolman's legacy. Woolman embraced the Quaker moral reform movement with his entire being, so much so that he pursued Quaker simplicity and more quiet time for communion with God by giving up a career as a merchant to make a living as a farmer and tailor; he walked instead of riding in a coach drawn by overworked horses; he ate no sugar because it was produced by slave labor; he refused to eat or drink from silverware because silver was mined by exploited laborers; he demurred from bunking in a ship's cabin because it had wasteful ornamental carving; and he dressed in undyed clothing because the dye served no useful purpose and weakened the cloth. Woolman, empathizing with the downtrodden and exploited, sought to convince others of slavery's immorality by helping them imagine themselves in the situation of slaves. In his publications, he traced for his readers the causal connections between slavery and the greed and excessive consumption of those who did not own slaves. George Walton did not mirror Woolman's otherworldly self-denial, but he shared his imaginative empathy with the slave's condition. Not a profound or original thinker, Walton reflected the values of his adopted religion and questioned the compatibility of the career of a merchant sea captain with the simplicity of a true Christian. He imitated Woolman in using gentle persuasion to bring others to see the wickedness of slaveholding. By the time of his death, Woolman had helped shape the character of the Society of Friends; when Walton and others embraced the Quaker religion, they embraced antislavery as well.

The motivation and thought processes of George Walton, an obscure and ordinary Quaker, are probably more representative of those of most of the Friends who were his contemporaries than are those of famous antislavery leaders such as the saintly John Woolman and the socially and politically prominent Moses Brown. Thus, studying Walton's writings should help us understand why the antislavery movement found adherents among the common people of North Carolina's Quaker community.

The decision of North Carolina's Friends to end their involvement with slavery and the means they chose to do so presented a series of difficult challenges. Individual North Carolina Friends underwent private struggles between consciences awakened to the evils of slavery on the one hand and their habitual way of life and economic interests on the other. Individuals convinced of the sinfulness of slaveholding worked to persuade their monthly, quarterly, and yearly meetings to promote manumission. Once committed to manumission, Friends' meetings employed various means to overcome the resistance it met among members reluctant to let go of their human property.

In addition to the challenge of persuading fellow Quakers, the manumission movement faced the opposition of the State of North Carolina at every turn. State law limited the circumstances in which slaves could be set free and then required that freed slaves leave the state.

This latter provision led eventually to interstate and national confrontations. Soon after ratification of the Constitution of the United States, North Carolina's Friends and the men and women they set free faced the Fugitive Slave Act.

The texts included in this volume document at every level—personal, communal, state, and national—the difficult struggles that North Carolina Friends underwent in seeking to end their involvement in the ownership of fellow human beings. Beginning at the personal level, the writings of George Walton carry the story through the communal and state levels.

Walton's private journal also illustrates how his antislavery activities were integrated with his daily life and benevolent activities as a public Friend.

A Note on the Transcriptions

The texts reproduced in this volume retain the spelling, capitalization, and punctuation of the original documents. Within the texts, materials enclosed in braces in roman type {thus} represent my reconstruction of text missing from the original; material enclosed in braces and italic type, such as {*manuscript torn*} and {*illegible*} represent either explanatory information about the text that I have provided or indicate that I have added a word to improve the sense of the passage.

PART I

An Individual

George Walton Confronts Slavery

Perquimans County in the last half of the eighteenth century was a rural society of white farmers of middling economic status and their slaves. In 1766, taxables in the county numbered 1,544, a figure that can be translated to a total of about 5,400 inhabitants. The region produced corn principally, wheat secondarily, and cotton and flax in modest amounts. Perquimans County's farmers had gradually moved away from tobacco over the course of the century. Residents also exported livestock, naval stores (tar, pitch, and turpentine), and lumber, staves, and shingles. Their markets were mainly in New England and the West Indies.[1] Perquimans resident George Walton participated in this economy as master of a ship engaged in the trade with the West Indies and as a landowner who possessed one or more slaves.

Walton married Sarah Earls in 1764 in Perquimans and had a daughter with her, Elizabeth, who was born in 1768. George and Sarah were not Quakers. By December 1772, Sarah had died and Walton was engaged to Mary Newby Winslow, the widow of Timothy Winslow. Mary belonged by birth to the extensive and prominent Newby Quaker clan. Mary could not become the wife of a non-Quaker and remain in unity with the Society of Friends. Early in 1773 Walton applied to the Perquimans, North Carolina, monthly meeting and was welcomed in unity on 2 June. George and Mary wed with the meeting's blessing on 4 August. Their union produced three daughters and a son, all born in the years 1775 to 1781.² George Walton became active in the manumission movement immediately after joining the Society of Friends and quickly emerged as an antislavery leader.

1

1772–1773

George Walton's Accounts of Two Dreams

During the night of 17 December 1772, George Walton dreamed an extended dream that began with his walking along through a town, looking for a Quaker meetinghouse. His account of that dream follows below. At the time of that dream, Walton was in the process of joining the Society of Friends.

George Walton Becomes a Committed Friend

Like many of his contemporaries, Walton seems to have used dreams to help make or confirm life-altering decisions. Such a practice was characteristic of Quakers in particular in the late eighteenth and early nineteenth centuries.[3] Walton's own interpretation of the first dream he records placed it in the context of what his decision to become a Friend would mean for his way of life. The dream suggested to Walton that he had to give up his occupation as a merchant in order to escape the love of material things, earthly pleasures, and a worldly reputation that separated him from a godly Christian life, concluding, "I must forsake all trade and the Way of life I am now in."

Six weeks after this dream, Walton had another about a wheat field and a grape arbor. Walton interpreted this second dream as having a similar meaning to the first—that is, it confirmed him in his profession of the principles of the Society of Friends.

A Dream or Night Vision 17th 12th Mo 1772

Source: Papers of George Walton, Accession No. 3988, Americana Collection, National Society Daughters of the American Revolution, Washington, D.C.

In the Night laying on my Bed, I dream't I was going along a Town looking for a Meeting house, at last I came to a large Building which by the outside appeard to be one, there was a large End door open and I went in, but I thought there were Merchants writing, and two Gentlemen walking about the Room; one of them seeing I only just enter'd the Door, Spoke to me very pleasantly, Capt won't you come in; But I seeing it was not a meeting house as I wanted to find one, gave them no Answer, But took up a Small Trunk I thought had some Goods in, and went out. I then Seed another large House on the Top of a Hill, but could See no path but I climb'd up by long Grass which grew out of the Rock (for the House Seemd to be Set on a Rock) and so got up very easy. When I got up I thought there was no meeting held at that time, but there were Some people without waiting that did not seem to be friends, one of the Women fell into Some discourse with me but I thought I did not like her, she call'd me Mr Walton Capt Walton &c. which I look'd upon as Hypocrisy; I then thought Instead of my Trunk I had a Bundle of Cloth, which this Woman wanted to buy, I told her my Price and She thought it Cheap, She took my Cloth, but I got nothing for it, I then Saw some Taylors sitting above me which Shewed me Some Cloaths they were making, and ask'd if none of that was my Cloth, I told them No. Then they all said they must go Home I said I must go Home also; I directly lost Sight of all them, and then I see'd a broad Road to the Top of a Mountain which Seem'd to be very wet and Slippy, but I thought it was not very Steep, for I was almost up it; As I went along the Road I overtook a Man which Appear'd to be a Gentleman, and I thought a Boy on his Right Hand which appear'd to be Black, I thought I did not like this Gentlemans Company and was going to run up the Hill, betwixt him and the Boy, The Boy on my right hand, and him on my left, upon which he having a great Stick in his hand went to Stop me, Saying I should not run in his Ground, I ask'd him the reason, he said I should make it rough and full of Holes so that others might come up also—Upon which the Boy on my right hand, (that till then I thought had been his Servant) gave me a Stick that I might fight my way, it was all woolded or bound round So that it could not be Split, then I went up to the Top of the Mountain with the Seeming Gentleman and he said no more to me, for I thought I could handle a Stick as well as him so went on boldly{.} Then I thought we had this large Mountain to go down again and the Top of it was very Slippy, we no Sooner set off, but the Gentleman Slip'd down as far as I could See him, and I thought he must be dash'd to pieces, as he seem'd to fall down a great Rock into a pit. I then went down the hill with the greatest ease, having fine grass all along to keep my feet from Slipping, as I was going down I overtook Several dress'd much in the Fashion of the World, who told me he was not kill'd but he troubled me no more. they seem'd to go down the Mountain very well too, and offerd to shake hands but I thought I had not freedom to do it, as I passed by them one of the Company, (I thought a Young Man) said to some Women that were along with him, what a pretty Man he would have been had it not been for Marrying that Ugly wife, meaning my Dear wife that was Dead, I made no reply but kept along till I came to the foot of the Mountain, where we were all Stop'd by Briers and thorns But I espied a narrow path by the Side of them, thro' which I went very easy, only once I thought I got a lash in my face but did not hurt me; (I left all the rest amongst the Briers & Thorns) Then I got into an open Grassy plain, and I thought two grave Men I had not seen before, came out after me I thought they were going along with me, or to the same place; but yet their seem'd to be a deep black pool of Water that kept us from being in our right path; along which there grew Briers and thorns and Different Sort of Bushes on both sides, I goes up along it, and soon found a place I thought I could jump over, upon which I took a Run, and very easily got over there being but one Bush in the way and that did not in the least stop me, after I was got over I waited for the other two, and they both got safe over, tho' one seem'd to wet his feet and when he jump'd had liked to have fallen on his Back{.} I seem'd to have Boots on so that my feet could not get wet. After we were all over I thought we were in plain Ground, but a very small Compass of it, we seed our Home, but we had Briers and Thorns on every Side; they told me I must be their Guide for they did not then know the way, I told them I was now got where I know'd, In the right path and could easily guide them for I thought I saw a plain narrow path, all along betwixt the Briers and Thorns; tho' it was not yet Seen to either of them—So I awakned out of my Sleep—

One of the Men appear'd to me to be Josiah White[4] the other a more Antient Man I did not Remember to know—This is a nigh as I can relate word for Word what I dreamt.

The Interpretation as was afterwards made appear to me was as follows—

The Town I was walking in is the World, and my looking for a Meeting house Signifys my thinking or expecting to find truth amongst Gaity and Pleasures of this life, the large House with Merch[ts] in, looking by outward Appearance to be a Meeting House, Shews the fair outside Appearance the people of this World make in Godliness but their inside's full of covetousness and Deceit my haveing a small Trunk shews I had in Some Measure Join'd with them, and their inviting me in, shews they were desirous I should Join farther, but my going away after I found it not to be a Meeting House, shews I have now seen the Deceitfulness of Riches and must leave them, but my taking my trunk with me shews me desirous to hold the truth and the World together, as I climb'd up to the Meeting house with it, but no one ever did or can Enjoy a true Meeting under Christs divine teaching, till all that Seem delightfull to them in this World is laid aside, the long Grass from the Rock is Christs Everlasting Gospel by which all true Believers must Climb up if ever they expect to be united in his heavenly Meeting The Woman that gave me the flattering titles and all the rest that were with her, are the People of this World which would fain be thought good Christians by going to Meetings and Religious Worship but by Deceit and Hypocrisy their is no entering admitted them, My giving her my Cloth Shews I must forsake all trade and the Way of life I am now in and leave it to people of this World As there was no Meeting because we all loved trading. The Slippery Mountain and broad path I had to go up is the World and the Gentleman in the Way to hinder my running up is the Devil which is afraid I should make his Deceit known to the World that others might come to the Blessed truth, therefore he attempted to hinder me, the Small Black Boy at my right hand is Christ Which was represented Black, to shew how much the Devil is exalted and Christ abased, the Stick he gave me was his Holy Spirit Bound round with truth So that it could not be Shaken by which I must fight against all the Slippery paths and Wiles of Satan The Being upon the top of the Mountain Shews my first Entring the World after having overcome; and the Gentleman's falling Down shews that Satan will have no more power over me, Going down the Mountain Shews my travail thro this Life and the Grass that keeps my feet from Slipping is the everlasting Gospel of truth, the People that are also seeming to go down Safe are the People of this World, which make a Shew of Godliness and would fain be accounted such by offering to Shake hands with me, But the Briers and thorns which are the Pleasures and Riches of this World, Stops them they can go no farther; This last Pool I had to get over signifys my being fully wash'd and Purify'd from all the filth and Pleasures of this World and in the Right Path for everlasting happiness, but the Path being so Narrow, and Briers and thorns on each Side shews it dificult to walk in tho' I plainly saw it, which I humbly Pray the Lord by his devine Spirit may direct me in least I should Err from his Blessed truth

    Geo: Walton

29th of 1st M^{o} 1773
In the Night laying on my Bed, I dream't I was in a large Wheat feild which belong'd to many People and was divided into different lots, and they all Seem'd Some to be Ripe, Some almost Ripe, and Some Green, I thought there were some more with me and we were to Reap it I thought their had been other Reapers before us, and had left at the Ends of the field some Green not fit to reap, then I thought I said to my fellow labourers let us go to work, here it looks Ripe, we must not be idle and I went in amongst it, and was Surprized when I found a great part of it Shaken out upon the Ground, and a great Part only an Appearance of Wheat without any Substance, but Some all amongst it was full Ripe and Good, I said this had been done by the Storms and Winds that had been—

Then I thought I went out of the Feild and went into an Arbor of Grape Vines, and I thought they were very Plenty, Some quite Ripe Some Red and Some quite Green, then I thought I pluckt Some of the Ripe and begun to eat, and Said I did not like Grapes before I Married, but my Wife had learnd me and I liked them as well as her now. So I awakned—

The Interpretation as Appear'd to me was thus
The large Wheat field is the World the Diff^t Shares, are the Diff^t Religions, to which I shall be Sent to be a Labourer amongst, Some being Reap'd and Some being left not fit to Reap, are those that some labourers have brought to the Blessed truth, and those that would not hear are yet left in the Ways of the World. Some being Shaken out, and Some but a Shew are those that have fallen away with temtation and trials, and the chaffy part that Stands are those that make a shew of Religion but have not the Substance tho' the{re} be good amongst them, being full and Ripe to receive the Blessed truth The Grape Vines Appear'd to me to be the People call'd Quakers, Some of Which are good, Some Luke Warm, and Some quite Green and without the knowledge of the Blessed Truth tho' they profess it, and my Loving Grapes thro marryin{g} my Wife, Shews thro her I first became aquainted with the Profession, in which I pray God of his infinite Goodness to make me Perfect—
                Geo: Walton

Interpretation of Dreams

It is reasonable to agree with Walton that his dream of searching for a meetinghouse was a product of his personal coming to terms with his new religious profession and the new way of life it demanded. Carla Gerona notes that among eighteenth-century Friends "much of the dreamwork featured something akin to a 'very spacious house' high on a hill that represented 'the mansion of rest and happiness' and signaled an individual's or a meeting's state with respect to God."[5]

We can also see that on a less conscious level the dream indicated that a focal point of Walton's new religious commitment would be his participation in the campaign to put an end to Quaker involvement in the injustice of racial slavery. Part and parcel of Walton's joining the Society of Friends was his taking to heart the belief in the equality of all people in the sight of God.

Walton dreamed that a black boy helped him defeat a man who threatened him with a big stick. He interpreted this part of his dream as Christ's enabling him to invoke the Holy Spirit and thereby defeat the wiles of Satan. Walton, however, appears to have been unaware of how revolutionary it was for an eighteenth-century North American white man to write the sentence, "The small black boy at my right hand is Christ."

In contemporary American culture, the color black, rather than being associated with the divine Savior who would lead one to paradise was more often associated with Satan, who would drag one to hell. Such was the case in a dream recorded just three years before Walton's—although it had been experienced many years earlier. When Walton's distinguished Quaker neighbor Thomas Nicholson was a young man, he dreamed of a "great & dreadful fire" out of which "proceeded something of a black colour," which he sensed was the devil. In the dream the black creature threw Nicholson into a lake of fire, which he took to be hell. Nicholson heeded this dream as a warning against wasting time in vain pursuits such as "Jesting . . . , fidling, & dancing, & singing." Yet given that elsewhere Nicholson argued that for the sake of their own souls slave owners should free their slaves even if they were likely to be re-enslaved, it is easy to interpret the thing "of a black colour" that cast Nicholson into the torments of hell as representing African Americans, the ownership of whom led to the destruction of the slave owner's soul.[6] In contrast to the general identification of the color black with the devil, Walton said that Christ was represented in his dream as black "to show how much the Devil is exalted and Christ abased."

While Walton's case seems to confirm historian Mechal Sobel's conclusion that Quakers made use of dreams to help them through life-changing decisions,[7] it also supports historian Carla Gerona's deduction that the dreamers "in turn recognized that their transformative experience might move others in the community to change themselves." The practice of writing down one's more powerful dreams and sharing them with others in order to influence them or solicit interpretations was an integral part of Quaker culture of the period. Friends regularly circulated these written dream accounts and even published those that were approved by the Society of Friends.[8] Walton shared his dreams with his fellow religionists in order to light in them the same fires of commitment to righteousness that had been enkindled in him.

Soon after he joined the Society of Friends, Walton became active in the movement among Friends to set their slaves free and took a leadership role in the movement for several years following.[9] Walton joined the Society of Friends when the agitation of the issue of slaveholding was reaching a pivotal juncture in the affairs of the North Carolina Friends Yearly Meeting.

That agitation centered on the Perquimans Meeting, which he was joining. In 1768, the North Carolina Yearly Meeting advised its members against buying and selling slaves for the purpose of engaging in the slave trade. In 1772, it forbade engaging in the commerce of slaves with non-Friends, "Excepting it be to Prevent the Parting of man and wife or Parent and Child, or for other good Reasons as shall be approved of by the monthly Meeting." Friends were to be careful not to "sell a slave to any Person who makes a Practice of Buying and Selling for the sake of Gain, without Regarding how the Poor Slave may be used, or the great Evil of Seperating man and wife or Parent and Child." In 1773, the yearly meeting required members to obtain approval of the monthly meeting before buying and selling slaves between Friends and forbade the buying of slaves from non-Friends under any circumstances.[10] Presumably disallowing the selling of slaves to slave traders but allowing such sales among Friends derived from the desire to avoid the cruelty of breaking up of families and the sexual promiscuity encouraged by the tearing apart of families.[11]

The yearly meeting had done little on the issue of the morality of holding slaves (as opposed to the issues of buying and selling them) before 1772 other than to state that owners should treat their slaves well. In that year, however, the yearly meeting took up the issue of how to advise Friends who wanted to free their slaves, despite the law that forbade manumission without the consent of the county court. They failed to resolve the problem in 1772, for they could not reconcile two competing claims on the conscience: that of the requirement of obeying the law and that of the requirement of loving all men.[12] Perplexed by their predicament, they wrote to the London Yearly Meeting, which advised the North Carolina Friends to follow the Lord's promptings.[13]

Walton interpreted his dream of searching for a meetinghouse to relate to his commitment to the principles of the Society of Friends. Its timing and imagery make it clear, nonetheless, that the dream relates as well to Walton's wrestling with the issue of the enslavement of blacks. When Walton took to heart the ideals of the Society of Friends, he embraced antislavery as well, convinced that "the Blacks being kept in Slavery how contrary it is to truth and Holiness and the Spirit of Christ."

2

1774

George Walton's Letters on Slavery, with an Account of a Dream

In 1774, the Perquimans monthly meeting brought the matter of slaveholding before the yearly meeting as a practical and immediate problem. In April, Thomas Newby, a prominent Quaker and member of the yearly meeting's Standing Committee, expressed his "uneasiness" to the Perquimans monthly meeting about owning slaves and asked the meeting's advice on how to go about freeing them. The monthly meeting referred the matter to the yearly meeting, which referred it to the Standing Committee. The Standing Committee determined that any Friend who wished to free his slaves could do so with the permission of his monthly meeting. The monthly meeting was to appoint a committee to determine if the persons for whom freedom was proposed were in a position to support themselves, and if they were, to draw up manumission papers. Thomas Newby's quandary was now returned to the hands of the Perquimans monthly meeting. But the committee that the monthly meeting appointed to consider the matter found it too weighty a matter to decide in haste and postponed a decision. Newby continued to own slaves and his conscience remained troubled.[14]

George Walton Promotes Manumission

During the summer of 1774, George Walton wrote a letter to Newby, a fellow member of the Perquimans Friends' Meeting, regarding Newby's inclination to free his slaves. In the letter, which is reproduced below, Walton attempted to persuade Newby to proceed with freeing his slaves, even if that action was contrary to the law. He explained to Newby, "I have been

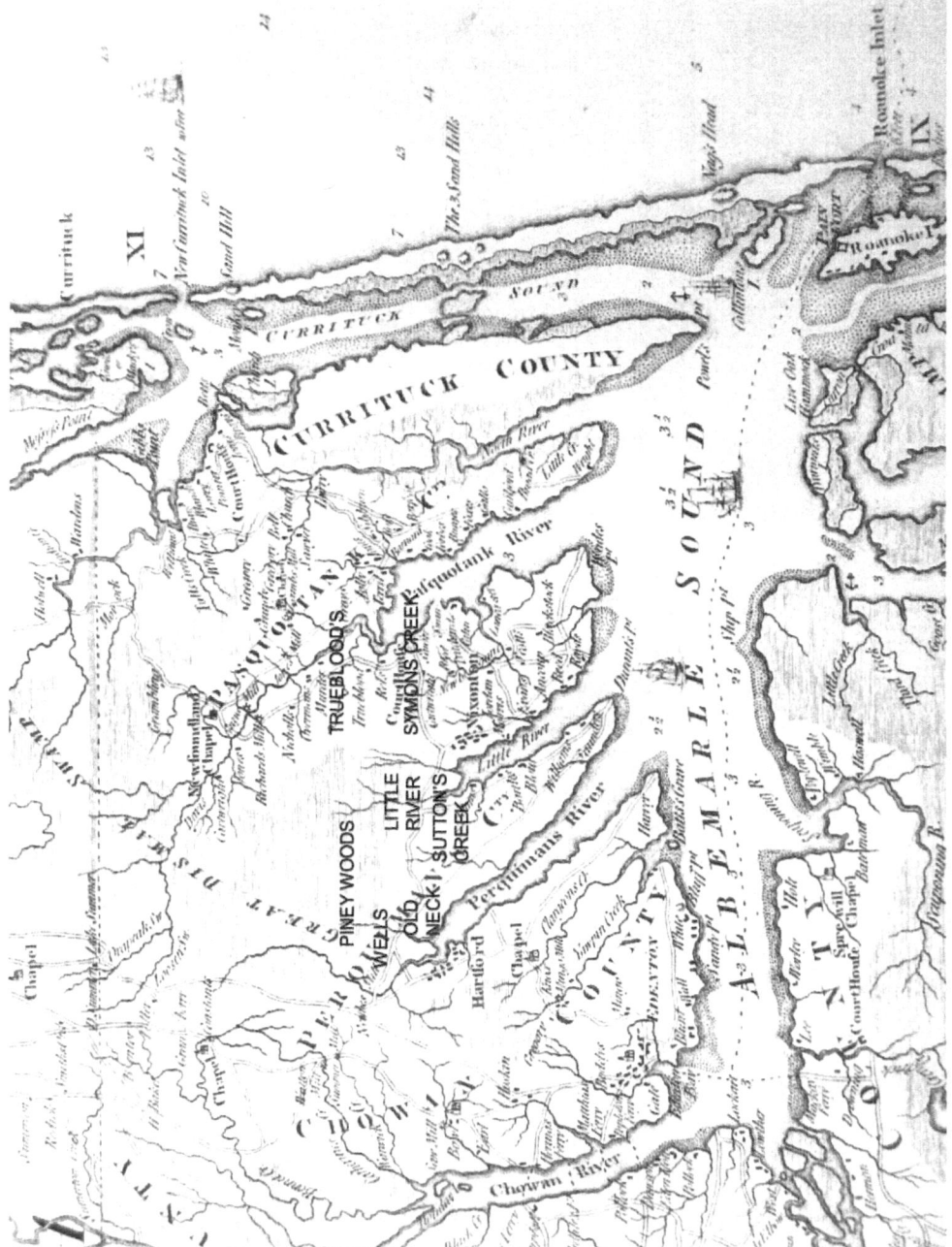

"Eighteenth-Century Quaker Meetinghouses in Pasquotank and Perquimans Counties," by Michael J. Crawford, using a detail from "An Accurate Map Of North And South Carolina With Their Indian Frontiers. . . . From Actual Surveys By Henry Mouzon And Others. London," Printed for Robt. Sayer and J. Bennett . . . May 30th 1775. In his journal, George Walton mentions seven meetings and their meetinghouses in Perquimans and Pasquotank Counties. All were located along rivers or creeks. The Perquimans River, which runs from northwest to southeast, bisects Perquimans County. Three of the meetinghouses were strung along the river's east bank, beginning near its headwaters: Piney Woods, Wells, and Old Neck. These were all meeting places of preparative meetings—that is, local meetings—of the Perquimans monthly meeting. Little River Meetinghouse stood on the west bank of the Little River, which is the boundary between Perquimans and Pasquotank counties. Although it was located on the west bank of the Little River and in Perquimans County, the Little River Meetinghouse was the meeting place of the Pasquotank monthly meeting, which included preparative meetings at the remaining three meetinghouses Walton mentions, all of which were in Pasquotank County: Symons Creek, on a tributary of the Little River; Newbegun Creek, on a tributary of the Pasquotank River, the eastern boundary of the county; and Trueblood's. The last is probably the Trueblood located to the west of the Pasquotank River above the point where it dramatically narrows.

brought under a grea{ter sen}se of the poor Blacks captivity then ever I was before; and I {believe it} my duty to communicate it to thee, hoping it might be of some {use} for the propagating of truth and their freedom." Walton reported finding Newby "fully convinced and a true promoter of" black manumission. "But," Walton continued, "I still labor under a fear that self interest or the desire of not getting the ill will of men of Account (as they are called in this world) will hinder him and many more from persevering in the work they have begun."

Immediately after delivering the letter encouraging Newby to free his slaves, Walton began a campaign to persuade other Quakers to set their slaves free. The day after delivering the letter to Newby, he informed Francis Jones, a public Friend,[15] that he had done so in a letter duplicated below. Walton urged Jones to share the letter to Newby with other Friends who might be encouraged to free their slaves.

Just four days after delivering the letter on slavery to Thomas Newby, Walton had another dream about enslaved blacks. A central figure in this dream was a black man recently arrived from Africa "who could Scarcely Speak English." Walton would have had frequent contact with blacks born in Africa; during this period, roughly a third of North Carolina slaves were Africans.[16] Walton reported this dream in a second letter to Jones. The dream reflects the important place that blacks and their enslavement had taken in Walton's psyche, for the dream, he reported, "has brought me under deep thought concerning the workings of divine providence, and my firm belief {that the} Blacks will become a people in which God will be glorified, and show forth his power."

Letters on Slavery

Source: Papers of George Walton, Accession No. 3988, Americana Collection, National Society Daughters of the American Revolution, Washington, D.C.

{Epistle to Thomas} Newby, concerning the Blacks being kept in Slavery, how contrary it is to truth and Holiness and the Spirit of Christ—

Most Esteemed Friend
   Since my Departure from North Carolina I have been brought under a grea{ter sen}se of the poor Blacks Captivity then ever I was before; and I {think i}t my Duty to communicate it to thee, hoping it

might be of some {use} for the propagating of truth and their freedom; God has heard their cries[17] and seen their Affliction and will certainly deliver them from under the Yoke of Bondage; Therefore bow down before him while he Mercifully calls unto you by his Servants, and handmaids as he did unto Pharaoh, by Moses and Aaron; and harden not your heart as he did, lest you also be in like manner Afflicted. for it Seems to me their Bondage may be very rightly compared to the Children {of Isra}els; for the Children of Israel were a free People in their own Cou{ntry as} are the Blacks. Joseph was Sold by his Brethren to the Ishmalites, and they sold him into Egypt, a land of Darkness. The Blacks were also Sold by their Brethren, to Some Merchants who may Justly be compared to the Ishmalites and they brought them to Sell amongst us. Oh, is our land to become like Egypt, and are we to be like Egyptians, to dwell in a land of darkness; Open your Eyes my {bre}thren and see where you are lest the judgements of God come upon you unawares, and there be none to deliver. Remember God Sufferd the Egyptians to afflict them four Hundred Years, and in that time no doubt but the Egyptians look'd upon them to be their lawful Servants, as well as you do the Blacks; therefore they harden their hearts, and thought they could not loose so much Worldly Interest, they would rather Suffer the Judgements of God, tho' they were often warn'd, yet the love of Worldly Interest kept them from yeilding to the Commands of God tho' they knew his Anger was kindled at their hard heartedness and Rebellion.—And it is much to be fear'd, there are Some in this our land whose Eyes it has pleas'd God to open, yet they rebell against the light made manifest to them, and Say thus within themselves; I can't part with So much Worldly Interest lest become Poor, my Children must Suffer Want, tho' I know {*line missing*} and myself require it, {I pray God} will forgive me if it be wrong. It is to be feard I say there are some such as those in the land. Oh! Deceive not yourselves with such vain delusions, for this is the Work of the Enemy, who is striving to keep you still in your Sins, and is as unwilling to let you out of Spiritual Bondage, as you are to let the Blacks out of outward Bondage. But the blessed truth will have no Such coverings, all worldly {*manuscript torn*} must be trodden under foot and all excuses that tend to {*manuscript torn*} Interest laid aside, that the everlasting truth may be ex{alted a}bove all. Woe! to the Rebellious Children that take counsel but not of me, and cover with a

Covering but not of Spirit Saith the Lord, that they may add Sin to Sin.[18] And Remember our blessed Lord Said, Seek ye first the Kingdom of God and his rightousness, and all other things shall be added unto you;[19] and he says again he that loveth father or Mother, Son, or Daughter, Wife or Children, or even his own life more then me is not worthy of me;[20] O{n the} contrary this is to the Royal law our Blessed Lord gave, ({*manuscript torn*} weigh it in your own Breasts) To do unto all men as you would have them do unto you.[21] Would not you think it very hard to be forced from your Native Country, and carried into a Strange land, and there to be kept in Bondage during life and consider by Birthright the Blacks are a free people as well as we, and God created all mankind for his honour, and Glory, and to Shew forth his Power; therefore we are not to Judge them because {they} are Black, or to bring into Bondage those whom God created free for we do not read one man was to be in Bondage to another, but every man was free for himself and to get his Bread by the Sweat of his Brow.[22] And if some Wicked man who had not the fear of God in him brought them first from their own Country, being Greedy of worldly Gain, is that any reason that we who have the fear of God in our hearts, should join in this unchristian Action, for there are neither bond nor free, Male, nor female, but all one in Crist Jesus, for the Spirit of Christ opens the Prison Doors, and Sets the bond Servant free.[23] I^h 61st[24] and if it has pleas'd God to open our Eyes, and Enlighten us by his divine Spirit, we ought to become as a City Set on a hill that can't be hid,[25] and Manifest ourselves to the World, that others being thereby convicted in themselves, may follow our example, Seeing our good Works, and Glorify our Father which is in Heaven, for tho' the Wicked Join hand in hand he Sha{ll} not go unpunished,[26] for God is of purer Eyes then to behold In{iquity.}[27] Oh! strip yourselves of all Worldly coverings and do not weave the Spiders Web, for it shall not become Garments, all Worldly coverings are to Short and to narrow, to hide you from the Eyes of the all wise God for he Searches the Heart and the veins; all outward shew or formal Cerimonies avail nothing if the Heart is not right with God, and be asured if any man Suffer his Heart to go after this World, or Set his Affections on any thing below, his heart is not excepted with God For remember that it is Written If any man love the World, the love of the Father is not in him[28] and what would it Advantage a Man to gain the Whole World and loose his own Soul.[29] Consider how Precious the Soul of Man is in the Eyes of God, that his only Son forsook his throne of Glory, and came down amongst wicked men Suffering Persecutions, revilings, mockings, Scoffings, Spittings Buffetings Scourgings, and even the Painful, and Shamefull Death of the Cross, to Redeem Sinners and Do we so lightly regard his Sufferings, and manifold Mercies {he} from time to time bestows on us; and the Salvation of our own Souls that we cant obey his divine Commands, and follow the Meek and humble example he set us, forsaking all the fading and transota{ry allur}ements of this World which must Perish, and Striv{e to store} up treasure in Heaven[30] that is lasting, and our Joy not man taketh from us.[31] And not always live in Sin and transgression contrary to his divine Command, for Christ says if you die in your Sins where I am you can't come[32] for nothing that is impure or unclean can enter into the Celestial city. Therefore Pursue the Work you have well begun in proclaiming liberty to your Brethren and turn not back again in your hearts as the Jews did and bring them again into Bondage therefore God proclaimed them to the liberty of the Sword of the Pestilence and of the famine, Jer^h 34th 15. 16. 17. For be asured the hire of the labourers who have reap'd down your feilds which is of you kept back by fraud crieth;[33] and the cries of them which have reaped are enter'd into the ears of the Lord God of Sabaoth, who will reward every one according to his Works for there is no respect of Persons with God.[34]— Some may be ready to say the Law is against our Seting them free, So that if we are willing the law wont let us. But know this O Man whoe'er thou art the law of God is not to be Subject to the law of Man, if contrary to truth & holiness, for God by his covenant of Grace has put his law in every mans heart and writ it in his inward Part, So that we are all left without excuse, from the Greatest to the least, and if Man for Worldly Interest has made a law contrary to the law of God writ in our hearts we can't be Subject to it for consience Sake, lest we fall into condemnation—We read that King Darius made a Decree that no one Should ask any Petition of any God, or man, but of him for thirty days Yet we find Daniel did not regard it, but Prayed unto God three times a day as usual, altho' the Decree was that whoever broke it, Should be cast into the Lions Den, but he feared God and chused rather to obey him then Man, knowing that he was able to deliver him from the Jaws of the Lion's,[35] And the three Children chused rather to be cast into the burning firery furnace then to fall down and Worship the Golden Image which Nebuchadnezzer has Set up, because it was contrary to the law of God writ in there Hearts, therefore they could not be Subject to it[36]—Look at our Blessed Lord, and his Apostles, how they were Persecuted for the truth's Sake; And look at the first rise of friends, how they were Persecuted, Imprisoned, Stock'd Whip'd, Suffer'd the Loss of lands, and Spoiling of Goods because they could not for Consience Sake be Subject to the corrupt laws, and vain Customs and traditions of Men, contrary to the law of God writ in their hearts, therefore they took the Spoiling of their Goods joyfully, counting them all as Dung, So that they might win Christ; knowing that this light affliction, which is but for a Moment worketh for them a far more exceeding and eternal weight of Glory whilst they lookd not at things that are Seen but at things that are not Seen, for the things that are Seen are temporal but the things that are not Seen are Eternal.[37] And they Remembred our blessed Lord Said, if they have persecuted me, they will also Persecute you[38]—for they that are born after the flesh Persecute them that are born after the Spirit. Therefore let me intreat you to take example by those Apostles and Saints that are gone before, and fear not them that after they have killed the Body have no more that they can do, but fear him, that after he hath killed, can cast both Body and Soul into Hell; Yea I say unto you fear him, and Stand Stedfast, unmoveable always abounding in the Work of the Lord, for as much as you know that your labour is not in vain in the Lord;[39] and quit yourselves like men, and be Valient Soldiers for the truth under Christs Banner; for I firmly beleive their is a day of firery tryall coming upon the land; that the Children of God may be purg'd and purify'd from the filth and Corruptions of this Wicked world, by the Spirit of Judgment and by the Spirit of Burning,[40] So with my Prayers to the most high God to uncover every heart, that they may See their own Corruptions; I wish Grace, Mercy, and truth, to all that love our Lord Jesus Christ in Sincerity—

    Geo: Walton

P.S. If thou think it worthy, I should be willing it might be communicated to Friends, for I travail much in Spirit for Sions Prosperity, tho' I have too long conceald it I ought to have manifested myself to the World long ago—and not have left the Lords work undone to the last—

I did not Send this Epistle to him from the West Indies, for I neglected the first Opportunity that offer'd, by being busied about worldly Affairs; so was not admitted another Oppertunity; but I deliver'd it to him the 11th of the 8th M^o 1774 before I Saild for Philadelphia for I could not be easy in my mind, or go to Sea contented till I did it—

A Coppy of a Letter to Francis Jones (a publick Friend) before I Sail'd to Philidelphe; on Delivering the Epistle to Thos. Newby—12th 8th M^o 1774

Most beloved Brother in Christ Jesus our Lord

I congratulate the{e} with this, to Inform thee I have deliver'd that Epistle to Thos Newby, which upon delivery I read to him, as he seem'd to have a desire to know what was in it, but upon reading it, made no reply I remember only a Sigh; But after Some pause we enterd into discourse on the Subject, and I find him fully convinced and a true Promoter of it. He has sent a Letter by me to David Ferriss[41] to know his Oppinion how to proceed, which he deliver'd to me before I deliver'd mine, So that he had no colour or Pretence in the Matter. But I still labour under a Fear that Self Interest or the desire of not getting the ill will of men of Acc^t (as they are call'd in this World) will hinder him and many more from Preservering in the Work they have begun. Therefore in the Name of Christ Jesus our Lord (for whom my flesh is Dead, being bound and crucified from the Alurements and Pleasures of this World) I beseech thee as a true Yoke Fellow in the Vineyard of our great Master not to Flinch from the heat of the Day, but put in thy Sickle and cut down those weeds or Evil Spirits that may be Obsticles or interpose in the Way of truth; for if the Children or those that are brought into that State hold their tongue, the very Stones will Speak; For now is the time of tryal that the Kingdom of Christ must be exalted, and the Whore and false prophet cast into the lake that burns with fire and Brimstone—Therefore fear not, but proclaim aloud the day of the Lord, and warn them to Speedy repentance, that thou may redeem thy Soul, for if thou hold thy peace their blood will be required at thy hands. Therefore let me intreat thee if he neglect to shew it to any Friends, that those would add one Spark to increase that light that now So dimly Shines, and According to the Ability given to thee, move all those that profess the truth, to put Speedily in practice what they have So long hessitated about, lest the day of their Vissitation be withdrawn; for I firmly believe if they Slight and neglect Gods favours from time to time, they, like the Jews, will be cast off, and another people will come in and finish the Work that is now begun; God has Said it, and will not Repent, that he will not give his Glory to another, neither his Praise to Graven Images;[42] Therefore he is Glorified by none but those that perform his will, in truth Sincerity and humbleness of Spirit, and Atributes all Praise Glory and Honour to his Name; to such as those he does and will manifest his Glory, But those that put aside the day of their Visitation and follow the desires of their Hearts and the Work of their own Hands, he will not Manifest himself; for by such Worshippers he is neither Praised or Glorified acceptably; but all such, as unprofitable Servants must be cast into outer darkness[43]—

If I err in any part, or Seem to Speak too Severe, excuse me for it is not to Shew myself, or to exalt the flesh, but as the Spirit giveth utterance So I speak—

I salute thy family and all Friends in Love in Christ Jesus our Lord, and Greet thee with a Kiss of Love in the truth remaining one that labours in Spirit for Sions Prosperity

    Geo: Walton

A Coppy of a Letter wrote to Francis Jones from Oakrecock Bar upon my Dream on the 15th Inst—

Most Beloved Friend   18th 8th M^o 1774—

In a Measure of that Seed which changeth not, I salute thee with Brotherly Love, to inform thee of my good Health for which I return daily Praises, to Almighty God, and pray that thou, and all Mankind may enjoy the Same, but especially those that beleive in the truth as it is in Christ Jesus our Lord, for we are commanded more especially to love the Brethren. Since my Departure from thee I have had a Dream, or rather I may Say a Vision, that deeply affect{ed} my mind, and I thought it would give me Some releif to communicate it to thee, knowing thy gift is great in Spiritual things.—

On the 15th Inst In the day time laying upon my Bed (as I had been up great part of the Night) I dream't a black man Seemingly one that had not been long from his own Country, who could Scarcely Speak English, came up in a very humble Manner, to two Ancient Friends, who Seem'd to be Elders, whom I thought I was well aquainted with, but I do not remember their Names, the Black Seem'd to be Weeping, and told them he was very much troubled at those Wars, and fightings, and beg'd them to keep out of them; So departed{.} I standing just by thought I did not understand him distinctly therefore ask'd the Friends what he Said, and they told me over again, to which I answered (being under great trouble of Mind, So that my heart Seem'd So full I could hardly Speak) this is come upon them for their pride, and haughtiness, and Setting at nought that meek and humble Spirit, that would have preserv'd them from those things, and have forsaken the Lord the fountain of Living Waters, and hew'd themselves out broken Cistrens, Cistrens that will {not} hold Water;[44] upon which the Mate awaked me, for which I was very Sorry, for my Dream Seem'd Sweet and refreshing to me, I felt the devine presence of the Lord to be nigh unto my Soul. This my Beloved Friend has brought me under deep thought concerning the Workings of Devine Providence, and my firm belief {that the} Blacks will become a People in which God will be Glorified, and Shew forth his Power, for the Knowledge of the Lord must cover the Earth as the Water's cover the Sea—And concerning those fightings and Divisions amongst the People it is because they have erred from the Spirit of God, and gone a Whoring after there own inventions, therefore God has given them over to a Reprobate Mind,[45] and they follow the lusts of their own hearts, Remember my Blove'd friend, Boston in a more Rigouros Manner Persecuted the Servants of the Lord, then any other place, So the judgments of God are come upon it more severely. But be asured there is a day of firey tryall coming upon the Land, that the Children of God may be tryed and purified, purer then Gold Seven times try'd in the fire; for they have liv'd in Pleasure and fulness of Bread, and So are become Wanton, and done despite to the Spirit of grace;[46] I could write much for my Spirit is heavy Buthened, but time won't permitt, therefore I shall conclude, recomending thee to that Seed of God in thy own Breast, to Interpret fully those lines, and Remain thy Sincere friend and a lover of truth.

    Geo Walton

I salute thy family in Brotherly love, and Greet thee with a Kiss of Love; Farewell for I am in great hast, the Vessel is now under Way.—

In the 10th M^o 1774 It pleas'd God of his infinite Mercy and tender Love to my soul, to open my mouth in Publick to Set forth the praises due to his great and Glorious Name, and declare to his People what he had done for my soul, and to Warn the Wicked from the Evil of his Ways, that they might flee from the Wrath to come;[47] O, the strivings that was in my Breast before I gave up, but the peace I felt afterwards is unspeakable and not to be conceived by any, that has never tasted thereof.—

May I never forget his Mercies nor blot the Remembrance of his tender Love out of my Mind but declare his Wonderful Works to the Generations to come—

3

1775–1777

George Walton's Journal from 2d, 6th Month, 1775,
to 12th, 10th Month, 1777

George Walton played a leading part not only in the movement to persuade Friends to free their slaves but also in the confrontation with North Carolina's government that the manumissions precipitated.

Night Patrols

In mid-1775, hoping to prevent slaves from responding to Loyalist urgings to rise and free themselves, local authorities in North Carolina's Albemarle region decided to increase the number and frequency of night patrols and called on all adult male residents, including Quakers, to participate in the patrols. When he was appointed captain of one of the company of patrollers, George Walton refused to serve and counseled fellow Quakers to follow his example.

The colony of North Carolina had formally established slave patrols in 1753.[48] In the earlier part of the eighteenth century, when the free white population outnumbered the more than two thousand slaves by a factor of two or more, the colonial government deemed more casual forms of control adequate. When the economy expanded in the middle of the century, the proportion of slaves in the population increased; in some areas there came to be twice as many enslaved persons as free whites. To the white residents, an established mechanism for preventing slave rebellion appeared essential to their security.[49]

In North Carolina the county courts appointed slave patrollers, drawing their names from county tax lists and militia rosters. Only property owners were appointed. The original duty of North Carolina's patrollers was to search slave quarters for weapons. Eventually their responsibilities expanded to include dispersing slave gatherings and patrolling roads in order to question slaves on the roads and detain those that did not have the pass required by law.[50]

When the county court appointed members to a patrol, it named one of them the unit's captain. The captain exercised responsibility for deciding on which nights, in which locations, and by what routes the unit would operate. He also kept a record of participation in patrols. That the county court appointed George Walton a patrol captain indicates that the court recognized in him leadership abilities and a degree of social importance. By turning down the appointment, Walton exposed himself to fines for noncompliance and sacrificed a 40-shilling tax exemption as well as exemption from militia, jury, and road work duty. In 1779, the assembly increased the penalty for not serving to one hundred pounds.[51]

Walton objected to Quaker participation in the patrols since it was wrong to deny fellow human beings their natural freedom and because participation in the patrols would inevitably involve Quakers in the use of violence—in contravention of Quaker pacifism—while subduing blacks found violating curfew or when putting down blacks in open revolt. Quakers, Walton pointed out, had no more justification for taking up arms to resist blacks than they had for joining the army to resist British tyranny.

It is not known how many Friends followed Walton's lead and refused patrol duty. Records do indicate, however, that North Carolina Moravians, whose views on the resort to violence were similar to those of the Quakers, did not have scruples about stockpiling arms to use in case of a slave uprising during the Revolution or about serving on night patrols during the War of 1812, even though in both wars they refused to take up arms against the British.[52]

The journal is published here in its entirety.

The Journal Begins

Source: Papers of George Walton, Accession No. 3988, Americana Collection, National Society Daughters of the American Revolution, Washington, D.C.

2^d 6th M^o 1775 I went to the Yearly Meeting in Virginia in Company with our Friends Francis Jones, Moses Bundy, Joseph Newby, and Some other private Friends, and it was a time of great probation to our Ministers, they not having Certificates from the Monthly meeting (as it had not been customary to require one only to go to a Meeting in Virginia and so streight back) met with cool reception; from the Elders of that Meeting. there was there Saml Hopkins[53] from Philedelphia Hannah Reves from the Jerseys and another woman freind from the Jerseys I don't Remember her Name, all Publick, Benjamin Sharper, Joshua Thompson[54] and Joseph Jenny their Companions.—

Sixth Mo. 1775} About this time there was a great {*illegible*} the People about Negros Rising, and they appointed Patrollers to go about in the Night to {watch} them; I had an Order given me to act as Capt of one of the Companys, and all Friends in General without any Exception to Age or Quality (unless Minor's) were Appointed to Act; which brought a Concern on my mind lest Some might be drawn in without considering the Consequence of it, And I found it my Duty to lay it before Freinds; which I did after the Following Manner—

To all Friends that beleive in our Lord Jesus Christ and Love his inward Appearance—
Dear Friends
It is not to Shew myself Singular, or to Appear forward in the Affairs of the Church (but to ease my mind of an unexpected burthen I am brought under, and in Obedience to my Great Lord and Master the Prince of Peace) that I Salute you in this Manner; And I heartily wish that all that profess to be followers of him may in like manner be brought to a true Sense and feeling of the Darkness of the times and the Spirit of AntiChrist that now rules in the hearts of many—

What now lays heavy upon my mind, and I am about to lay before Friends' consideration according to the Ability given me Is concerning Friends undertaking to Act as Patrollers, without Strictly weighing and considering where it may end, and also from what Spirit it Proceeds, for it most certainly can't proceed from the Spirit of Christ Jesus to Usurp the Liberty of our fellow creatures, so far as not to Suffer them to go to See their Wives, or neares friends, but to take them up and have them Whip'd without committing any other crime, but only walking peacably along the Road, or being at Home (as it may Justly be call'd) with their Wives; Remember the Spirit of Christ is full of Mercy and Compassion, and tender Love to all Men, opens the

Prison Doors, and let the Captive go free, And how far is this from that Royal rule our Blessed Lord gave us, to do to all men as we would have them do to us.[55]

{We t}hat have So long profess'd to the World that we wanted to give them their entire Liberty, and now to usurp them in the Smallest part of it, and that with Rigour. But some may say this care is Necessary, lest they should rise, and take both our lives and Property's—This is so Shallow and naked an excuse for those that profess to be the true followers of Christ the King and Prince of Peace, who declares that his Kingdom is not of this World else would his Servants fight, that it may well be compared to fig leaves, to hide them from the Eyes of the all seeing God. And it comes so nigh doing our Endeavour to protect ourselves from any other outward Enemy by strength of Arm that for my part I can Scarce See any Difference; it all proceeds from one Spirit, even the Spirit of Anti-Christ; The same plea might with as much reason be made in Joining in all those Resolves that are made to protect ourselves against the King of England's invading our Propertys and Perhaps our Lives, and if it comes to that to take up Arms also.—But some may be ready to say there will be no need of taking up Arms in this Affair, I Answer, how is that Known. Suppose any one met with Negroes that resisted, and would not be dispersd what would be done then, would not they try to do it by Violence, Yea certainly, otherwise they would not be true in their Office and would disobey their Master that set them to Work; And if they did offer Violence, they certainly would disobey their Heavenly Master, who says we must Love and pray for our Enemies, and if any man Smite us on the one Cheek, turn the other also; and John tells the Soldiers to do Violence to no Man. But Suppose those Blacks Should openly Rise, when we had been Acting as Gaurds over them, would it not justly be expected that we should take up Arms to Subdue them, Yea certainly, for the Gaurds of all places are in the same rank with Soldiers, whether they be for the King or Commonwealth and where is the Difference in taking up Arms against one Enemy more then against another.—

Those that have truly known {co}ming to the Mountain of the Lord their Swords are beaten into plowshares and their Spears into pruning hooks, they can't kill nor destroy neither learn War any more,[56] but their Spirits that before were like Lions, Bears and Wolves, killing and destroying, are become as Lambs {le}d and Guided by the Spirit of Child that neither does, nor thinks harm to any one.

I wish Friends would weigh it d{ee}ply before they Join with it, and Consider where it may end; for it seems to be a Key to open a Door to bring friends to be more deeply connected in those troubles and Commotions that are now in the Nation, which I think we ought all to endeavour to keep out of.—

The Patrollers did not much concern me before, as not thinking Friends would have been requested to Act in any such Office, till first day last I had a ticket given me to act as Capt of one of the Companys, which I did not except, but returned it to the Person gave it me; but hearing since that Some Friends have begun to Act in that Office, and perhaps without deeply weighing what might be the Event, brings this burthen upon me and I am led to clear my mind after this manner—

For my part I beleive I can never act in any such Office with a cler Consience, and I hope thro devine asstance, not to do any thing that may bring Guilt to my Consience whatever I may Suffer, for according to the Apostles words, I am perswaded that neither Life nor Death principallitys or powers thro' devine Assistance, can be able to Seperate me from the Love of God which is in Christ Jesus our Lord.—[57]

If any should think I am too Severe, bear with me, for since it has Pleas'd the Capt of my Salvation to call me to the Battle of the Lamb, thro' his Assisting arm I am willing to be a Valient Soldier under his banner, and faithfully to obey his Command, And I pray that many more Valient Soldiers may list themselves under his Banner, and Stand faithfull for his Great Name, in this Day of Firey tryal and fierce Wrath of the Lord;—

If his wrath is gone forth the Plague is begun and it greatly behoves the Servants of the Lord to Stand between the Living and the Dead, Offering holy {Incense} to his great and Glorious Name, with Prayers and Intercessions, that he would be pleas'd to Spare his People and not cut them off in his Wrath.—So with my prayers to the most high God, to open the Blind Eyes, unstop the Deaf Ears, unloose the Dumb tounge and Soften the Hard hearts I bid you farewell, Directing every one to the Word of his Grace, which alone is able to Guide You in true Judgment, And remain a Sincere friend to all Mankind, and well wisher to Sions Prosperity

   Geo Walton—

P.S. I am perswaded if all Friends would do their utmost indeavour, to keep their Negroes at Home, and likewise to Order those from their Houses that were not on lawfull Business there might be a great Regulation in a Loving and Friendly Manner and without danger of Embrueing our hands in Blood.—

"Inconsistant with righteousness"

In the autumn of 1775, the Yearly Meeting determined that slaveholding was "inconsistant with . . . righteousness," and advised "all the members . . . who hold slaves . . . cleanse their hands of them as soon as they possibly can." George Walton's interest in the slavery question was by now apparent to the Quaker leadership, for he was appointed to the committee that drafted this resolution.[58]

Following the 1775 Yearly Meeting's resolution that all members end their involvement with slaveholding as soon as possible, the committee appointed by the Perquimans monthly meeting in 1774 to help Thomas Newby finally acted. It produced a document setting ten of Newby's slaves free, which Newby signed on 3 March 1776.[59]

The Journal from 17 June 1775 to 24 May 1776

17th of the 6th M^o 1775

About this time their was great Disturbance Between England and America and several Battles were fought at or nigh Boston which seems to be a fullfilling of the Dream I had on the 15th of the 8th M^o 1774. The Continent Enter'd into many Resolves against England and would Gladly have friends to Join with them, but by the mercy of the Lord and his Protecting Arm, they were preserv'd from medling with them{.} the Resolves were enter'd into Soon after their begun to be Disturbance between England & America in 1774—[60]

I now Continued at Home frequenting only our own Meetings and did not yet find it my Duty to travail abroad for as Yet I was but a Child in the Work of the Ministry—

On the 25th of the 8th Month 1775 begun our Quarterly Meeting at Pasquotank for Ministers and Elders, but I not being yet Recommended to the Quarterly meeting as A Minister, was not there on the 26th and 27th. the Meetings of Worship were very large and Many Weighty truths were declare'd amongst them, and I believe it was a humbling time to Some, tho there Seem'd to be many there that had a Spirit of lightness, & Airiness, and what was Said by way of Reproof Seem'd like water pour'd upon Rock it could find no Entrance in them{.} Religion being at a low Ebb with many nothing but outward Performances being left, nothing of the true Power or life to be felt in them—

On the 2^d of the 9th M^o We had a most Violent Storm of Wind & Rain So that no Person could ever Remember any like it Blowing down many Houses and Trees in Abundance the Corn was very much Destroy'd and fother {fodder?} was tore So that but very little was to be got, this brougt me under a Weighty Concern of Mind and I was humbly bow'd before the Lord under a Sense thereof, then it was open'd to me that God Judgements was over the Land for their Disobedience and Since the People would not bow in Mercy, he would cause them to bow in Judgement, for he would be Glorify'd by the Work of his Hands.

On the 2^d—4th day in the 11th M^o I went to Western Branch in Virginia[61] and was at their Monthly meeting on 5th day, on 6th begun their Quarterly Meeting for Ministers & Elders and Continued 7th & 1st days for Worship and I beleive it was a time of Comfort & refreshment, to the faithfull tho there were many of other {con}fessions; & Some Seem'd light & Airy—

On 2^d day I was at a Burial at Summerton[62] of a Child belonging to our Friend Elisha Copeland; that was burnt to Death, it was a very Solemn time, and many Weighty truths were Spoken to the Comfort & Encouragement of the faithfull, and Sharp Reproof to the Backsliders, warning them to prepare for their great & final Change, I think I never return'd from any Place with so great peace in my mind as I did from here. Glory be given unto God, to whom it is due—

The last 6th day in this Month our Quarterly meeting for Ministers & Elders begun at Well's and Continued 7th & 1st days for Worship I believe it was a time of Refreshment to many tho' there were many light & airy ones that seem'd to be dry & Barren, and did not know nor witness a Spiritual Refreshment by Assembling themselves together—

I now kept Close to meetings about Home and was at Some Burials—

27th of 1st M^o 1776 I went in Company with our Friend Moses Bundy to Virginia to the Marriage of Thos Winslow, with Ann Jordan, Daughter of Robt Jordan and the Meeting was very Comfortable & Solemn altho' I felt very Heavy and much Burden'd before I went in, under a feeling Sense of the Darkness of many there, but when I sat down to wait upon the Lord I witness'd myself to be refresh'd and was made able to clear myself, I hope to the Comfort of the well minded, and to the Exhortation of those that were afar off, and did not Yet Witness Christ the Hope of Glory to be in them and to know him to be the Way, the truth and the Life and that no Man could come to the father but by him;[63] and by Yeilding true Obedience to the leading and Guidance of his holy spirit in them

The {*manuscript torn*} day in 2{^{d} M^o} 177{6} {I attended a meeting} at Little River which was Solemn & Refreshing {to} the welminded our Fr{ien}d Able Thomas from {Penn}silvania attending it whose Service in Love was Comfortable & Edifying—

The 24th of the 5th M^o begun our Quarterly Meeting at old Neck which was a {*manuscript torn*} time to some and caused Greif of Heart; the

Soldiers c{om}ing and behaving very indecent about the House; yet the fai{thfu}ll were preserved still & quiet Our Friends William {*manuscript torn*} from Penslvania {*manuscript torn*} & also had several more meetings in the Parts very Comfortable & Edifying—

The Progress of Manumission

The most significant acts of the 1776 Yearly Meeting prohibited Friends from buying and selling slaves and appcinted a committee of eleven to help any Friends who wanted to free their slaves. The Yearly Meeting also instructed monthly meetings to protect freed slaves from re-enslavement. The Yearly Meeting agreed to pay associated legal costs. On receiving this advice, the Perquimans monthly meeting added six more members to the committee. George Walton was included in that number.[64]

In late 1776 and early 1777 Walton and other members of the committee visited fellow Quakers, encouraging them and helping them free their slaves. During that time, at least fourteen North Carolina Friends, including Walton, joined Newby in setting free their slaves. The fifteen men together liberated some forty slaves. Other Quakers were sympathetic but hesitant, and still others were unwilling.[65]

The Journal from 25 October 1776 to 29 March 1777

The 25th of the 10th M[o] 177{6}
Begun our Yearly Meeting which was large, and Continued till the 29th Which was an Affecting time I believe to many and the presence of the Lord was livingly felt & Witnessed to by many; It was Attended by our Friends Samuel Emlen[66] & {Samuel} Hopkins from philadelphie Mark Reeves[67] from Salem in the Jerseys & George Dilwyn[68] from Burlington all publick; also our Friend Edw[d] Stabler[69] from Virginia and many Friends from the Westward both publick & private requesting the Yearly Meeting to be Circular one Yeare in Perquimons the other to the Westw[d] but, it was refer'd till the next Yearly Meeting there was an Order passed that no Friend in Unity should buy or Sell any Negroe Nor hire them for a Term of Years so as to prolong their Bondage Neither hire any of such as were not in Unity with us. Also it was Advised that all Friends should Endeavour

to Cleanse their Hands of them as soon as possible and a Comittee was Appointed to Assist Friends in preparing Manumissions; as several then declare they were Convinced of the Evill practice and were willing to Release them. And that Comittee was to be joined by some others appointed by Each Monthly Meeting that were thought fit for such a Service. At our Ensueing Monthly Meeting after the Quarterly the following Friends were Appointed to Join our Quater of the Comittee Viz Mark Newby Wm Albertson Josiah White Exum Newby, Moses Bundy & myself

On the Seventh Nin{th and} tenth of the twelfth M^o Visited {frie}nds Up the River And {*manuscript torn*} one Manumitted their Neg{roes on} the North Side of the River {*manuscript torn*} low as Wm White's which were in Number Sixty th{*manuscript torn*} only two people on the South Side Released Eight of them But we found a great openness in the people and their Minds tender on that Acc^t.

21st of 2^d M^o 1777 Begun Quarterly Meeting of Ministers & Elders at Littl{e Riv}er in which Divine Comfort {was} witne{ssed} {22^d & 23^d} {*illegible*} meetings {for w}orship & I believe it was a Seasoning time to Many

24th I was at a Meeting at Newbegun Creek in Company with our Friends Thos Saint {and} Francis Jones & it was a Very tender time I believe {for} many and I hope Instructive to the Enquiring Soul—

25th We had a Meeting at Truebloods[70] there were but few Friends there but Yet {I believe} that it may be Rember'd by some many good Cau{tions} & Admonitions being given not to depend too much on Outward forms or Will Worship but to come to know & taste of the Life & Substance—this Night I got home—

26th Was our preparative Meeting at pineny Woods

27th Thos Newby. Caleb White Moses Bundy & I Visited Several Familey of Friends on the South side of the River on Acc^t of their Setting their Negroes Free and it was to us a Time of hard Labour & Travail meeting with Some that were much Blinded by the gain of Oppression and very unwilling to do as they would be done by. Yet some were tender & three were set free—

On the 22^d of ye 3^d M^o 1777

Our Friend Sarah Metcalf Appointed a Meeting for the Blacks and desired that Moses Bundy & I would be there if we found freedom which Accordingly we both were and it was a very tender time many good Cautions and Advices being given and I hope might prove of Service to some—

On the 29th We had a Meeting for the Blacks at pineny Woods and many good Counsels & Exhortation{s} were deliver'd and I beleive Some of the Blacks were tender and I hope may Remmerber the good Advice given them—

Re-Enslavement of the Manumitted Blacks

Viewing the wholesale manumission of blacks as both unlawful and irresponsible, the North Carolina General Assembly condemned the freeing of slaves as an "evil and pernicious Practice . . . {that} ought at this alarming and critical Time to be guarded against." The legislature enacted a law authorizing the seizure and sale of illegally freed slaves.[71] The Yearly Meeting's Standing Committee engaged lawyers to contest in court the application of the law retrospectively to slaves who had been freed before its passage.[72]

On 18 June, Walton, with Thomas and Mark Newby, attended a meeting of the court at Edenton, where lawyers engaged by the ad hoc committee established by the Yearly Meeting were going to argue in favor of the freedom of several manumitted former slaves whom freeholders had seized and turned over to the sheriff under the new law. Because the prosecution lawyers did not have an attested copy of that law, the trial had to be postponed. When the court reconvened at Hertford several weeks later, the court ruled against the freed slaves and ordered that they be sold to the highest bidder.[73]

The Journal from 20 May to 10 October 1777

On the 20th of the 5th M^o 1777 The Standing Committee met to consider of, and inspect into an Act made by the Assembly to take up all free Negroes, and to be Sold at publick sale at Court;[74] many having been taken up and people going about daily to take them up, And after much consultation it was refer'd to a future Sitting, not coming to any Determination; only it was thought it might be necessary to try the Virtue of the Act by Law, as it Seem'd not to be against Negroes allready Set free, but against them that should be set free here after.—

On the 30th Begun our Quarterly Meeting for Ministers and Elders at Old Neck. And we were Accompanied by John Pemberton from philadelphia,[75] and Edwd Stabler from Virginia.—

On the 31st Before Meeting of Worship the Standing Comitee met to Consider further about the Case of the Negroes and after a Seasonable Conference on the Subject it was thought best & safest to leave the Management thereof to a Comittee of ten Friends choosen out of the Standing Comittee.—

After the Comittee broke up, begun the Meeting for Worship and Business which was large and Comfortable—

1st of 6th Mo 1777 Being 1st Day the Meeting was large there being many of other Societies but all I believe behaved Well and I hope Some were edified and comforted—

15th Francis Jones & I was at a Burying of a Child of John Shepherds in Hertford County, at which was many people chiefly not of our Society, but all behaved well, and Some were tender, and I hope it will not Soon be forgotten, the Name of the Lord, & his power, being exalted above all.—

18th I attended Edenton Court in Company with Thos Newby and Mark Newby, two Negro Women being intended to be Sold on that day (as Notice had been given to their former Masters) but when we got to Edenton our Lawyers that were employ'd by the Committee of ten friends, inform'd us that our ~~Persecutors~~ Adversaries had no Attested Copy of the Act. Therefore it was not in the power of the Court to Sell them or to go upon their tryall they having no law to go by, So that we need not Stay on that Acc^t.

Whilst we were in town the parson of Edenton, Earll, by Name[76] came to me and Mark Newby and asked us what was our Motive for Setting them free, what law or Scripture had we for it. Mark Newby made him Several Suitable answers I do not distinctly remember, & I told him our greatest motive was to fulfill the Command of our Blessed Lord by doing to others as they would be done by[77] which no person could do, So long as they kept them Slaves for I believed that none of us would be willing to be slaves from which he and I enter'd into a pretty long Argument in which I believe he'll have nothing to Vaunt on, I ask'd him, if Christ had not said that he that put away his wife committed Adultery and he that taketh her committeth Adultery[78] to which he readily Answer'd Yes. I Ask'd him then if he did not think that those that parted Man and Wife made them to Committ Adultery and the Sin would lay at their Door. He Answer'd Stop I know not, perhaps that fellow was such a Rogue he could not keep him, we must do a Small evill to keep from a Bigger—I told him a Christian ought to live in no known Evill and that committing evill that good migt come on it which the Apostle Says God forbid,[79] he Said God forbid Also, then C{h}ang'd the discours to some other Branch So the dispute Held I believe near an hour

On Seventh Day; being 12th Of 7th M^o 1777—I set off for Virginia in Company with Francis Jones & Rachel & {illegible} White; and on first Day we Attended two Burials at Saml Bufkins—his Wife's Mother and his Eldest Daughter the Meeting was large being many of other proffessions it was an humbling time to Many & the Everlasting truth was declared with great Power Glory to God alone—We had an Evening Meeting at the Same House, mostly Friends, it was a very tender Comfortable Meeting and Friends were encouraged to trust in the Lord in all trials & probations which he in {h}is Wisdom might permit them to be tried with—

Second Day; we had a Meeting over the Western Branch⁸⁰ within five Miles of Portsmouth, at one Widow Hugh's there were no Friends about there nor none at the Meeting but what went with us, but it was a Tender Meeting as ever I remember to be at, the people were greatly affected I believe there were few dry Eyes in the Meeting especially among the Women, at our parting the Widow Hughs was very tender and Desired we might not forget them but would come again She believed it would be of great Service among them—and I beleive if they are Visited and they are careful to keep to there first Love there will be a Meeting Settled there in time Glory be to the Lord who is able to tender the hardest hearts and make them bow under his Mighty Power. I writ a few Lines to one Wᵐ Taylor who was in a low Condition advising him to keep close by the Grace of God and witness in himself &ᶜ—That Evening we went to our Friend Robᵗ Jordans—

Third day. In the Morning we cross'd Nancemund River and had a Meeting at John Densons in Chuckatuck.⁸¹ The Meeting was small but very Comfortable. Friends about there are much gone back again into the World and but a Small Remnant left. I lodg'd that night with John Denson and had much Di{s}course with him and found him a very tender Young Man and much affected with a feeling Sense of truth altho he lives remote from Friends and being only just come to his Estate there are many allurements to draw him aside but I think he is a hopeful Youth—

Fourth Day, we were at the Weekday Meeting at Westren Branch (Isle Whight County) which was also small there is a great Declension among Friends in Virginia altho' I hope they'l soon begin to increase again for there are many tender People—

Fifth Day, we had a Meeting at Summerton⁸² which was tender and Comfortable, there are some tender friends about that place—going from meeting to our Friends Elisha Coplands we had as sharp a thunder Shower as ever I remember to have been in and the thunder was a {illegible} the lightning seem'd to Strike amongst our Horses—Oh the Wonderfull goodness of God to his People and how are his Judgments mixt with Mercy toward the Workmanship of his Hands O that the Inhabitants of the Earth would learn Righteousness and fear and tremble before him—that Evening we Rode nineteen Miles to our Friend John Whiteheads in Southhampton County

Sixth Day, we had a Meeting at Vix's and tho' there are but few Friends thereabout yet the Meeting was pretty large and the people Seem'd tender, there was the parson and his Wife, and two Daughters he seem'd Much Affected with the testimony of truth and Seem'd loving after Meeting I believe there is a good Seed in him if it was not too much Stiffled by the Briers & thorns—

That Evening we had a meeting at John Whiteheads which was very powerful and Affecting the Everlasting truth was Exalted and the Ways thereof largely treated of—there was a Woman who had been brought up a Friend but by unwatchfulness had fallen away and to her last husband Married out, but it had pleased the Lord to visit her and bring her to a Sense of her Backslidings which brought her very low almost to despairs then she joined with the Baptists but found no true peace there. I had much discourse with her after Meeting and she was very tender, her Husband also was very tender and confessed he beleived Friends were in the rightest way of any people but the Way seem'd so narrow. We had much discourse on Baptism Plainness of speech and Honouring of Men alwhich I was enabled to open clearly to there understandings and the Man confessed to the truth thereof, the Woman seem'd much bewildred in her Mind and did not say Much. Glory be given to God alone, Who give Wisdom to babes and Sucklings, & hides it from the Worldly Wise and prudent.—

Seventh Day I got home again and found my family much better in Health then I left them Praises be given to God for Ever for his abundant Mercies and tender Regard to the Sons of Men—

On 21st of the 7th M^o 1777 Begun the Court at Hertford on ye 22^d the Negroes that were taken up were brought to tryal and altho' the Lawyers pleaded {much} and clearly shewed they could not sell them by {that} Act, it not being intended to look Back but only to hinder any more to be set free, and that it was contrary to the Constitution that any law should look back and therefore they must Violate the Constitution otherwise set them at Liberty and to Sell them by the former law that could not be, it being void at the time they were set free, by the Declaration of Independency and that also it was to be executed by the Church Wardens which were also out of Office,[83] and further that they should have had by the old Act Six Months Liberty to quit the Country before they could be lawfully taken up which those had not; therefore they had no law to Sell them by. But altho' things were so plainly and Clearly Demonstrated; yet by a Majority of the Court Jud{g}ement was given they should be Sold their were five Justices on the Bench three of which gave it their Judgement they should be sold Viz Jethro Ballard Wm Skinner[84] Christopher Rite and Jessey Perry, two would not Consent to it; viz George Whitbee and Jesse Heason. Accordingly the Next day twenty Nine were sold at publick Vendue at the Court-House— *

{2}9th of the 8th M^o 1777 Begun the Quarterly Meeting at Simon's Creek for Ministers & Elders in which Friends were exhorted & encouraged to trust in the Lord in the time of trial and affliction and he would Preserve them and Support them {illegible} & hide them as in the Hollow of his Hand till the Calamities were overpast it was a Comfortable refreshing time—

31st We had a large Meeting for Worship & Business Which was Weighty & Solemn and Business transacted with great Condescension & love one to another—

---

* According to the minutes of the Perquimans County Court of Pleas and Quarter Sessions, the judges present when the court opened at 9 A.M. on 22 July 1777 were Jesse Eason, Jesse Perry, William Skinner, George Whedbee, and Christopher Wright, but when the court resumed business after an hour's recess, Jethro Ballard had replaced William Skinner. The court minutes that refer to the case of the manumitted blacks reads simply: "Ordered that the Sheriff of this County Tomorow morning at the Hour of Ten oClock Expose to Sale to the Highest Bider for Ready money at the Court House door the Several Negroes taken up as free and in his Custody Agreeable to Law." The court minutes for the following day include the following: "Ordered that the Sheriff Hire out to the Highest Bider until the Next Court one Negro man Abraham Taken up as free and one of the Owners not having lawful Notices—Under the following Restrictions the Person hiring to give Security to See him forth Coming to the Next Court and for Payment of the Hire." The minutes for the July 1777 term are the only known minutes of the court for the period of the War of Independence. "Minutes of Perquimans County Court, July Term 1777," in *Perquimans County Historical Society Year Book 1975*, ed. Raymond A. Winslow, Jr. (Ahoakie, N.C.: Perquimans County Historical Society, 1976), 16, 22, 24, 31.

1st Continued for Meeting of Worship in which were many people of other Societys the Meeting was very large and Solemn and People in General seem'd to be Affected with the Declaration of truth, tho' some seem'd uneasy in time of Silence it being a Mystery hid from the Worldly Worshipers—

11th Of the 10th M^o I Attended the Funeral of two Children of Zachariah Copelands at Summerton in Virginia In Company with Francis Jones (which were Scalded to Death by the Still Cap Blowing off) the Meeting was Solemn & tender and the people seemed much Affected with the Declaration of truth and the Solemnness of the Occasion in which we were gathered—

12th Being 1st Day we had a Meeting at Stephen Shepherds in Sarum,[85] which was very Solid & Comfortable, and tho' there were few Friends yet the people seem'd much Affected & well Satisfied—In the Evening Francis Jones being Sick, I in Company with John Shepherd, his Wife & Sarah Copeland Visited the Widdow Baker (one of their Neigbours but not Friend) who was thought near Death by having a Cancer on her Cheek & her son Capt Wm Baker was also Sick at her House and his Wife being under a Concern of Mind for her Future welfare had a great Desire to have been at our Meeting but could not Attend by reason of the Sickness of her Mother in law and Husband, this made me the more Willing to go to Visit the Sick feeling my mind Unusually Burthened but I knowed not whether for her sake or her Sick Mother in Law, And After I got there John Shepherd & I went into Wm Bakers Room and John Shepherd's Wife and Sarah Copeland into the Widow's Room, and I thought there would be no Opportunity for me to speak to either the Old Woman or Capt Baker's Wife as I did not yet know which I was Burthen'd for, but under this Anxiety of Mind I cried unto the Lord in Secret if he would be pleased to make way for me if he had any thing for me to do and I was Willing to Wait his time, then under this resignation I found peace, Soon after John Shepherd Mentioned to Wm Baker he had a Desire to See his Mother, but Wm Seemed to put him off by telling him the Sight was Affecting and the Smell most Intolerable, this brought me again under trouble thinking there was no hopes of Opportunity of Speaking to either but Soon after Capt Bakers wife came out of her Mother in laws Room and Sat with us, then John Shepherd mentioned again he had a great Desire

to see her and Capt. Bakers wife said She would be very gald {*glad*} if we would go in for her Mother took it hard if any one came there and did not go to See her this made me to rejoice, hoping my way would be opend if my great Master had any thing for me to Do—Then Capt Bakers wife got up and went in before us and we followed, when we came to her Bed Side John Shepherd took her by the hand and asked her how she was, and if She knowed him, She said she was very poorly but she knowed him well. he said Some more words to her but she was to weak to talk much; So he bid her Farewell and took his leave of her. This deeply Affected my Mind as thinking perhaps it might be a last Farewell, and I could not refrain Weeping then I stept to her Bed Side and took hold of her Hand and Bid her farewell and Said altho' I was unknown to her in person, I travell'd with her in Spirit and my prayer was when she had done in this World she might find a resting place for her Soul, or words nigh to that Affect (for my mind was so Overwhelmed with grief I could scarce remember what I said) this made I believe every one in the Room burst out in crying, and Capt Bakers Wife standing by the foot of the Bed I took her by the Hand and bid her Farewell She wept greatly and held my Hand and would hardly let it go this filld my Heart so full I could no longer contain myself but snatchd my hand from her and stept out of the Door into a Middle passage to pour out my tears in Secret before the Lord. She soon came out into the passage to me and Said O she Wished she could have been at Meeting I said I wish she could; then my Heart was Enlarged towards her and the Opportunity I found was presented to clear my Mind of that Burthen I had felt. I then Declar'd to her that the True Worship which God required was Spiritual and not Carnal for God was a Spirit & must be Worshiped in Spirit, and it was the Spirit and Soul of Man that was to be cleansed and must enter into rest & not the Carnal Body therefore it
{*The journal ends here.*}

Aftermath

In 1778, the Superior Court reversed the 1777 County Court decision (see Part III, document 5). In 1779, however, a joint committee of the legislature found that "the conduct of the said Quakers in setting their slaves free when our open and declared enemies were endeavoring to bring about an Insurrection of the Slaves, was highly criminal and reprehensible," and the legislature specifically legalized the 1777 seizures and sales of the slaves the Quakers had freed and eliminated the six months' grace period.[86]

In 1779, the Yearly Meeting responded to the legislature's libel on the Quakers' motives for freeing their slaves by drafting a petition in which they explained that they had acted on their convictions that freedom was a natural right the blacks had not forfeited and that slaveholding was unchristian. The fifteen who had freed their slaves in 1777, including Thomas Newby and George Walton, signed on behalf of the meeting. However, on the recommendation of sympathetic legislators who advised that passions on the issue were at a high pitch, the Yearly Meeting chose not to present the petition. As the petition merits quotation at length and bears Walton's signature, its text is included in Part III, document 7, below.[87]

In 1777, the Perquimans Monthly Meeting recommended George Walton to the Quarterly Meeting of Ministers and Elders as "a minister with whom we have Unity," and each of the next three years selected him as their representative at the Quarterly Meeting. By 1778, Walton had risen so high in the esteem of his co-religionists that they appointed him to the Standing Committee of the Eastern Quarter, where they kept him through 1782. In his first two years on the Standing Committee, Walton served as clerk. In 1779 and in 1783, Walton was appointed to committees entrusted with presenting petitions on behalf of the blacks to the General Assembly. In 1779, the Quarterly Meeting appointed him to a committee charged with visiting families to encourage reformation of departures from order. In 1781, the Yearly Meeting asked him to serve on a committee to determine whether some writings of the late Thomas Nicholson[88] should be approved and circulated, and the Quarterly Meeting added him to a committee to which monthly meetings could apply for assistance in laboring with members who persisted in the practice of slaveholding. The following year, his monthly meeting put him on a committee that sought to persuade slaveholding members to free their slaves. And in 1785, Walton was a member of a committee appointed to lay before the Quarterly Meeting an account of expenses of some Friends who were seeking relief for certain slaves freed by Friends in North Carolina but imprisoned in Virginia and sold to pay prison fees.[89]

At the end of his dream of searching for a meetinghouse in December 1772, Walton dreamed that his fellow Friends asked him to lead them through the briars and thorns that blocked their way home. Walton subsequently not only became a member of the Society of Friends but also, as his dream foreshadowed, met the challenge of leadership in a time of difficulty, acting prominently in the movement to free the slaves his fellow Quakers held.

PART II

The Community

The Society of Friends in North Carolina Chooses Manumission

The Society of Friends in North Carolina had its origins in the 1670s in the Albemarle region. One hundred years later, the society had grown by natural increase and immigration to twenty-three monthly meetings. North Carolina's Friends gathered in two quarterly meetings, eastern and western. The North Carolina Yearly Meeting of Friends convened at Old Neck Meeting House in Perquimans County and communicated at least yearly with the Philadelphia and London yearly meetings.¹

The Quakers who lived in substantial numbers in the counties bordering the North Carolina sounds in the middle of the eighteenth century were mostly descendants of native-born converts to the faith rather than Quakers who had emigrated from elsewhere. Like their parents and grandparents, they were mainly simple farmers who grew up with slavery and accepted it as normal. Beginning in the 1750s, however, admonitions about the immorality of trading and owning slaves reached North Carolina from Quakers in the northern British colonies. Philadelphia Quaker abolitionist John Woolman, for instance, paid a visit to several North Carolina Friends' meetings in 1757. Although at first, according to his own report, he was diffident about speaking publicly against slaveholding—"[At Simon's Creek Monthly Meeting] I was silent during the meeting of worship, and when business came on, my mind was exercised concerning the poor slaves, but did not feel my way clear to speak"—he discussed the condition of the slaves privately with individual Friends. By the time he reached the Albemarle region, he had found more freedom to speak out, until, at Piney Woods, his last stop in North Carolina, he "was drawn forth into a fervent labour amongst them."[2] The response of the North Carolina Yearly Meeting to such outside influences was mild; it merely encouraged its members to examine themselves on the question of treating their slaves well.

During the 1760s, the antislavery sentiment emanating from Pennsylvania and other centers of Quaker influence in the North gradually awakened the consciences of North Carolina's eastern Quakers on the evil of slavery. Thomas Nicholson, one of the more influential Friends of Perquimans County, maintained a correspondence with Quaker reformers in Pennsylvania.[3] He had probably encountered Woolman during the reformer's visit to the Albemarle region in 1757. Later the same year, as a visitor to Philadelphia representing the North Carolina Yearly Meeting, he served with Woolman on a committee that considered the division of opinion among Pennsylvania Friends on the payment of taxes imposed to support the war with the French and the Indians.[4] In 1767, Nicholson issued an open letter urging his co-religionists to adopt a policy of gradual emancipation (see document 1, below). A second event that followed in quick succession brought about a change in the advice issued by the North Carolina yearly meeting. In 1768, the Western Quarterly Meeting at New Garden asked the yearly meeting whether it was permissible to buy and sell slaves. Many of North Carolina's western Quakers were immigrants from Pennsylvania and carried with them a strong antislavery sentiment. In response, the yearly meeting advised against buying and selling slaves for the purpose of engaging in the slave trade. In contrast, the Pennsylvania yearly meeting forbade the buying and selling of slaves for any reason.

In 1772, the Western Quarterly Meeting requested a clarification of the yearly meeting's stand on slavery, and the yearly meeting adopted a statement that forbade engaging in the commerce of slaves with non-Friends without good reasons approved by the monthly meeting. Friends were bid to avoid selling slaves to professional slave traders. That same year, in imitation of the Virginia Yearly Meeting, the North Carolina Yearly Meeting sent a memorial to the North Carolina House of Burgesses recommending a petition to the Crown against the importation of African slaves.[5]

The North Carolina Yearly Meeting hesitated in advising Friends who wanted to free their slaves in the face of the colony's law that forbade manumission without the consent of the county court. The court was restricted to granting such permission when a slave had earned freedom by some meritorious act or service. An even more restrictive law in force in Virginia during the period 1723 to 1782 likewise discouraged Quaker manumissions in the Old Dominion.[6]

1

1767

Thomas Nicholson Urges Gradual Emancipation

Thomas Nicholson (1715–1780), a prominent landowner, merchant, Quaker missionary, and author in Perquimans County addressed the following open letter to his co-religionists a year before the Western Quarter requested that the Yearly Meeting clarify the society's position on slave trading. The contents of Nicholson's letter, with its dual focus on the wrong that slavery does to the slave and the harm it does to the slaveholder, reflects the reform sentiment then spreading through American Quakerdom. Nicholson acknowledges the difficulty that the law presents to anyone seeking to free his slaves, but his proposal of a form of gradual emancipation does not offer a truly practical way around the legal hurdle.[7]

Thomas Nicholson's Open Letter to North Carolina Friends

Source: Society Miscellaneous Collection, Box 11, Historical Society of Pennsylvania, Philadelphia, Pennsylvania.

    6 mo. 1st: 1767
To any judicious and enquiring Friend
    I have for many Years been much distressed in my mind on account of Negroes remaining Slaves in our Society for several Reasons,
    First, being convinced in my Judgment that the Slave Trade is a very wicked and abominable Practice, contrary to the natural Rights and Privileges of all mankind, and against the Golden Rule of doing to others as we would be done unto.—
    Secondly, fully believing that they prove a Snare to Friends' Children, by being made use of as Nurseries to pride, Idleness and a

Lording Spirit over our Fellow Creatures, and oftentimes by their contrary Behaviour prove Provocations to Masters and Mistresses to anger Passion and unsavory Expressions to the wounding of their Spirits.—

Thirdly it appears to me to be a Contradiction to our peaceable Principle and Testimony against Wars and Fighting, under a Gospel Dispensation, to keep Captives taken by the Sword against their own free will and Consent, and that if our own negroes should ever be concerned in rising to endeavour to recover their Freedom it would be ungrateful in us towards our Fellow Subjects to refuse our Assistance to subdue them.

Fourthly where true Endeavours have been used to inculcate Principles of true Religion Piety and Virtue in them for the good of their Souls, it hath appeared to me to have had but a small effect and looks to me that it will remain to be the Case with all such in whom the Seeds of Discontent and uneasiness remain under a Sense of their State of Bondage and Slavery.—

Now let any thoughtful person seriously consider whether it is not reasonable to suppose that any person convinced in their Judgment of the above Evils and Difficulties, and at the same Time in possession (mostly by Inheritance and breeding in their Families) of eighteen or twenty of them aggravated by the Laws of the province to sell them at public Sale to the highest Bidder, and the Mony to be put to the use of the Parish, if freed by their Master or Mistress, excepting for meritorious Causes to be allowed of by the County Court, and I think they must Sympathize with me in my Distress of mind,

Upon the whole I think I can honestly say that on the Terms of any Expedient being fallen upon to let them have their Freedom on reasonable and lawful Terms I am willing to give up mine, and until such a Method can be fallen upon there is nothing that appears to me to be more safe and expedient in the present Distress than for those that have them (that are willing to live with them and behave themselves well) to keep them and use them well, and after a reasonable number of Years of Servitude to defray the Cost or Charges of raising them, to make them free under proper Guardians and Restrictions to keep them from becoming a public Charge or Offense to Government, and such as behave badly, and are not content to live with their present Masters or Mistresses, to be sold to other masters or mistresses, in which all reasonable Regard ought to be paid to the Choice of the said Slaves with their new master or mistress.

And as it is evident that the burnt Child dreads the Fire, and none knows so well where the Shoe pinches as those that wear it I should think it expedient for Friends to discourage the practice as much as possible, by advising those who have their Hands clear of them, to keep them so, and by no means to involve themselves in a Difficulty that they will find hard work to extricate themselves from if ever they come rightly to weigh the matter in a true Ballance.

    Thomas Nicholson

2

1768–1773

Evolution of the North Carolina
Yearly Meeting's Policy on Slave Trading

Extracts from the Minutes of the North Carolina Yearly Meeting, 1768–1773

Source: Minutes of North Carolina Friends Yearly Meeting, 1768–1773, North Carolina Yearly Meeting Archives, Friends Historical Collection, Guilford College, Greensboro, North Carolina.

1768 (pp. 97–98)

{T}he discipline & Queries relating thereto ought to be understood as a prohibition of Buying Negroes to trade upon or of them that trade in them; and as the having of Negroes is become a Burthen to such as are in Possession of them it might be well for the meeting to advise all friends to be careful not to buy or Sell in any Case, that can be reasonably avoided, with which advice & Judgment this meeting Concurs.

1769 (pp. 99–100)

{I}t appeard to this meeting from representation of the western Quarter that friends there, were Still uneasy, respecting friends purchasing Negroes, They desiring there Should be an absolute Prohibition in that respect, which this meeting taking into solid Consideration do agree to refer it to next yearly meeting.

1770 (pp. 103–4)

The referrence respecting Negroes from Last yearly Meeting coming under the solid Consideration of this Meeting and after weightily Considering the Consequences that might arrise from an absolute Prohibition of Purchasing Negroes, in any respect whatever—do unanimously agree to Substitute the following Query as the 7th Instead of that which hitherto has fill'd that Place (Viz) Are all friends carefull to bear a faithful Testimony against the Iniquitous Practice of Importing Negroes; Or do they refuse to Purchase of those that make a trade or Merchandize of them; and do they use them which they have by Inheritance or otherwise well Indeavouring to discourage them from Evill and Incouraging them in that which is good.

1772 (pp. 107, 117–19)

Friends of the Western Quarter Made a Motion for some Notice to be taken in respect to the Querie Relating to buying and selling Negroes, and Friends appoints a Committee to Consider the same and make Report to the next Sitting of this meeting. . . .

We the Committee afforesaid met according to appointment, and haveing weightily Considered the Evil Practice of Buying and Selling Negroes whereby the Slave Trade is kept up and Encouraged, and the number of them Increased in the society, do give it as our Judgement that no Friends in unity, shall Buy a Negroe or other slave of any other Person then a friend in unity, Excepting it be to Prevent the Parting of man and wife or Parent and Child, or for such other good Reasons as shall be approved of by the monthly Meeting, and it is Earnestly advisd that all Friends who are Possessed of slaves by Inheritances or otherwise, use them well in Every Respect, Endeavouring to discourage them from Evil and Encouraging them in them in that which is good, and that they do not Sell a Slave to any Person, who makes a Practice of Buying and Selling for the Sake of Gain, without Regarding how the Poor slave may be used, or the great Evil of Seperateing man and wife or Parent and Child.—Which Report is approved and Confirmed by the Meeting. . . .

The Standing Committee Report that they haveing had the Slave Trade under their Consideration; had Drawn up their Sentiments thereon which was Read and approved in this Meeting and ordered to be Recorded they had Likewise wrote an Epistle to Friends of the Meeting for Sufferings in London which they Produced at this Meeting for the approbation thereof, which said Epistle is approved and Ordered to be forwarded to the said Meeting and Likewise to be Recorded.—which are as followeth.—

The Standing Committee's Sentiments Being fully Convinced in our Minds and Judgements beyond a Doubt or Scruple, of the Great Evil and Abomination of the Importation of Negroes from Affica: by which Iniquitious Practice Great Numbers of our fellow Creatures with their Posterity are Doom'd to Perpetual and Cruel Bondage; without any Regard being had to their Haveing forfeited their Natural Right to Liberty and freedom, by any act of their own or Consent thereto otherwise then by meer force and Cruelty, Impresses our minds with such abhorence and Detestation against such a Practice, in a Christian Community; where Experience fully makes it manifest that Instead of their Embracing true Religion, Piety, and vertue, in Exchange for their Natural Liberty, that they are become Nurseries to Pride, and Idleness, to our youth in such a manner that Morallity, and true Piety is much wounded where slave keeping abounds; to the great grief of true Christian minds.—And therefore we cannot but Invite our fellow Subjects; and more Especially the Representatives in North Carolina (as much lies at their Doors for the Good of the People and Prosperity of the Province) to Joyn Heartily with their President Brethren the Burgesses of the Collony of Virginia in Presenting addresses to the Throne of Great Brittain in Order to be as Eyes to the Blind, and Mouths to the Dumb; and wheither it succeeds or not we shall have the Secret Satisfaction in our own minds of haveing used our best Endeavour, to have so Great a Torrent of Evil, Effectually Stoped, at the Place where it unhappily had the Permission to begin.—

Signed By	Caleb Trueblood	Ralph Fletcher
Thomas Nicholson	John Symons	John Sanders
Samuel Newby	Abel Trueblood	Matthew White
Thomas Newby	Joshua Morris	John Anderson
William Albertson	Mark Newby	Zachariah Toms

Jacob Wilson	Lancelot Bell	John Morris
John White	Joseph White	Zachariah Nixon
	Benjamin White	Joseph M^cadam

1773 (pp. 127–28)

Querie 7th are all Friends Carefull to bear a faithfull Testimony against the Iniquitious Practice of Importing Negroes, or do they Refuse to Purchase of those that make a Merchanize of them; or of such as are not in unity with Friends, Excepting it be to Prevent the Parting of man and wife—or Parent and Child, or for other Good Reasons as shall be approved of by the monthly Meeting, and do they which have them by Inheritance or otherwise use them well, in Every Respect Endeavouring to discourage them from Evil and Incourageing them in that which is Good?

3

1772–1773

Advice from London

It was standard practice among Friends when confronting difficult and controversial decisions to wait for the guidance of the Holy Spirit, to seek consensus within the affected meeting, and to consult other Friends' meetings. American Quakers particularly valued the advice of the London Meeting for Sufferings. On behalf of the North Carolina Yearly Meeting, the Standing Committee of North Carolina Friends sent the London meeting a yearly epistle. In their 1772 epistle, North Carolina Friends sought guidance on the moral and legal dilemma they faced in the matter of slaveholding.

Extract from the North Carolina Friends Standing Committee to the Meeting for Sufferings in London, 8th mo. 28th day 1772

Source: Minutes of the Standing Committee, Eastern Quarter, 8/28/1772, North Carolina Yearly Meeting Archives, Friends Historical Collection, Guilford College, Greensboro, North Carolina.

As there is an Act of Assembly in this Province which is a prohibition to any Person setting a Negro Free, for any cause, excepting meritorious causes, to be allowed of by the County Court under the pain of said Negro's being seized and sold to the highest bidder and the money arising from such Sale to be applied to the use of the Parish; so that such Friends as are desirous to set them at liberty, from Principals of Justice & Christianity are under a great difficulty on that account so that we should be very glad of your Friendly advice and assistance on that account: also if any steps appear to you that might be taken with Prudence and safety.

Extract from London Yearly Meeting, ca. 6th mo. 5th day 1773, to Friends in North and South Carolina

Source: Correspondence of the London Meeting for Sufferings, microfilm, Friends Historical Collection, Guilford College, Greensboro, North Carolina.

With respect to some Difficulty Friends labour under in your Province about setting your Slaves at Liberty, we desire to remind you of that weighty Saying of our Lord, vizt *If thine Eye be single, thy whole Body will be full of Light.*[8] Abiding in this Light, we doubt not you'll clearly see in the Lord's time, the way to be delivered from this Difficulty and Burthen, either by a proper Application to your Legislature, laying the weight of your Uneasiness before them, or otherwise as you may be directed by the wonderful Counsellor, & Everlasting Father of his people.

4

1774–1775

Evolution of the North Carolina Yearly Meeting's Policy on Slave Ownership

Extracts from the Minutes of the North Carolina Yearly Meeting, 1774–1775

Source: Minutes of North Carolina Friends Yearly Meeting, 1768–1773, North Carolina Yearly Meeting Archives, Friends Historical Collection, Guilford College, Greensboro, North Carolina.

1774 (pp. 132–33)

{I}t appeared there was a Case Laid before Perquimans Monthly Meeting by our friend Thomas Newby, Relating to keeping Negroes in Bondage and Slavery and Likewise of his being uneasy in that Practice and he desires the advice and assistance of friends on so weighty and Important an affair as giving them their Liberty, and they thought proper to refer the case to the Standing committee for their advice and assistance therein and the Committee having weightily considered thereon, Give it as their advice and Judgement, that all friends that find them Selves under a Burden and uneasiness on account of keeping them in Slavery may Set them at Liberty by applying to the monthly Meeting, and Likewise the monthly Meetings to appoint Proper persons to assist such friends in drawing Instruments of writing for that Purpose, and Likewise to Judge wheither the persons proposed to be set free is able to get their own Livelyhood, and the Clerk is desired to send copies of this Judgement to Each Monthly Meeting.

1775 (pp. 136–37)

Friends of the western Quarter being uneasy under the Consideration of keeping our fellow men in Bondage and Slavery desire this Meeting May Revise the Querie Relative thereunto and make such alteration thereon as may Relieve some Distressed minds, and the Meeting appoints a Committee to Consider thereon and make Report to this meeting whose Names are Thomas Nicholson, Thomas Knox, Samuel Newby, Mark Newby, Joshua Skinner, Thomas White, John Knox, George Walton, Moses Bundy, Humphry Park, Zachariah Nixon, John Talbot, John Unthank, Thomas Jessep, James Newland, Isaac Beeson, Samuel Holliday, Zachariah Dick, John Carter, Thomas Thornbrugh, Peter Dillon, Jacob Hunt, Thomas White son of Thomas, Josiah White, Job Parker, Chalkly Albertson, John Overman, and Gabriel Cosand. . . .

The Committee . . . being Generally met and after much Conference finding that the alteration that at Present would give Ease of mind to Several Friends, is that the Querie should Extend to a Prohibition of Either Buying or Selling Negroes.

5

Circa 1775

Thomas Nicholson Urges Immediate Emancipation

In his 1767 open letter to Friends (document 1, above) in which he advocated a form of gradual emancipation, Thomas Nicholson stated that he was willing to give freedom to all his slaves if a legal expedient by which it could be done could be found. In 1774, with the approval of the Standing Committee, he circulated an essay called "Liberty and Property." No copy of this composition has been located, and it most likely was never printed but circulated in manuscript form. The piece apparently promoted a change in the law that would loosen restrictions on manumission.[9] Shortly thereafter, Nicholson determined that it was neither necessary nor desirable to wait for a change in the law. He wrote the following brief essay in which he urges slaveowners to end their association with the sin of slavery immediately, in defiance of the law and despite the likelihood that those they set free would be returned into slavery by the state courts. Nicholson copied the essay into his private journal.[10]

Considerations on Slavery, by Thomas Nicholson

Source: Journal of Thomas Nicholson, typescript, Friends Historical Library of Swarthmore College, Swarthmore College, Swarthmore, Pennsylvania.

Having been deeply distressed in my mind for several months Principally on account of the unjustifiableness of the Practice of keeping Negroes in Bondage, and Slavery in which time of trial, I have met with many strong reasonings, both for and against, the Practice, untill I have been brought into, and for sometime have felt that condition described in the 116 Psalm V. 3, the sorrows of death compassed me, and the pains of Hell got hold upon me, I found trouble and sorrow, in which condition I have had to consider, of the following scriptures, in a very close and awful manner, Isaiah at Verses, 15, 16, and 17[11] when we make many prayers. I will not hear; your hands are filled of blood, wash ye, make you clean, put away the evil of your doings from before mine Eyes, cease to do Evil, learn to do well, seek judgment believe the Oppressed, Micah VI, 8. He hath shewed to thee, O man what is good, and what doth the Lord require of thee, but to do Justly, and to love mercy, and to walk Humbly with thy God; Matthew VII. 12. Therefore all things Whatsoever ye would that Men should do to you, do you even so to them; for this is the Law and the Prophets, Matthew XVI. 26. For what is a Man profited, if he should gain the whole World, and lose his own Soul? Or what shall a Man give in exchange for his soul? Revelations XVIII. 2. Babylon the great is Fallen, is fallen, and is become the Habitation of Devils, V. 4. come out of her my People, that ye be not partakers of her sins, and that ye receive not of her plagues: V. 13. Her Merchandize, among other things, was in Slaves and Souls of Men V. 24 In her was found the Blood of Prophets, and of Saints, and of all that were Slain upon the Earth. As I have been very deeply dipped in a state of Sufferings in the Case, I have gradually, been lead into the following considerations, and Views.

First: Supposing a Law made by Mortal Men, to allow one man to lay hold of another, his fellow, Mortal and Brother by creation, and Intail Slavery, on him, and his posterity, forever without his consent; or any forteiture of liberty on his part to be contrary to true Christianity and a Violation of that Golden Rule, commanded by the great Law giver, Christ Jesus, all things whatsoever ye would that Men should to you, do you even so to them.

Second: If another law is made by Mortal Men to escape this slavery, by ordering, that if any person set a Negro free, excepting for Meritorious causes, and that they shall be sold and without paying any regard to a tender Scruple of Conscience, in keeping them, in slavery, would it lay us under the Guilt of obeying Men more than God, if we should forbear setting them free, on account of that law, when our conscience condemned us for keeping them in slavery and Bondage?

Third: Supposing the case, to be as above stated, whether, such as do hinder those that would set them free from conscience motives, will not be in danger of a falling under that woe pronounced against such as will not {enter} in the Kingdom of Heaven, themselves, and such as would enter, the{y} endeavoured to hinder?[12]

Fourth: Supposing by setting them free, contrary to the law of the Country, we might open a door for a more crucial Bondage, to be Intailed upon them, by their being sold into the hands of others, that will not use them with so much tenderness, as their present Masters would do?

Fifth: If that should happen to be the case, will not the burden and sin lie on the heads of those that are the cause thereof, and be required at their hands, and those that have set them {free} be clear, when they have done all that is in their power to do?

Sixth: Whether such as do clear themselves, as above, may not answer all their opposers, we have faith to believe, that the God whom we endeavour to serve is able to preserve those whom we do set free, from falling into the hands of cruel and wicked Men, but whether he will or not, we will no longer be concerned in that cruel Babylonish Practice, which is only by Human Laws allowed of, nor partake with you in that Merchandise, as it is in slaves and Souls of Men.

6

1776

Thomas Newby's Manumission Paper

Thomas Newby, who owned fourteen slaves, was one of the wealthiest men in Perquimans County in 1775.[13] In fact, he owned more slaves than any other taxpayer in the county. Only two others owned as many as twelve slaves, and of the 145 slaveowners listed on the county tax rolls, only nine held eight or more. When a man of Newby's prominence freed his slaves, he set an example whose influence reverberated, at least among his fellow Quakers. His act of manumitting his slaves promised to change the lives not only of his own slaves but also of the slaves of all Quakers who followed his lead.

When Newby freed ten of his slaves on 3 March 1776, he had been contemplating the move for at least two years. His yearly, quarterly, and monthly meetings had deliberated long before offering Newby practical help in freeing his slaves. The terms of the manumission underscore how tentative and experimental this first step was for conscience-stricken Friends. The manumission paper drawn up by the Quaker committee that had been appointed the task by the Perquimans monthly meeting did not free the slaves absolutely and unconditionally. Rather, it bound the freedmen to a yearly payment to Newby, which the former owner could enforce by selling the labor of his former slaves.

Thomas Newby's Manumission of Ten Slaves

Source: Perquimans Monthly Meeting Minutes, 3/6/1776, North Carolina Yearly Meeting Archives, Friends Historical Collection, Guilford College, Greensboro, North Carolina.

{T}he friends that were appointed the 4th of 5th month—1774—to assist Thomas Newby in drawing Manumissions and Likewise to Judge whether the persons proposed to be Manumited were able to get their Livelihood—Produced to this Meeting A Manumission in the following words—[14]

Know all men by these Presents that I Thomas Newby of the County of Perquimans and Province of North Carolina of my own free will and out of a tender Scruple of Conscience in Relation to keeping my fellow Creatures in purpetual Bondage and Slavery Notwithstanding the practice is allowed of and perpetuated by human Laws—I do by this manumission or Instrument of Writing so far as is in my power for the Ease and peace of mind hereby Publickly Declare to all whom it may Concern that I do by Virtue of these presents in behalf of my self my heirs administs. or assigns from this time forward most freely Set at Liberty Six Negro men on their paying me or my heirs the Sum of twenty Shillings a year and on the terms of good behaviour and Remaining so (viz) Tom Glasco Jack Cudger James and Harry—Also four Negro Women (viz) Judah, Sue, Patience, and Hager and their Increase that they may hereafter have but in case they or Either of them Should behave bad or not pay their Leveys in due time then they he or She so offending to be Sold by me or my heirs for as Long a time as will make full Satisfaction for the offence Commited and all Charges that may arise thereon

Witness my hand and Seal the 3rd day of 3rd month March 1776
Signed sealed in presents of   Thos. Newby
Jacob Wilson
Caleb White

7

1777

Thomas Newby's Petition to Free His Slave Hannah

According to the Perquimans County tax list of 1775, Thomas Newby owned eight male and six female taxable slaves. In March 1776, by the manumission paper reproduced in Document 6, he freed six of the males and four of the females. Hannah was not one of the females freed at that time. She does not appear on the list of taxables in the Perquimans County tax list of 1775, but she does appear on the 1772 list.[15] According to the following petition to the county court for permission to free her, Hannah had "grown old." These last two facts suggest that Hannah had become too old to be a taxable asset.

The circumstances of Hannah's case raise speculations about why Newby appealed to the court for permission to set Hannah free rather than freeing her by means of a private instrument similar to the one by which he had freed the original ten slaves. It is possible that Newby sought a court order not only because it would secure Hannah's freedom in the eyes of the law but also because, given her age, Hannah did not meet the yearly meeting's requirement that a slave had to able to support him or herself before it would approve a Friend's application to manumit him or her.

The terms of the 1776 manumission and the circumstances of the 1777 petition to free the superannuated slave Hannah suggest that while Thomas Newby was convinced that slaveholding was wrong he was nonetheless willing to derive some economic benefit from freeing his slaves. When he freed able workers, he obliged them to make a yearly payment; by seeking to free Hannah, he may have sought to relieve himself of the obligation of supporting an elderly woman.

Although the court denied Newby's petition, he did give Hannah her freedom, for she appears in a list of emancipated blacks who were later seized and sold by order of the county court.[16]

Thomas Newby to the Court of Pleas and Quarter Sessions

Source: Robert M. Calhoon, Religion and the American Revolution in North Carolina (Raleigh, N.C.: North Carolina Department of Cultural Resources, Division of Archives and History, 1976), 46.

To the Worshipful Court of Pleas & Quarter Sessions to be Held in Hertford on the Second Monday in February 1777. I Thomas Newby of the County of Perquimans and State of North Carolina, Humbly prayeth that Your Worships Will take this my petition into Consideration & Grant this the said petition (to Wit) The Liberating of A Certain Negro Woman belonging to me, Your Humble petitioner, by the Name of Hannah, for this my Reason. In the first place, She being Grown ould And Can be Very little Service to me, as to any Hard Work or Drudgery. She being an Excellent Midwife Called on Every hand turn to Both White Women & Black and from Account has performed her Duty With as Much Scill as any of that profession. Moreover She being A peaceable Negro Woman haveing lived in this place for the Space of forty Years With one Certain Husband & Raised A Number of Children Which Are at present Divided amongst the Heirs to Whom they fell. And your Humble petitioner, from being Satisfied and Contented With the Services Which I have Received from her, the said Hannah, Humbly prayeth that your Worships May take in Consideration & Set the Said Negro free by your order. & further your Petitioner prayeth not.

Thomas Newby

{*Endorsement:*} Thomas Newby Petition to Liberate Negro Hannah Rejected

8

1776–1789

The Progress of Manumission

After the North Carolina Yearly Meeting decided that Friends should cease holding slaves, it set up a formal process for persuading individual Quaker slaveholders to set their slaves free. The minutes of the Standing Committee and of the Perquimans monthly meeting document that process in practice. They indicate that many Friends found the decision to let go of their human property difficult to make and that the Society had to use patient persuasion over the course of years. A dozen years after the yearly meeting condemned slaveholding as contrary to Christianity, some North Carolina Friends, despite the threat of being disowned, had still not agreed to set their slaves free.

In her examination of slave manumissions in Virginia in the first decade after American independence, Eva Sheppard Wolf finds that individual leaders and community pressure were crucial for translating personal belief in the immorality of slavery into decisions to free slaves. Manumissions by Virginia's Quakers, Baptists, and Methodists as well as by persons motivated by secular Enlightenment ideology took place when influential men took the lead in persuading their neighbors and when the community with which particular slaveholders identified pressed the cause of antislavery.[17] The writings of George Walton (in Part I) and of Thomas Nicholson (above) and the extracts from the minutes of the North Carolina yearly and Perquimans monthly meetings that follow here bear out Wolf's findings in North Carolina. Individuals and community played essential roles in converting conviction into action.

Extracts from the Minutes of the North Carolina Yearly Meeting, 1776–1789

Source: Minutes of North Carolina Friends Yearly Meeting, 1768–1773, North Carolina Yearly Meeting Archives, Friends Historical Collection, Guilford College, Greensboro, North Carolina.

26/10/1776

We the committee appointed to take under solid consideration the reference from the Eastern Quarter in Relation to buying and selling Negroes and the method of Dealing with such as might prove deficient therein Generally met and after much Brotherly & Sympathizing conference and Consideration do unanimously agree to report as our Judgement that the minute of Last Yearly meeting relative thereto needs a revisal or Reconsideration and that monthly meetings may stand in need of further assistance therein, which after several weighty remarks being made thereon is refered to a future sitting of the meeting....

{28/10/1776}

{A}fter a time of weighty deliberate Conference on the subject, and feeling persuasion that Keeping our fellow men in Bondage is inconsistant with the Law of Righteousness in which divine goodness was evidently felt to be near and by the seasoning power thereof several were enabled very affectingly to Express their Sentiments and to declare their willingness and resolution to set all their negroes fully Free—It was the Unanimous sense of the meeting, that all the members thereof who hold slaves be earnestly and affectionately advised to Cleanse their Hands of them as soon as they Possibly can, and in the mean time that none of the members of this meeting shall be permitted to buy or sell any slaves or hire any from such who are not in membership with us And in the cases which now Lie under the consideration of Pasquotank monthly meeting or any member or members of this meeting who may hereafter Buy sell or Clendestinely assign for Hire any slaves in such manner as may perpetuate or prolong their Slavery the monthly meeting to which such belong after due Labouring with them if they refuse to take such steps as their friends may think Necessary and condemn their conduct to the

Satisfaction of the meeting, shall Testifie against them as in other Offences against the Church. . . .

This meeting having a further and free conferrence on the subject under consideration in the morning respecting the Freedom of the Negroes it is unanimously concluded to appoint a Committee from this meeting to Visit and Assist friends in setting their Negroes Free as the way may open for them to proceed and that each monthly meeting is advised to nominate such friends in their respective meetings as they may judge most suitable to Join the said Committee. The following friends are appointed for the above service {Vizt}
Thomas Nicholson, Thomas Knox, Thomas Newby, Jacob Wilson, Caleb White, Joseph Henley, Zachariah Nixon, Zachariah Dicks, David Vestal, Eleazer Hunt and William Coffin Junr. who are desired to render a particular account of their proceedings to the Next Yearly meeting. And if any of the slaves set free by the members of this meeting should be interupted in their Freedom or any attempts made to bring them again into Bondage it is recommended to the standing committee to have that or any other matter respecting them Particularly under their care and Notice and to appear on their behalf and take such steps for their assistance and preservation as they may apprehend Necessary; and any expence that may arise on their accounts this meeting agrees to Repay.

24/10/1777

{I}t likewise Appears that no friends amongst us are Concerned in Importing or Buying Negroes, altho' some have Sold which is under the Care of Friends, and there seems to be a fear of some who have them in possession not using them so well in every Respect as might be desired.

{25/10/1777}

The Committee Appointed last Yearly Meeting to assist such Friends as Appeard disposed to Release their Negroes from a State of Bondage being called on to render an Account of the progress made therein, Report, that they found a great Willingness, even beyond their Expectation to promote the Work and that a Considerable Number have been set free by those who had them in possession, about forty of which have Since been taken up and sold in Consequence of an Act of Assembly passed at Newbern in the 3d or 4th Mo. last (which was after Said Negroes were Manumitted) which seems to put a stop to that Work at present,[18] altho they believe Several friends who yet have Negroes in their possession, are very uneasy in remaining in a practice they are Convinced is not consistant with Justice, or doing as they would be done unto. . . . .

The Case of the Manumitted Slaves who have bound themselves to friends during Life, haveing been a Matter also under the Consideration of the Committee, it was their Unanimous Sense, that such a Practice ought to be discouraged, as a Matter tending to lay Wase {waste} the Testimony of Universal Liberty. for though the Conduct of some friends may in that Respect have been Influenced by Motives of Compassion, Yet, in case of Death such Negroes might be deemed as part of the Estate of such Deceased friends, and of Course involve their Posterity in the Same Difficulties that we have endeavoured to remove by such Manumissions—With which Judgement the Meeting Unites.

{25th day, 10th month, 1779}

They also Report they have had farther to Commisserate with those in Bondage, and the Necessity of doing Justice to those Oppressed People, and are free to give it as their Sense, that the good Work begun should go forward, and Strict Justice extended towards all such Negroes as are Unmanumitted, and that their Owners Act as Guardians to protect them from Suffering by the Hands of evil & designing Men—Of which this Meeting Approves, and Recommends it to the Care of the Quarterly Meetings.

{10th month, 1780}

The case of friends hireing Negroes coming before this meeting and after a time of Solid consideration and conference thereon it is concluded that no friend in unity hire any Negro from any Master or Mistress whatever except such as are Manumitted & Yet in a State of Minority or the property of orphans in unity, also that no friend in unity hire out any Negro or Negroes for any term of time whatever, to any person or persons, Except such Negroes as are in minority & Manumitted or the property of orphans.

{30th day, 10th month, 1781}

The committee appointed to take into consideration the Cases of friends taking tests & holding Slaves Report that . . . taking under solid & deliberate consideration the case of friends holding negroes in Slavery do give it as our Judgement that monthly meetings shall continue to visit & Labour with Such in love & Tenderness, Endeavouring to convince them of Iniquity thereof; but after Such care has been fully extended & to no purpose then the monthly meeting shall apply to a Committee appointed out of the Quarterly meeting for that Purpose, which shall assist them in Labouring with Such, but if after all, their endeavours prove fruitless, and they Still persist on to hold them in Slavery, the monthly meeting may with the consent of said committee testifie their Disunion with them.

And after being Several times Read and considered the meeting Concurs therewith & confirms the same and Recommends it to the care of the Quarterly & monthly meetings & Requests the Quarterly meetings to hand up an Account of their progress therein to next yearly Meeting.

{26th day, 10th month, 1782}

Agreeable to a Recommendation of last Yearly meeting it appears by accounts from the Quarterly meetings that friends have visitted such of their members as were in the Practice of Slave holding the effect of which is a Considerable Number have been Manumitted Since last year with a Comfortable Prospect of the Releasment of several more Erelong and this meeting Recommends to the Quarterly & monthly Meetings to still continue their Care agreeable to the order of last yearly meeting and Report their Progress to the Next yearly meeting.

{27th day, 10th month, 1783}

The Committee appointed on Seventh day to take under their Consideration the State of the Society, Report that having deliberately Considered the Case of friends holding Slaves, do give it as their Since and Judgment that monthly meetings sould {should} Continue in a further labour with all such as are Slave holders; and have any Right of membership with us; and where any members still continue to reject the advice of their Brethren & Refuse to Execute proper Instruments of writing for fully Releasing from a State of Slavery All Such as are in their power whether arrived to full age or in their Minority; and no hopes of the Continuance of friends being profitable to them, that monthly meetings after having fully Discharged a Christian Duty to such; may proceed to testifie their disunion with them. and that the following Querie be Substituted instead of the Sixth (Viz) Querie 6th. Are friends Clear of Importing, Purchasing, Disposing of, or holding mankind as Slaves, and do they use those well who are sett free, and are under their care through nonage or otherwise, Endeavouring to Incourage them in a virtuous life? . . .

The Quarterly meetings are Recommended to Dissolve their Committees that were appointed to be applyed to in Respect to Dealing with friends that held Slaves.

{31st day, 10th month, 1787}

We the Committee . . . do give it as our Sense & Judgment . . . that the Yearly Meeting Recommend to the Quarterly Meetings that they appoint suitable Committees in each Quarter to Visit & labour with all such Friends as remain in the practice of holding their fellow Men in a State of Slavery, Endeavourng to Convince them of the Iniquity of such a practice; and should they still reject the advice of their Friends, that monthly Meetings ought Speedily to testify their disunity with them.

{28th day, 10th month, 1788}

A Report was handed up from the Eastern Quarter, which is in Substance as follows, That the Committee appointed by the Quarterly Meeting in Consequence of the advice of our last Yearly Meeting, have reported that they have Visited all the monthly Meetings belonging to this Quarter, & had the satisfaction therein; also nearly all the Members thereof that were in the practice of holding Slaves, & that a Considerable Number have been Liberated since their appointment. . . . And as it appears that all Friends have not yet cleansed their hands of Slaveholding this Meeting directs the Inferior Meetings to put the former advices of our Yearly Meeting in practice respecting such who still continue to hold them as Slaves, & hand up a Report of the Service to the next Yearly Meeting.

{16th day, 10th month, 1789}
Reports were received from the Several Quarterly Meetings in Substance as follows, That Friends have proceeded so far in putting in practice the former advices of this Meeting respecting such as continue in holding Slaves that such have been visited, some have been disowned on that account, and Complaints lie against others; & this Meeting agrees that advice be handed down to the Inferior Meetings, for Friends to continue their Care therein, & to proceed agreeable to the former advices of this Meeting towards such as continue in that practice; also respecting the Education of such Negroes in minority which are under Friends Care.

Extracts from the Minutes of the Perquimans Monthly Meeting, 1781–1789

Source: Perquimans Monthly Meeting Minutes, North Carolina Yearly Meeting Archives, Friends Historical Collection, Guilford College, Greensboro, North Carolina.

{5th day, 12th month, 1781}
The following Friends are appointed by the Quarterly Meeting as a Committee for the Monthly Meetings to apply to for Assistance in Labouring with those who are in the practice of Slave Holding, that the Monthly Meetings cannot prevail on to free them, Viz Thos. Newby William Albertson, Mark Newby, Caleb White, George Walton, Matthew White, Ephraim Overman, Joshua Perrishoe, Joseph Hendley, Humphrey Parke, Aaron Morriss Jnr. & Zachariah Nixon, and the Monthly Meetings are desired to hand up an account to the Quarterly Meeting, preceeding the Yearly Meeting what Progress hath been among them in freeing Slaves.

{2nd day, 1st month, 1782}
This Meeting thinks proper to recommend to the preparitive Meeting to Visit and Labour with those of their Members who are still in the practice of holding Slaves in Love and Tenderness and report their progress therein to a future Monthly Meeting.

{3d day, 7th month, 1782}
By Accots. handed from the Several Preparitive Meetings it appears that they have Visited and Laboured with most of their Members that

was in the practice of Slaveholding agreeable to the recommendation of the Monthly Meeting and report they found a disposition in some friends to Comply with the order of the Yearly Meeting, and that some others were willing their Negroes should have the full benefit of their Labour, And in some others they found a Disposition to continue in the practice of holding them in Bondage—This meeting therefore appoints the following friends as a Committee to Visit and Labour with all such of Its Members as do continue in the practice of Slave Holding Vizt. George Wilton {*Walton*}, Benjamin Albertson, Humphrey Parke, Caleb Winslow, Job Parker, Thos. White, Gabriel Newby, Reubin Wilson, John Sevice, Joseph Draper, William White, & Silas Draper, and report there progress therein to the Next Monthly Meeting.

{*7th day, 8th month, 1782*}

The Committee appointed to Visit and Labour with such friends as wear in the Practice of Slaveholding Report they have Generally complied therewith and that Several Friends have Manumited there Negroes Since Last Monthly Meeting, and a Considerable number seem inclineable to Provision the there Negroes Slavery May not be perpetuated, And that in some others their appeared a Disposition to hold them in slavery as heretofore. . . .

But few Negroes Manumitted Since Last year.

{*4th day, 12th month, 1782*}

An Extract from the Quarterly Meeting Minutes being Read is as followeth—This Meeting recommends to the Monthly Meetings to still continue their care towards those who have not manumited their slaves agreeable to the order of the Yearly Meeting and report their Progress to Next Yearly Meeting—

{*2nd day, 7th month, 1783*}

A part of the Committee appointed in the third Month Last to Visit and Labour with such of their Members as continue to hold their Negroes in Slavery Report that they have nearly complyed therewith and only Two Friends have Manumited those under there care, And that Yet there are Many among us who still continue to hold them several of whom contend for the practice of holding them in Bondage—

{*3d day, 12th month, 1783*}

Agreeable to the recommendation of the Quarterly Meeting, This Meeting appoints the following Friends as a Committee to Visit such of Its Members as Hold Slaves Vizt. Mark Newby, Caleb White, Wm. Albertson, Caleb Winslow, Benjamin Abertson, Jnr. Josiah White, Humphrey Parke, Job Parker, Matthew White, Jacob Wilson, Benjamin Albertson, Jnr. & William White, and report there progress therein to a future Monthly Meeting.

{*3d day, 11th month, 1784*}

{T}he State of the Meeting appears nearly as followeth . . . Ansr. 6th {*Query*} Clear of Importing Purchasing or Selling Mankind. Tho some Continue to hold them in Bondage & their proper Education much Neglected.

{*7th day, 1st month, 1789*}

That Part of the Extract respecting those that hold Slaves Comeing before this Meeting—It is recommended to the Preparitive Meetings to Labour with all those Members that are In that practice & if any should continue Obstinate & Refuse to take the advice of these Friends that Complaints be handed up to this Meeting against them.

9

1777–1797

List of Emancipated Blacks Who Were Re-Enslaved

Early in 1792 the Standing Committee of the North Carolina Yearly Meeting for the Western Quarter wrote to the Philadelphia Meeting for Sufferings regarding the plight of manumitted persons who had been re-enslaved under the laws of North Carolina. The Meeting for Sufferings, believing it would be useful to publicize such cases, requested a written copy of accounts of those cases that could be collected. The Western Quarter's reply went astray and was never received in Philadelphia; late in 1796, the Meeting for Sufferings repeated its request. The Pennsylvania Quakers wanted to present a memorial to the U.S. Congress in order to provoke discussion "of the iniquitous practice of enslaving free men within your state." They believed that to do so "it will be requisite to prove the existence of so enormous an evil by authentic documents." For this purpose, the Meeting for Sufferings sought "a particular statement of such cases as can be well attested" and a statement of the full number of those who had been thus re-enslaved.[19]

The Western Quarter answered on 29 July, stating,

> there is but few Blacks within the Compass of our western Quarters, out of which Two instances call for our attention, to inform, (to wit) one friend some years past liberated all his Negroes to the amount of Eight, and in a short time after he sold them all into a state of bondage for which gross Evil he was disowned. The other was a friend who liberated Seven Blacks and died not long after leaving directions by Will for his heirs to be Guardians for them untill there should be a Law tolerating their freedom who have reduced them all into a State of slavery.[20]

Whereas the Western Quarter's report was of little use for the purposes of the Philadelphia meeting, the report the Standing Committee for the Eastern Quarter sent contained specific and pertinent information. The Eastern Quarter's report, dated 9 January 1797, provided an accounting of 134 blacks whom North Carolina Quakers had freed since the 1770s and who had been re-enslaved, saying that there were more whose cases could not be documented with the available records. One of the 134 emancipated slaves who had been seized and sold was a woman named Dinah whom George Walton had set free.[21]

To the Meeting for Sufferings in Philadelphia

Source: The Memorial and Address of the People Called Quakers, from Their Yearly Meeting Held in Philadelphia, by Adjournments, from the 25th of the 9th Month, to the 29th of the Same Inclusive, 1797 (Philadelphia: Philadelphia Meeting of the Religious Society of Friends, 1797), 2–4.

To the MEETING for SUFFERINGS in Philadelphia.

DEAR FRIENDS,

YOUR Letter dated the 17th of the 11th month last, came safely to hand. Notwithstanding our epistolary correspondence has for some time past ceased, yet we hope, as occasion may require, the same may be revived. We have taken the matter respecting the distressed circumstances of the emancipated Blacks into consideration, and made application to the Clerks offices of the counties of Perquimons and Pasquotank, where all (except a few) have been sold, and cannot procure any authentic account from the records, as the courts have for the most part only ordered the free Blacks in the custody of the sheriff to be sold. A copy of two of their orders is enclosed.[22] Our Standing Committee have from their own knowledge collected a number of the names of those sold, and who they were freed by; a list of which is also enclosed: yet we are fully satisfied that there are others that have been emancipated, sold as slaves again, and many instances of children born after their mothers were freed, sold with their mothers; in some cases sold and parted from their parents when small. Many of those mentioned in the enclosed list have been separated from their nearest connexions in life; as the wife from the husband, and husband from wife, and children from parents. Many of the Blacks included in the enclosed list, were emancipated prior to the passing of the act in

1777; and the proceedings of the county courts in the sale of some of which, were removed to the supreme court of the district, by *certiori*, and a judgment obtained in their favour: notwithstanding the same persons were again reduced to slavery, in consequence of another act of the General Assembly, passed in the year 1779.[23]

We hope this may come timely to answer the end proposed: for we may add, that the distresses of the free Blacks yet continue. Our late petition from last yearly meeting hath not met with the desired effect.

We also enclose a copy of an account of the trial and sales of a number of the said emancipated Blacks at Perquimans, July term, 1777, being preserved by Friends at that time.[24]

With the salutation of love we conclude, and are your affectionate Friends.

Signed on behalf and by direction of the Standing Committee for the Eastern Quarter of the Yearly Meeting in North Carolina, 9th day, 1st mo. 1797.

    THOMAS JORDAN, *Clerk.*

A LIST *of sundry* EMANCIPATED BLACKS, taken up and sold by order of the County Courts of Pasquotank, Perquimons and Chowan, in consequence of several acts of the General Assembly of the state of North Carolina, since the passing of the first act in the year 1777, to the present time.

	Blacks.	By whom emancipated.	
	David,	William Albertson.	Parted from his wife & children.
	Abram,	Benj. & Chalkly Albertson.	Carried to South-Carolina from his wife & children.
	Joan,	William Albertson.	
	Tom,	John Anderson.	
5.	Jem,		
	Jacob,		
	Harry,		
	Ceasar,	Elihu Anderson.	
	Jupiter,		

10.	Dublin,	Jeremiah Cannon.	
	Cuffee,		
	Candace,	Samuel Charles.	
	Jack,	Isaac Elliott.	
	Pleasant & 3 children,	James Elliot and wife.	Carried into the back country.
	Tom,	William Griffin.	
	Mingo,	John Haskitt.	
20	Juda,		
	Rose,	Joseph Jones.	
	Sarah,	Josiah Jordan.	
	Dick,	Isaac Lamb.	
	Candace,	George and Sarah Metcalfe.	
25	Anna & child,	Samuel Moore.	Said child born after its mother was manumitted.
	David,	Charles Morgan.	
	Esther & child,	Aaron Morris, jun.	
30	Rebekah & chilr.		
	Jaob and Penny,		
35	Ben,	Zachariah Newby.	
	Sam,	Thomas Newby, of Pasquotank.	
	Hannah,	Kezia Nixon.	
	Glasgow,	Thomas Newby, of Perquimons.	Glasgow and Jack carried a very considerable distance from their wives & children. Tom and wife sold from their children.
40	Jack,		
45	Cudgo,		
	Tom and wife,		
	Susanna,		
	Patience,		
	Hannah,		
	Priscilla,		
	David,	Robert Newby.	
	Peggy,		
	Priscilla,		
	Jenney,		
50	Jem,	Mark Newby.[25]	
	Zango,		
	Ned,		
	Phebe,		

	Samuel,	Mary Nixon.	
55	Ann,		
	Hagar,		
	Francis,	Zachariah Nixon.	
	Charity,	Tho. Nicholson.	Richard carried
60	Francis,		into the back
	Sarah,		country from his
	Richard,		children.
	Pompey,		
	Dill and child,	Nich. Nicholson,	Jenny carried into
65	Jenny,		the back country
			from her children.
	Rose,	Thomas Newby, of	
		Pasquotank.	
	Jonas.	Christopher Nicholson.	
	Bofor,	Cha. Overman.	Hagar carried to
70	Job,		South Carolina
	Haga,		from her husband
			and children.
	Tobey,	Matthew Pritchard.	
	Tamar & child,	Henry Palin.	
	Hagar,	William Robinson.	
	Fanny,		
	Job,		
	Dick,	Samuel Smith.	
77	Patience,	John Sanders.	
	Dick,	John Smith.	
	Lemuel,		
	Frank,		
	Ruth & child,		
	Dorcas,		
	Easter,	Jesse Symons.	
85	Ephraim,	Elizabeth Symons.	
	Hagar,		
	Jenny & child,	William Townshend.	
	Aaron,	Joseph Thornton.	
90	Juda,	John Trueblood.	
	Samson,	Josiah Trueblood.	
	Nero,		

95	Moses, Charles, Benjamin,	Caleb Trueblood.
	Sawney,	Aaron Trueblood.
	Jacob, William, Sibba, Hagar,	Benjamin White.
101 105	Cuffee, Hannah, Rose, Jane, Ruth, Candace,	Thomas White.
110	Luke, Zilpha, Nancy Priscilla, Mingo,	Caleb White.
115	Lyddai, Peter, Robin, Patience,	William White.
	Cancer,	Margaret White.
120	Ned, Violet, Fanny, Quea,	Josiah White.
	Rebekah,	Benjamin Winslow.
	Jane, Rose,	Matthew White.
125	Robin, Dinah,	Jacob Wilson.
	Dick, Judah,	Lydia White.
	Dick,	Rachel Williams.
	Dol,	Caleb Winslow.
	Nancy,	Jacob Winslow.
	Rose,	Joshua White.
	Dinah,	George Walton.
134	Jenny & child,	Matthew White.

PART III

The State

North Carolina Thwarts Quaker Manumission

The manumission movement among North Carolina's Quakers arose contemporaneously with the coming of the American Revolution to the colony: While North Carolina Quakers were moving toward liberating their slaves, North Carolina Patriots were moving toward liberating the colony from British rule. As a result, the manumission movement was ill timed to benefit the blacks that were set free.

North Carolinians joined other British North American colonists in protesting taxation by Parliament and rejoiced with fellow Americans at the repeal of the Stamp Tax (1765) and all of the Townshend Duties (1768) except those on tea. But when a new royal governor, Josiah Martin, took up his duties in North Carolina in 1771, the difficulties he had with the General Assembly owed more to the assemblymen's traditional jealous defense of their legislative prerogatives than to revolutionary opposition to British rule. However, news of the Coercive Acts (1774), which were Britain's official retaliation against the city of Boston and the Massachusetts Bay Colony for the destruction of East India Company tea during the Boston Tea Party, fanned the flames of revolutionary sentiment in North Carolina. If Parliament could close the port of Boston to commerce and alter the bay colony's charter, North Carolina Patriots reasoned, what was to prevent it from applying the same arbitrary power against other colonies, including North Carolina?[1]

A committee of correspondence established by the General Assembly to maintain contact with leaders in other colonies declared that the cause of Boston was the common cause of all Americans and endorsed the idea of a Continental Congress of representatives of the mainland colonies to decide on a united response to what many agreed were "Intolerable Acts" of British tyranny. To prevent the North Carolina General Assembly from sending delegates to the Continental Congress, Governor Martin refused to call it into session. North Carolina Patriot leaders gathered instead in a provincial congress that elected delegates to the Continental Congress and created a colony-wide Committee of Safety.

Martin finally called the General Assembly into session in April 1775. The assembly promptly approved sending delegates to the Second Continental Congress in May, and the governor angrily dissolved the assembly. On May 6, news arrived in North Carolina that armed conflict had broken out at Lexington and Concord, Massachusetts, on 19 April and that the Massachusetts militia was now besieging the British army in Boston. In North Carolina, the militia began taking its directions from the Committee of Safety. On 2 June, Martin fled for protection to Fort Johnston, located at the mouth of the Cape Fear River, where a Royal Navy sloop supported the fort with additional firepower. In July, from the safety of the sloop, Martin watched helplessly as the militia burned Fort Johnston to the ground. In August, the provincial congress reconvened and created a provisional government in place of the royal government.

By this time, the Continental Congress, meeting in Philadelphia, had established the Continental Army and appointed George Washington commander-in-chief. North Carolina's provisional government duly agreed to pay its share of the army's cost and to send a regiment to join the Continental Line.

Although many in North Carolina were Loyalists, North Carolina's Patriots were better organized and seized the initiative. The Patriots harrassed those who remained faithful to the royal government and in December made an expedition into the South Carolina backcountry to capture Loyalists who had besieged a fort and seized a supply of gunpowder.

White revolutionaries in North Carolina viewed any encouragement of black aspirations for freedom as a threat to their movement, for they suspected the British authorities of planning to use slave insurrection to help put down the Revolution. By the summer of 1775, rumors had spread that the crown had promised "every Negro that would murder his Master and family that he should have his Master's plantation." Royal governor Josiah Martin wrote that the Royal government could employ some of the large numbers of blacks in many of the colonies to force the white residents into obedience to the king. In a letter that accidentally became public, he stated that he would advocate a slave revolt only in the case of "the actual and declared rebellion of the King's subjects, and the failure of all other means to maintain the King's Government."[2]

Evidence of slave conspiracies confirmed white fears. In July 1775, a posse jailed more than forty suspected black ringleaders of a planned revolt in Beaufort County, and in Craven and Pitt counties, patrollers pursued a group that they estimated at 250 blacks. Then, in November 1775, Virginia's royal governor, Lord Dunmore, proclaimed freedom for indentured servants and slaves belonging to rebels who would join the king's troops to help put down the rebellion. In response, blacks from North Carolina as well as Virginia joined Dunmore's forces and donned uniforms emblazoned with the phrase "Liberty to Slaves." On 1 January 1776, North Carolina's troops joined those of Virginia to defend Norfolk against the assault of Dunmore's troops, white and black.[3]

1

1777

An Act to Prevent Domestic Insurrections

The North Carolina government, suspicious of the Quakers' Loyalist leanings and fearful of slave rebellion, reacted in alarm when Friends began setting slaves free. Even when Thomas Newby sought to comply with the legal requirements by petitioning the county court in February 1777 for permission to free his slave Hannah as a reward for her services as a skilled midwife to both blacks and whites, the court denied the petition.[4]

To counteract the manumission movement, the legislature authorized any freeholder to apprehend illegally freed slaves to be delivered to the county sheriff, who was to sell them at the next session of the county court. As an incentive, one-fifth of the sale price went to the freeholders who apprehended the freed slaves; the balance went into the state treasury.[5]

An Act to prevent domestic Insurrections, and for other Purposes.

Source: Laws of North Carolina for 1777, Chapter VI, in The State Records of North Carolina, collected and edited by Walter Clark, Vol. 24, Laws 1777–1788 (1905; reprint, Wilmington, N.C.: Broadfoot Publishing, 1994), 14–15.

An Act to prevent domestic Insurrections, and for other Purposes.

I. Whereas the evil and pernicious Practice of freeing Slaves in this State, ought at this alarming and critical Time to be guarded against by every friend and Wellwisher to his Country:

II. Be it therefore enacted by the General Assembly of the State of North Carolina, and by the Authority of the same, That no Negro or Mulatto Slave shall hereafter be set free, except for meritorious Services, to be adjudged of and allowed by the County Court, and

Licence first had and obtained thereupon. And when any Slave is or shall be set free by his or her Master or Owner otherwise than is herein before directed, it shall and may be lawful for any Free holder in this State, to apprehend and take up such Slave, and deliver him or her to the Sheriff of the County, who, on receiving such Slave, shall give such Freeholder a Receipt for the same; and the Sheriff shall commit all such Slaves to the Gaol of the County, there to remain until the next Court to be held for such County; and the Court of the County shall order all such confined slaves to be sold during the Term to the highest Bidder.

III. Provided always, That the Sheriff, upon committing any such Slave or Slaves, shall at least five Days before such Sale, give Notice in Writing to the last Owner or Owners, or the reputed Owner or Owners of such Slave or Slaves, of the Time and Place of Sale, and of the Name and Names of such Slaves, to the End that such Owner or Owners may, if he or they think proper, make his or their Claim to the same; but if such Owner or Owners shall neglect or refuse to appear on the Day of Sale (due Proof of the Service of such Notice being made to the Satisfaction of the Court) such Owner or Owners, so neglecting or refusing, shall be forever barred from making any Claim to such Slaves.

IV. And be it further enacted by the Authority aforesaid, That the neat Proceeds of the Money arising by such Sale shall be disposed of in the following Manner, that is to say, That one-fifth Part thereof shall be paid to the Takers up of such Negroes or Mulattoes, and that the remaining Part of such Money be paid into the Hands of the Public Treasurers, to defray the contingent Charges of Government, and to no other Intent, Use or Purpose, whatsover.

V. And be it enacted by the Authority aforesaid, That if any Slave or Slaves shall hereafter be allowed by his or her Master, Mistress, or Overseer, or other Person having the Care of such Slave or Slaves, to hire out him or herself, such Slave may be taken up by any Magistrate or Freeholder, and kept to hard Labour, for the Use of the Poor of the County, for any Time not exceeding Twenty Days; any Law, Usage, or Custom, to the contrary notwithstanding.

2

1777

The Trial of Several Negroes Manumitted by Friends

The North Carolina Yearly Meeting's Standing Committee believed that the new law should apply only to slaves set free after the Act to Prevent Domestic Insurrections was passed. They determined to use the courts to win freedom for manumitted blacks who were already being seized. At the end of May, the Standing Committee referred the matter to a committee of ten of its members. The committee engaged lawyers on behalf of blacks who had been apprehended and jailed.

All three lawyers were prominent North Carolina jurists who were active in the resistance to British oppression. James Iredell (1750–1799) moved from England to Edenton, North Carolina, where he studied law under Samuel Johnston. He eventually wed Johnston's sister. Licensed to practice law in 1770, he was a deputy king's attorney by 1774. In 1776, the provincial congress appointed him to review North Carolina's statutes for revision, and in December 1777 he accepted election as a judge of the state's superior courts. In 1790, he became an associate justice of the Supreme Court of the United States. Samuel Johnston (1733–1816) emigrated from Scotland to North Carolina as an infant. After attending Yale College, he moved to Edenton and read law and received his license. He served in the General Assembly from 1759 to 1775 and in the Provincial Congress from 1774 to 1776. As president of the Provincial Congress, Johnston became North Carolina's chief executive when the royal governor fled the colony. He served as state governor from 1787 to 1789 and as U.S. senator from 1789 to 1793.[6]

When the court convened at Hertford on 22 July, the lawyers for the blacks argued that because North Carolina's constitution prohibited ex post facto laws, slaves freed before the new act passed could not be seized and sold under its terms. They also argued that according to the act of 1741 that had set the requirements for manumission, including meritorious service by the slave and approval by the county court, manumitted slaves should be allowed six months to leave the state before they could be re-enslaved. Three of the five judges rejected the defense's argument.

An account of the trial of several Negroes that had been manumitted by Friends

> Source: Memorial and Address of the People Called Quakers, from Their Yearly Meeting Held in Philadelphia, by Adjournments, from the 25th of the 9th Month, to the 29th of the Same Inclusive, 1797 (Philadelphia: Philadelphia Meeting of the Religious Society of Friends, 1797), 5.

An account of the substance of the trial of several Negroes that had been manumitted by Friends subsequent to an Act of the General Assembly of the state of North-Carolina, passed at Newbern in the month of April or May last.[7]

The 22d. of the 7th month, 1777

At a County Court held at Hertford, in Perquimons North-Carolina, Jesse Eason, George Whidbee, Christopher Wright, Jesse Perry, and Jethro Ballard, active Justices on the bench.

Jasper Charlton, James Iredell, and Samuel Johnston attornies at law, employed by the Negroes.

1st. Jasper Charlton Introduced the business by allowing that Friends did not deny the manumitting those that were manumitted, and would make no claim to them, to whom they had relinquished all pretensions of claim, commending Friends honesty and Integrity therein.

2d. He introduced and read in court the substance of Friends reasons for what they had done, and commented notably upon it.

3d. He shewed that the former act of Assembly was not pleadable against the Negroes from the alteration in the constitution, and that there was now no church wardens to sell them and apply the money arising from the sale to the use of the parish.—

4th. He made it evidently appear that the act on which the Negroes were taken up expressly saying "that no Negro or Mulatto slave shall hereafter be set free excepting for meritorious services &c." could not affect those that were free before that act was made, and that the acts afterwards saying "is, or shall be set free" cannot with any propriety of speech be construed to look back and include them—and that such a construction would contradict the twenty-fourth section in the Bill of Rights, which saith that retrospective laws, punishing facts committed before the existence of such laws, and by them only declared criminal, are oppressive, unjust and incompatible with liberty,— wherefore no ex post facto law ought to be made. And that in section forty-fourth in the constitution or form of government that the declaration of rights is hereby declared to be part of the constitution of this state, and ought never to be Violated on any pretence whatsoever.[8]

The other lawyers fully agreeing with him in the strength of what he had advanced, and James Iredell producing sundry instances wherein other laws had the words is, or shall, in them, and were not, nor could not, be construed to look further back than the time present, was interrupted by justice Wright by denying that that was any thing to the purpose; to which Iredell replied, or to that effect, that he thought it to the purpose, for the information of the court that the words *is or shall,* were understood in other laws not to retrospect, and could not be otherwise understood in the present case, without a reflection upon the assembly, that they had violated the constitution, which he could not suppose they would do, and hoped the court would not give a judgment that would in its nature say they had; to whom Wright replied, that the Assembly were to form the constitution.

Samuel Johnston, after having by strong reasons and arguments supported the beforegoing arguments, and endeavoured to shew the court that they had not power by that act of Assembly to sell those Negroes, that were manumitted before it was made, concurred with the Assembly in thinking that under the situation of some of the southern provinces with respect to Negroes, that there was a necessity to guard against their being free, which he supposed was sufficiently guarded against, by understanding that Act to have power to prevent the freedom of such only as should be manumitted after it was made, and replied to justice Wright's supposition that the Assembly had a right to form the constitution, that the constitution was already settled by the members chosen for that purpose,[9] under which the General Assembly was to proceed, and that the Assembly had no more power to alter the constitution, than the court had to make laws that they were to act by, in courts of justice. And the Assembly being bound and limited by the constitution, as the court was bound and limited by the law and oath that they had taken, or to that purpose, and that the court had no right by that law to order the Negroes that were manumitted before the passing that act to be sold, which he expected they would order to be discharged.

Matters being managed and pleaded as is before related, or to that purpose, the large number of persons who were present upon the occasion being very quiet and attentive, the court proceeded to judgment, and after some time of conference among the justices, said it was carried by a small majority for the Negroes to be sold; it appearing afterwards that Christopher Wright Jesse Perry, and Jethro Ballard, were for the sale, and Jesse Eason and George Whidbee, against it.

3

1777–1778

Accounts of Sales of Blacks Emancipated by Friends

The day following the trial at Hertford, the county court sold to new owners twenty-nine of the manumitted who had been seized. When the yearly meeting convened in the autumn of 1777, it noted that all the slaves that the North Carolina Friends had freed had either been or would soon be apprehended and sold by the county court.

Court Order for the Sale of Emancipated Blacks

Source: Memorial and Address of the People Called Quakers, from Their Yearly Meeting Held in Philadelphia, by Adjournments, from the 25th of the 9th Month, to the 29th of the Same Inclusive, 1797 (Philadelphia: Philadelphia Meeting of the Religious Society of Friends, 1797), 4.

Perquimans County, July Term at Hereford, A.D. 1777.
THESE may certify, that it was then and there ordered, that the sheriff of this county, To-morrow morning at ten o'clock, expose to sale to the highest bidder for ready money, at the Court-house door, the several Negroes taken up as free, and in his custody, agreeable to law.
    Test. W. SKINNER, *Clerk pro tem.*
A true Copy, 25th August, 1791. *Test.* J. HARVEY, *Clerk*[10]

An Account of Sale of Negroes Sold at Hertford, North Carolina

Source: Records of the Pennsylvania Yearly Meeting, Meeting for Sufferings, Friends Historical Library of Swarthmore College, Swarthmore, Pennsylvania.

An account of Sale of Negroes Sold at Hertford July 23^d 1777.

Thomas Newby's	Glasgo	to Robt Salter	£88.—
	Tom & Susanna	Benjamin Edwards	136.10
	Jack	Josiah Granberry	131.—
	Cudgo	Ambrose Knox	136.—
	Patience	Thomas Smith	126.10
	Hannah	Josiah Granberry	119.—
8	Silla	Col^o Burton	142.10
Mark Newby's	James	Joseph Smithwick	184.10
	Ned	do do	253.10
	Zango	Colo Burton	260.10
4	Phebee	Turner Bindham	125.10
Benjn White's	Jacob	Josiah Grandb^y	140.—
	Will	do do	200.10
4	Sibba & Peter	Benjn Hawkins	242.10
White's	Cuffee & Rose	Thos· Hawey Jun	225.—
	Hannah	Joseph Richardson	92.15
4	Rose	Jos^h Grandberry	130.—
John Haskits	Judah	Col^o Burton	112.10
Matthew White's	Rose	do do	130.—
Lyddia White's	Dick & wife Jane	do do	250.—
Thos Nicholson's	⎫ Rich^d· & wife ⎬ Turner Bindham ⎭ Nicholas Nicholson's Jane		163.10
Tho Nicholson's	Pompey	John G Blount	162.—
William Albertsons	David	Robert Salter	130.—
10 Caleb Whites	Zelpha	Col^o Burton	<u>115.10</u>
			£3797.5

		April 23ᵈ 1778	
White's	Violet	Benjⁿ Phelps	306.7
	Fanny	Doctor Riddick	325.—
			631.7

		October Court 1777	
	Dick	Abraham Wilson	
4	Abram	Aleˣ MᶜLane	

		October Court 1788	
Townshend's	Jenny	Thomas Creecy	£50.
Robᵗ Newby's	Peggy	Nathan Creecy	78.—.6
	Jenny	Charles Moore	68.—
Smith's	Richᵈ	Willᵐ Askill	98.5
Robinsons	Hagar	Tho Creecy	27.10
	Fanny	do do	41.2
Albertson's	Caesar	Wᵐ Knowles	52.7
Haskitt's	Mingo	Wᵐ Hollowell	83.13
9 Thornton's	Aaron	Nathan Creecy	<u>90.5</u>
			687.17.6

4

1777

Friends' Reasons for Releasing Their Negroes from a State of Slavery

After the act of the North Carolina legislature that established grounds for re-enslaving those the Quakers had set free and after the county court proceedings that went forward under the terms of the act, the Standing Committee of the North Carolina Yearly Meeting believed it was important to promulgate the true motives behind the manumissions. In their October 1777 assembly, the yearly meeting formally placed the statement adopted by the Standing Committee on the record.

A Just and Righteous Plea in Behalf of Liberty & Freedom

Source: Minutes of North Carolina Friends Yearly Meeting, 25 October 1777, North Carolina Yearly Meeting Archives, Friends Historical Collection, Guilford College, Greensboro, North Carolina.

A Just and Righteous Plea in behalf of Liberty & freedom

If we are called in question concerning the good Deed done to the much Injured Africans in Restoring to them that Liberty and Freedom which is a Natural and Unalienable Right of all Mankind the Cause is too good to deny it—And therefore are Willing to Inform all whom it may Concern the true Cause and Motive that induced us so to do in Order that if any are found fighting against God they may be left with out excuse—

That from Mature deliberate Consideration And the Conviction of our own Minds, being fully persuaded that freedom is the Natural right of all Mankind, and that no Law Moral or Divine has given us a

Right to or property in the persons of any of our fellow Creatures any longer than in a State of Minority, And being desireous to fulfill the Injunction of our Lord and Saviour Jesus Christ by doing as we would be done by—

The above laudable Motives prevailing on our Minds beyond all Selfish and Worldly Considerations, we believe that our Conduct therein hath the Sanction of Divine Approbation and ought to be Approved by all Reasonable Men—

For having endeavoured to steer clear from the least Stain or Guilt in that guiltless Blood shed on the Earth, when that awfull day shall come in which the * "Earth shall disclose her Blood and no more cover her Slain"; fully believeing that the trade in Slaves & Souls of Men is justly chargeable with a large share there in, and that those who do remain partakers with Murtherers and Men stealers, will be involved in their guilt; and therefore, whatever Ignorance may surmise to the Contrary, haveing thro' Divine assistance done what we believe was our Duty to do; if Men should be permitted to Reduce them to a State of Bondage and Slavery, the guilt will be laid to the charge of those that are the cause thereof; and we shall appeal to him that Judgeth righteously without respect to Persons.

* Isa. 26 c. 21 v.

5

1778

The Superior Court Annuls Re-Enslavements

In November 1778, the superior court of the district of Edenton heard on appeal the case of the blacks manumitted by North Carolina Quakers. Just as three leaders of the North Carolina bar had represented the blacks in the lower court, another prominent North Carolina attorney argued their case before the superior court. Their advocate was notable Whig politician William Hooper, delegate to the Continental Congress and signer of the Declaration of Independence. Concurring with the defense that the act regarding manumissions could not be applied retrospectively without violating both the state constitution and natural rights, the superior court reversed the order of the Pasquotank and Perquimans county courts that the blacks be sold and re-enslaved.

James Iredell, who had been one of the lawyers for the blacks in the Perquimans County court, heard the appeal with two other judges of the superior court. Iredell personally delivered the superior court's decision to the clerks of the Pasquotank and Perquimans county courts. It was publicly read in the December 1778 term of the former court and in the April 1779 term of the latter court.[11]

Order of the Superior Court of the District of Edenton

Source: Memorial and Address of the People Called Quakers, from Their Yearly Meeting Held in Philadelphia, by Adjournments, from the 25th of the 9th Month, to the 29th of the Same Inclusive, 1797 (Philadelphia: Philadelphia Meeting of the Religious Society of Friends, 1797), 6.

STATE OF NORTH-CAROLINA.

At a superior court of law, begun and held at the court-house in Edenton, for the district of Edenton, the first day of May, in the year of our Lord one thousand seven hundred and seventy-eight, before the honourable Samuel Ashe, Samuel Spence, and James Iredell, esquires, justices.

On motion of William Hooper, esquire, attorney at law, in behalf of the following Negroes, viz. Glasgow, Tom, Susanna, Jack, Cudgo, Patience, Hannah, Silla, James, Ned, Langa, Phœbe, Jacob, Will, Sibb, Cuff, Rose, Hannah, Peter, Rose, Dick, Jane, Richard, Jane, Pompey, David, Zilpha, Violet, Fanny, Dick, Abraham, Judy, Rose, Hannah, David, Charles, Toby, Nero, Precilla, Rose, Judith, Jane, Samuel, Hagar, Ann, Sarah, on a suggestion that the said persons though free subjects of the state, were sold and enslaved, by order of the county courts of Perquimons and Pasquotank, in express violation of the constitution of this state, and contrary to natural justice, and that there are manifest errors, and irregularities in the said proceedings. Ordered, that a Certiorari issue, unless sufficient cause to the contrary be shewn within the three first days of the next term.

And at the superior court of law, begun and held at Edenton court-house, for the district of Edenton, on the second day of November, one thousand seven hundred and seventy-eight, before the honourable Samuel Spence, esquire, one of the justices of the said court.

On motion that the rule to shew cause granted last term, why a writ of Certiorari should not issue, directed to the justices of Perquimons county, to remove all the orders and proceedings of the court of the said county, relating to the sale and enslaving of the following Negroes, to wit; Glasgow, Tom, Susannah, Jack, Cudgo, Patience, Hannah, Silla, James, Ned, Langa, Phœbe, Jacob, Will, Sibb, Peter, Cuff, Rose, Hannah, Rose, Dick, Jane, Richard, James, Pompey, David, Zilpha, Violet, Fanny, Dick, Abraham, Judy, Rose, might be made absolute, affidavit having been made of the due service of the said rule upon the said justices in open court, and they failing to shew cause, and it is further ordered, that a writ of Certiorari issue, *instante,* directed to the clerk of the said county court, commanding him to certify a transcript of the said orders and proceedings immediately. Ordered, that such a writ of certiorari issue to the said clerk according.

On motion that a writ of certiorari should issue to the justices of Pasquotank county, to remove all the orders and proceedings of the court of the said county relating to the sale and enslaving of the following persons, or either of them, viz. Hannah, David, Charles, Toby, Pritchard, Nero, and Precilla, Rose, Judith, Jane, Albertson, Samuel, Hagar, Ann, and Sarah, on a suggestion that the said persons, though free subjects of the state, were sold and enslaved by order of the said court, in express violation of the constitution of this state, and contrary to natural justice, and that there are manifest errors and irregularities in the said proceedings. Ordered, that a Certiorari issue accordingly, unless sufficient cause to the contrary be shewn, within the three first days of the next term.

On motion that a writ of certiorari should issue to the justices of Perquimons county, to remove all the orders and proceedings of the court of the said county, relating to the sale and enslaving of the following persons, or either of them, viz. Dinah, Robin, Luke, and Nancy, on a suggestion that the said persons, though free subjects of the state, were sold and enslaved by order of the said court, in express violation of the constitution of this state, and contrary to natural justice, and that there are manifest errors and irregularities in the said proceedings.

In obedience to a Certiorari issued from this court, by order thereof, to the clerk of the county of Perquimons, directing him to certify certain proceedings had in the said court of Perquimons, relative to the sale of certain Negroes manumitted by divers persons of the sect called Quakers, the said proceedings being duly returned and certified, and arguments having been offered and fully heard, the court, for divers and manifest irregularities in the face of the record certified, and because it appears to them, that the said county court, in such their proceedings have exceeded their jurisdiction, violated the rights of the subjects, and acted in direct opposition to the Bill of Rights of this state, considered justly as part of the constitution thereof, by giving a law, not intended to affect this case, a retrospective operation, thereby to deprive free men of this state of their liberty, contrary to the law of the land {, *Ordered therefore, that the proceedings so Certifyed by Quashed, & held as null & Void.*}[12]

I William Blair, clerk of the superior court of law for the district of Edenton, do hereby certify the above and subjoined to be a true copy from the records of the said court. Given under my hand and seal of office at Edenton, the fourteenth day of October, Anno Domini, 1796.

    WILL. BLAIR, Clk.

I Spruce Macay, esquire, senior judge attending the superior court of law for the district of Edenton, do hereby certify that the above attestation of William Blair, clerk of the said court, is in due form. Given under my hand at Edenton, the fourteenth day of October, Anno Domini, 1796.

    SPRUCE MACAY, J.S.C.D.E.

Note—*That part of the Record, which expresses the reversal of the judgment of the lower court, is by mistake omitted in the transcript.*

6

1779

New State Legislation Annuls the Superior Court's Judgment

During the 1778–1779 session, a joint committee of the legislature found that "the conduct of the said Quakers in setting their slaves free when our open and declared enemies were endeavoring to bring about an Insurrection of the Slaves, was highly criminal and reprehensible," and the legislature specifically legalized the seizures and sales in 1777 of the slaves freed by the Quakers. It also eliminated the six months' grace period the law had allowed for manumitted slaves to leave the state.[13]

An Act for Apprehending and selling certain Slaves set free contrary to Law and for Confirming the Sales of Others, and for other purposes.

> Source: Laws of North Carolina for 1778, Chapter XII, in The State Records of North Carolina, collected and edited by Walter Clark, Vol. 24, Laws 1777–1788 (1905; reprint, Wilmington, N.C.: Broadfoot Publishing, 1994), 221.

An Act for Apprehending and selling certain Slaves set free contrary to Law and for Confirming the Sales of Others, and for other purposes.

I. Whereas, by an Act entitled an Act to prevent Domestick Insurrections & for other purposes, it is provided, that no person shall liberate his or her slave except for meritorious Services, to be judged of and allowed by the County Court, and by the said Act, it is Directed in what Manner and for what purposes such liberated slaves shall be apprehended and sold; and whereas, before the passing of the said

Act, and since the sixteenth day of April, one thousand seven hundred and seventy five, divers evil minded persons, intending to disturb the public peace, did liberate and set free their slaves, notwithstanding the same was especially contrary to the Laws of this State and the County Courts of Perquimans and Pasquotank, conceiving they had power to proceed against all such liberated slaves, did order them to be sold to the highest bidder, and whereas, doubts have now arisen whether the purchasers of such slaves have a good and legal title thereto, for remedy whereof,

II. Be it Enacted by the General Assembly of the State of North Carolina, and it is hereby Enacted by the Authority of the same, that all such sales made bona fide and for valuable consideration shall be deemed good and valid to all intents and purposes, and as many negroes are now going at large to the terror of the good People of this State, who were liberated in manner aforesaid previous to the passing of the said recited Act,

III. Be it further enacted by the Authority aforesaid, That the same proceeding shall and may be had against all such illegally liberated slaves as is directed in the said recited Act intitled, An Act to prevent domestic insurrections, and for other purposes, in the same manner as if such negro slaves had been set free after the passing of the same; Provided, that nothing herein contained shall deprive of Liberty any Slave who having been liberated & not sold by order of any Court has inlisted in the service of this or the United States previous to the passing of this Act.

7

1779

Memorial from Friends Who Manumitted Slaves to the North Carolina General Assembly

In 1779, the yearly meeting responded to the legislature's libel about the Quakers' motives in freeing their slaves by drafting a petition that explained that they had acted on their convictions that freedom was a natural right that blacks had not forfeited and that slaveholding was unchristian. The fifteen Friends who had freed their slaves in 1777, including Thomas Newby and George Walton, signed on behalf of the meeting. However, on the recommendation of sympathetic legislators who advised that passions on the issue were at a high pitch, the yearly meeting chose not to present the petition to the assembly.

Minutes of the North Carolina Friends Standing Committee

Source: Minutes of the Standing Committee, Eastern Quarter, 10/25/1779, North Carolina Yearly Meeting Archives, Friends Historical Collection, Guilford College, Greensboro, North Carolina.

The Committee met at Old Neck the 25th of 10th M^o 1779 and made choice of George Walton Clerk for this time. And taking under Consideration the destres'd Situation of the Negroes that had been Set free, & again Reduced to Bondage by a late Act pass'd for that purpose, thought it Expedient to present a Memorial to the Assembly on their Acc^t and one being prepared, and Deliberately Read & Consider'd Was Approved and Signed by Sundry Friends who had Mannumitted their Negroes which here follows—To the General Assembly of North Carolina now sitting at Hallifax, The Memorial of Sundry persons who had Manumitted their Slaves, Respectfully Sheweth, That, whereas the last General assembly held at Hallifax passed an Act for "apprehending & Selling Certain Slaves set free contrary to Law, and to distract the publick peace, & for Confirming the Sales of others," referring to the act to prevent Domestick Insurrections.—In answer to which, we declare it was from mature deliberate Consideration, & the Conviction of our own Minds, being fully persuaded that Freedom is the natural right of all Mankind, & that no Law moral or Divine has given us a right to or property in the Persons of any of our fellow Creatures, any longer than they are in a State of Minority, and being desirous to fulfill the Injunction of our Lord & Saviour Jesus Christ by doing to others as we would be done by; these motives prevailed on our Minds beyond all Selfish & Worldly Considerations, and We believe our Conduct therein hath the Sanction of Divine Approbation. And we are So far from doing any thing to distract the publick peace, that we do heartily wish & ardently pray for the peace & Happiness of all Mankind.—The passing of the aforesaid two Acts of Assembly, & the proceeding upon them, we fully believe to be not only a Violation of the full & Explicit Declaration of the Congress on the Subject of Universal Liberty & the Common Rights of Mankind, publish'd at the first entering upon the present Contest with great Britain;[14] But manifestly contradicts the Declaration & bill of Rights on which your right to make Laws depend, which expressly declares, Sect: 24th, "That retrospective Laws punishing Facts committed before the existance of such Laws, & by them only declared Criminal, are oppressive, unjust & incompatible with Liberty, wherefore no Expost Facto Law ought to be made." And in the Constitution or form of Government, it is expressly declared, Sect: 44th "That the Declaration of Rights is hereby declared to be part of the present Constitution, & ought not to be violated on any pretence whatsoever."—

The Superiour Court held at Edenton have publickly declared on record, (Nov[r] 2nd '78) That it Appear'd to them, that the County Court (who ordered the Sale of several of the Negroes) "in Such their proceedings, have exceeded their Jurisdiction, Violated the Rights of the Subjects, and acted in direct Opposition to the Bill of Rights of this State, considered justly as a part of the Constitution thereof, by giving a Law, not intended to effect this case, a retrospective Operation, thereby to deprive free Men, of this State, of their Liberty, contrary to the Law of the Land, Ordered therefore, that the proceedings so

Certifyed be Quashed, & held as null & Void." In Virginia many Negroes have been Manumitted since the Year '75, & none of them been taken up & sold, that we have heard of, except one for Misbehaviour. In Maryland there is an Act of Assembly (as we are Credibly informd) prescribing a Method for Manumitting Slaves, by which any Person has liberty to Set free any Slave or Slaves they are in possession of, provided Such Slave or Slaves are under Fifty Years of age—and Sound in Mind & Body, & that it is not in prejudice of Creditors without any other Restrictions. In Pennsylvania, the Jerseys, New York, Rhode Island & New England, Manumitting Slaves is frequent by many of other Societies, as well as our own, without offense to Authority.—We believing that Awful day will come, in which the Earth shall disclose her Blood, & shall no more cover her stain Isa^h 26 Chap. 21st ver. and apprehending the Trade in Slaves & Souls of Men hath a Large share therein, Wherefore we earnestly intreat you to take the whole matter under your Several considerations & relieve the oppressed.—

Signed the 25th of the 10th Mo. 1779,

By

Zachariah Nixon	George Walton	Thomas Nicholson
Benjamin Albertson	Thomas White	William Albertson
Caleb Winslow	Caleb White	Thomas Newby
William White	Matthew White	Mark Newby
Josiah White	Joseph Henley	Chalkley Albertson

And Thos Nicholson Thos Newby Mark Newby Joseph Henley Zachariah Nixon & George Walton are Appointed to present the Same, and make Report to this Committee."

8

1779

Thomas Nicholson Upbraids an Informer

Two weeks after signing the 1779 memorial to the General Assembly, Thomas Nicholson wrote the following letter in which he harshly rebuked a man who had informed the state authorities of the identity or location of slaves that Nicholson had privately freed. Perhaps "B. H." was the Benjamin Hawkins identified in the "Account of Sale of Negroes Sold at Hertford July 23^d 1777"(document 3 above) as the purchaser of two slaves, Peter and Sibba, who had been seized and sold back into slavery after Benjamin White had freed them.[15]

Thomas Nicholson to B. H.

Source: The Friend 18 (October 1844): 13–14.

> Perquimons county, the 6th of the
> Eleventh month,1779.
> Friend B. H.—As I have long borne with patience thy frequent, cruel, barbarous and unjust behaviour towards myself and family, I am now determined to break silence in great plainness, in order to be clear of thy blood, if thou dies in thy sins. Open rebuke is better than secret love. I have ever retained a great regard and love for the name of thy family, which I believe that thyself and two brothers have greatly lessened by your violent and shameful conduct towards the poor oppressed negroes. I suppose you justify yourselves under the pretended sanction of a cruel and barbarous human law, which is a violation of the present constitution, and a shame and reproach to our great pretensions to liberty and freedom. In considering the subject,

the following questions and answers do very pertinently arise, viz. Can law, human law, change the nature of things? can it change darkness into light, or evil into good? By no means! Notwithstanding ten thousand laws, right is right, and wrong is wrong. As to the law under which the negroes were sold, it is evident to every wise and impartial man that fully considers it, that it hath not the strength of a spider's web in it, and is void of itself. I am fully satisfied that the courts which ordered the sales of the negroes, had no more legal power or justice on their side, to support their proceedings therein, than I have to order thyself and wife to be sold for slaves during your natural lives, and to entail cruel slavery and bondage upon your posterity to the end of time. I have been informed that as thou was once passing by my plantation, thou said that it made thy heart glad to see so many young negroes. If thy gladness arose from an expectation of a further prey to thy greedy, if not bloody hands, and if thou expects to get thy living by freebooting and the gain of oppression, it is time to turn thy view some other way. I fully believe that thou never hereafter will be able to drink any more that [than] deadly poison in the one-fifth of the sale-money of any more of the negroes that I have manumitted, as I shall endeavour to guard them from ever falling into thy avaricious hands. As thou hast put thyself upon a level with some of the lower class to carry on thy cruel purpose, I do tell thee plainly, that although hand hath joined in hand therein, the wicked will not go unpunished. Therefore it is my advice to thee, to submit thyself to so deep a purgation, as to cause thee to vomit up again the portion of the gain of oppression, which thou hast greedily swallowed, otherwise I much question whether thou ever dies in peace of mind. That thou may happily experience this by true godly sorrow, which works repentance to salvation, never to be repented of, is the hearty prayer of thy sincere friend,

  Thomas Nicholson.

9

1788

Memorial from the North Carolina Yearly Meeting to the North Carolina General Assembly

The yearly meeting regularly sent memorials to the General Assembly seeking a change in the law of manumission that would protect the slaves they set free from re-enslavement. The version of these memorials submitted in 1788 was short and poignant and, borrowing language from the Declaration of Independence, combined appeals to the principles of the American Revolution with appeals to compassion and religion. As is demonstrated in the revision of the law the General Assembly passed in the session that convened the following month (see document 10 below), this memorial did not soften the hearts of the legislators.

The Remonstrance and Petition of the people called Quakers

Source: Minutes of North Carolina Friends Yearly Meeting, 30 October 1788, North Carolina Yearly Meeting Archives, Friends Historical Collection, Guilford College, Greensboro, North Carolina.

To the next General Assembly of the State of North Carolina to be held at Fayetteville.—The Remonstrance and Petition of the people called Quakers from their Yearly Meeting held at Wells's in the County of Perquimans by adjournment from the 27th day of the 10th month to the 30th of the same, inclusive, 1788.—

Respectfully Sheweth,

That as there are two acts of the General Assembly now in force for the prohibition of the freedom of Slaves, which we humbly apprehend is in no wise Consistant with the principles of the Established Constitution, & contrary to the Declaration of Independence of the United

States of America.—Notwithstanding we believe those Laws are not Constitutional, Yet they have been rigorously prosecuted against Several Negroes which were Liberated, by which they are again reduced into a State of Slavery, being dragged from their lawful Occupations, and Exposed to public Sale like brute Beasts to the parting of Man and Wife, and parents & Children, against the Laws of nature & of nature's God: We being again religiously concerned to lay their Suffering Case before you, ardently desiring that you may take the Case into Serious Consideration, & repeal the aforesaid Acts, & grant an Act of toleration to such as may be Emancipated.—And Your Petitioners, in duty bound, shall ever thankfully acknowledge, &c.—

Signed by order & on behalf of the Yearly Meeting aforesaid,
> by Levi Munden Clk.
> to the Meeting this Year.

10

1788

An Act to Amend an Act Entitled "An Act to Prevent Domestic Insurrections"

Despite the frustration that North Carolina Friends must have experienced when the men and women they liberated were re-enslaved, they continued to free slaves. In response, in 1788 North Carolina's legislature strengthened the enforcement provisions of the law forbidding manumissions unsanctioned by the courts. The new law rewarded not just freeholders (landowners) who apprehended improperly freed slaves, but also any freemen, freeholders or not, whose information led to the apprehension of such slaves. The act also required county sheriffs to act on such information freemen provided.

An Act to Amend an Act Entitled "An Act to Prevent Domestic Insurrections"

Source: Laws of North Carolina for 1788, Chapter XX, in The State Records of North Carolina, collected and edited by Walter Clark, Vol. 24, Laws 1777–1788 (1905; reprint, Wilmington, N.C.: Broadfoot Publishing, 1994), 24: 964.

Whereas by the before recited Act it is Enacted, that no person shall liberate or set free his or her slave except for meritorious services to be adjudged and allowed of by the county court, and by the said Act it is directed in what manner and for what purpose slaves illegally liberated shall be apprehended and sold: And whereas divers persons from religious motives, in violation of the said law, continue to liberate their slaves, who are now going at large to the terror of the people of this State: And whereas the mode prescribed for apprehending such slave or slaves is found by experience not to answer the good purposes by the said Act intended, the power of apprehending liberated slaves being confined to freeholders only, and optional in them whether they will exercise the authority or not; and it appearing the said law is not fully adequate to the good purposes intended: Therefore,

I. Be it Enacted by the General Assembly of the State of North Carolina, and it is hereby Enacted by the authority of the same, That from and after the passing of this Act, if any slave hath been liberated contrary to the before recited Act, should be still within the limits of this State, and all slaves liberated after the passing of this Act should be known or suspected to be lurking in any of the inhabited parts thereof, then and in such cases, on information made to any justice of the peace by any freeman of such liberated slave or slaves going at large or lurking about, contrary to the true intent and meaning of the said Act, then and in such case the justice to whom such information is made, is hereby impowered and required immediately to issue his warrant, directed to the sheriff of the county, commanding him to make diligent search and to apprehend all such slave or slaves, and to commit him, her or them to the gaol of the county, there to remain until the next succeeding court of the county, on which warrant all procedings shall be regulated in the same manner as is directed by the before recited Act; and that the person or persons apprehending any such slave or slaves by virtue of any such warrant, shall be entitled to the emoluments as is allowed to freeholders by the before recited Act. Provided nevertheless, That nothing in this Act shall be construed to debar any freeholder or freeholders from stepping forward in the execution of said law in the usual manner, or to divest them of the emoluments given by the said Act.

11

1797

A Bill to Thwart Quaker Manumissions

In January 1797, Thomas Jordan, clerk of the Standing Committee of the Eastern Quarter of the North Carolina Yearly Meeting, sent to John Elliott of the Philadelphia Society of Friends a printed copy of a bill that had been proposed in the North Carolina General Assembly but not adopted. Jordan wanted to show the Pennsylvania Friends "the disposition of some of our Legislators." Even though it never became law, the bill is of historical interest because the behaviors the bill's author intended to regulate suggest steps North Carolina Friends were taking to avoid the re-enslavement of blacks they had freed.[16]

A BILL to prevent the abuses of slaves and persons of colour, and to impose further restrictions on certain societies and others in this state, who endeavour to instil principles of emancipation in the minds of slaves.

Source: Records of the Pennsylvania Yearly Meeting, Meeting for Sufferings, Friends Historical Library of Swarthmore College, Swarthmore, Pennsylvania.

A BILL to prevent the abuses of slaves and persons of colour, and to impose further restrictions on certain societies and others in this state, who endeavour to instil principles of emancipation in the minds of slaves.

WHEREAS it has been made appear to this General Assembly by the presentments of the grand juries of the several county and superior courts of the district of Edenton, and the petitions and remonstrances of the Justices of the Peace and other respectable inhabitants of said district, that the same is in great and imminent danger from the diffusion of emancipation principles in the minds of the slaves:

> I. *Be it enacted by the General Assembly of the state of North-Carolina, and it is hereby enacted by the authority of the same,* That . . .

* * *

VI. . . . whereas sundry people under pretence of religious motives, send their slaves to the northern and eastern states, and having procured their emancipation in such states, return as freemen to this state: Therefore, *Be it enacted,* That all negroes of that description shall be held and deemed as slaves illegally emancipated, and shall be treated as such, agreeable to the directions of the several acts of Assembly of this state. Provided always, That the above recited clause shall not be in force until the first day of March next, in order that such black person, if they think proper, may return to the place where they were liberated.

* * *

XI. And whereas by the secret artifices of the Quakers, it is difficult in a variety of instances to discover and prove the actual emancipation of the negroes, and to carry into effect the act passed in the year 1788, Chapter XX, to prevent domestic insurrections;[17] *Be it enacted,* That if any negro shall be found to be going at large, or living in byeplaces, or not under the actual controul and service of the owner, and paying taxes for the same, such presumptive proofs, added to the general reputation of the owner or reputed owner on the subject of emancipation, holding such principles from motives of conscience (where positive evidence of the liberation cannot be had) shall be held as sufficient evidence of emancipation; and such negro shall and may be taken up and sold according to the directions of the several acts of Assembly relative to emancipated negroes. And in all cases of emancipated slaves, or of slaves taken up having hired their own time, under the act of 1784, Chapter IV, the costs shall always go with the judgment of the court against the person emancipating, or allowing the negro or negroes to hire his, her or their own time.

PART IV

The Nation

African-American Freedom and
the Manumission Debate in Congress

In the latter half of the eighteenth century, their religious beliefs led most Quakers as well as many Baptists, Congregationalists, and Methodists to conclude that slaveholding was a sin. Similarly, during and after the War of Independence, Enlightenment notions of liberty and equality, two central elements of the ideology of the American Revolution, caused many Patriots to question the justice of slavery. The revolutionary belief in a natural right to liberty raised the question of why blacks were denied their liberty. At the same time the revolutionaries' principled opposition to hereditary legal status raised the question of why some people inherited the slave status of their mothers. If all men are created equal, as the Declaration of Independence asserts, one could not justify the enslavement of blacks on the basis of their race. Furthermore, prominent examples of accomplished African Americans such as the Boston poet Phillis Wheatley and the Philadelphia mathematician, surveyor, and almanac maker Benjamin Banneker undercut the proslavery argument of racial inferiority.[1]

During the War of Independence, many white Patriots thus recognized the inconsistency of slavery with the ideology that justified their resistance to British oppression. In the North, where powerful economic considerations did not oppose it, states implemented emancipation. In some states such as Massachusetts, where the courts declared slavery incompatible with the state constitution, emancipation took place all at once. But many northern governments implemented a gradual process, such as freeing those born as slaves when they attained a certain age. Gradual emancipation took into consideration property rights of slaveowners and the notion that slaves had to be prepared for freedom. Pennsylvania's 1780 act was the earliest of the gradual emancipation laws adopted in the northern states and the most conservative. The act specified that anyone born into slavery within the state after the passing of the act would be free at the age of twenty-eight. If an owner failed to register his slaves, those slaves were to be free. Pennsylvania's law freed few slaves immediately. Although it ended the legal importation of slaves, it permitted the buying and selling of those who had been registered.[2]

A more complex situation developed in the South during and after the war. Emancipation societies did appear in several places in the Upper South, frequently led by Friends. In Virginia during the period 1782 to 1806, when the commonwealth had a liberalized manumission law in effect, masters voluntarily freed some ten thousand slaves. That phenomenon, however, does not mean that antislavery sentiment was widespread in the Old Dominion. Eva Sheppard Wolf argues persuasively that most manumissions in Virginia in the 1790s stemmed not from antislavery beliefs but rather from the realization that the hope of eventual freedom could act as an incentive to keep a slave faithful and diligent at his work or from the desire to reward a faithful servant. Such manumissions did not threaten the prevailing system of involuntary servitude but actually helped legitimize the institution of slavery.[3] Similarly, John Michael Shay finds that the antislavery movement in North Carolina "was more apparent than real, more an illusion than actuality." The Society of Friends was the only group in North Carolina whose commitment to antislavery was more than superficial. Even the Methodist General Conference rule (adopted in 1784) that clergy must emancipate their slaves and that no slaveholder could hold office in annual conferences and quarterly meetings did not apply to North Carolina's Methodists: the rule was to be enforced "no farther than is consistent with the laws of the states in which they reside."[4]

In fact, during the 1790s, even the minimal movement that had been made toward emancipation in the South was reversed. The Haitian Revolution of 1791, in which black slaves rose up, killed their masters, and took over the country, frightened whites in the southern United States, the more so in areas where a large percentage of the population was enslaved.

Whites feared that any encouragement of black aspirations for freedom would lead to servile insurrection and race war. Then, in 1793, Eli Whitney designed a simplified and easily constructed cotton gin that increased the speed at which cotton could be separated from its seeds and soon stimulated large-scale cotton production. The rapid spread of cotton cultivation in the Lower South called for a large, cheap labor force, creating a powerful economic incentive to perpetuate slavery.

In the 1790s, few southerners were prepared to argue openly that slavery was moral. Most took the position that it was an unavoidable evil. At the same time, most northerners were content to separate themselves from direct involvement in slavery. Their antislavery activism did not extend to eliminating slavery from the South. Southerners, though, were unconvinced that northern antislavery sentiment posed no threat to slavery's continuation in the South. Whatever their stance on slavery's morality, southerners were agreed on one thing with few exceptions—that slavery was an issue that must be left to southerners alone.[5]

As a consequence of emancipation in the North and its failure in the South, slavery emerged from the Revolution as a critical sectional issue. The divisions between the North and the South over slavery found embodiment in the compromises that produced the Constitution of the United States. The drafters of the Constitution found it either embarrassing or shameful to include the words *slave* and *slavery* in the fundamental law of the land, and so neither word appears in the Constitution of the United States. Nevertheless, slavery is the subject of numerous provisions in the Constitution, where it is referred to by euphemisms or circumlocutions.

The delegates to the 1787 Constitutional Convention agreed to include in a state's population three-fifths of the enslaved rather than all or none of them when apportioning representation in the House of Representatives and direct taxes (Article I, section 2, paragraph 3). This provision helped reassure the southern states that they would have a strong influence in Congress. The Constitution's prohibition on export duties (Article I, section 9, paragraph 5) provided economic protection to plantation crops (such as tobacco and rice) produced by slave labor. By denying Congress the power to outlaw the importation of slaves until 1808 (Article I, section 9, paragraph 1), the Constitution gave American citizens a full generation in which to import additional slaves.

One more compromise relating to slavery is Article IV, section 2, paragraph 3, which reads as follows:

No Person held to Service or Labour in one State, under the Laws thereof, escaping into another, shall, in Consequence of any Law or Regulation therein, be discharged from such Service or Labour, but shall be delivered up on Claim of the Party to whom such Service or Labour may be due.

The Fugitive Slave Law of 12 February 1793, enacted by the U.S. Congress, implemented the intent of this provision by providing a federal mechanism for apprehending escaped slaves and returning them to their owners across state lines.[6]

If slavery was not the preeminent sectional issue in American national politics before 1808, as one historian has recently argued,[7] the congressional debates in 1797 over manumissions by North Carolina Friends underscore the issue's explosive potential that would be realized beginning a decade later.

Quaker Antislavery Turns Outward

Since their principles forbade them from taking sides in an armed dispute or abetting a rebellion against constituted authority, most Quakers stayed neutral during the War of Independence. But after the Treaty of Paris was signed in 1783, in which Great Britain recognized the United States of America as an independent nation, Friends in America felt at liberty to submit to the authority of the state and confederation governments. Thus it was that in 1783, having eradicated slavery within the denomination, the Society of Friends turned its sights on eradicating that evil from their newly independent country. In that year, representatives of the Philadelphia yearly meeting presented to the Congress of the Confederation a petition bearing the signatures of 535 members of the meeting that urged the congress to put an end to the importation of slaves.[8] Six years later, in 1789, with the convening of the first U.S. Congress under the newly ratified Constitution, the society renewed its effort to get the national government to act against slavery, promoting an amendment to abolish the slave trade immediately. These efforts failed, principally because of the intransigence of the South and the unwillingness of the North to risk dissolving the bonds of union that held the sections together.[9]

1

1797

Petition of Freemen

In 1797, the confrontation between the Quakers of North Carolina and the state of North Carolina came to debate on the floor of the U.S. House of Representatives as the result of two petitions. The first was the following memorial from four former North Carolina slaves who had been manumitted by their Quaker owners and had taken up residence in Philadelphia. Fearing re-enslavement and forcible return to North Carolina under the 1793 Fugitive Slave Act, they sought the help of the Rev. Absalom Jones, one of the founders of the African Methodist Episcopal Church, who helped them draft the following memorial, "the earliest black petition to Congress."[10]

The Annals of Congress

Source: Annals of Congress, 4th Cong., 2d sess., 2015–18.

To the President, Senate, and House of Representatives.

The Petition and Representation of the under-named Freemen, respectfully showeth.—

That being of African descent, late inhabitants and natives of North Carolina, to you only, under God, can we apply with any hope of effect, for redress of our grievances, having been compelled to leave the State wherein we had a right of residence, as freemen liberated under the hand and seal of humane and conscientious masters, the validity of which act of justice, in restoring us to our native right of freedom, was confirmed by judgment of the superior court of North Carolina, wherein it was brought to trial;[11] yet, not long after this decision, a law of that State was enacted, under which men of cruel disposition, and void of just principle, received countenance and authority in violently seizing, imprisoning, and selling into slavery, such as had been so emancipated; whereby we were reduced to the necessity of separating from some of our nearest and most tender connexions, and of seeking refuge in such parts of the Union where more regard is paid to the public declaration in favor of liberty and the common right of men, several hundreds under our circumstances, having, in consequence of the said law, been hunted day and night, like beasts of the forest, by armed men with dogs, and made prey of as free and lawful plunder. Among others thus exposed, I, Jupiter Nicholson, of Perquimons county, North Carolina, after being set free by my master, Thomas Nicholson, and having been about two years employed as a seaman in the service of Zachary Nickson, on coming on shore, was pursued by men with dog and arms; but was favored to escape by night to Virginia, with my wife, who was manumitted by Gabriel Cosand, where I resided about four years in the town of Portsmouth, chiefly employed in sawing boards and scantling; from thence I removed with my wife to Philadelphia, where I have been employed, at times, by water, working along shore, or sawing wood.—I left behind me a father and mother, who were manumitted by Thomas Nicholson and Zachary Dickson;[12] they have been since taken up with a beloved brother, and sold into cruel bondage.

I, Jacob Nicholson, also of North Carolina, being set free by my master, Joseph Nicholson, but continuing to live with him till, being pursued day and night, I was obliged to leave my abode, sleep in the woods, and stacks in the fields, &c., to escape the hands of violent men who, induced by the profit afforded them by law, followed this course as a business; at length, by night, I made my escape, leaving a mother, one child, and two brothers, to see whom I dare not return.

I, Job Albert, manumitted by Benjamin Albertson, who was my careful guardian to protect me from being afterwards taken and sold, providing me with a house to accommodate me and my wife, who was liberated by William Robertson; but we were night and day hunted by men armed with guns, swords, and pistols, accompanied with mastiff dogs; from whose violence being one night apprehensive of immediate danger, I left my dwelling locked and barred, and fastened with a chain, being at some distance from it, while my wife was by my kind master locked up under his roof. I heard them break into my house, where, not finding their prey, they got but a small booty, a handkerchief of about a dollar value, and some provisions; but, not long after, I was discovered and seized by Alexander Stafford, William Stafford, and Thomas Creesy, who were armed with guns and clubs. After binding me with my hands behind me, and a rope round my arms and body, they took me about four miles to Hartford prison, where I lay four weeks, suffering much for want of provision; from thence, with the assistance of a fellow-prisoner, (a white man,) I made my escape, and for three dollars was conveyed, with my wife, by a humane person, in a covered wagon by night, to Virginia, where, in the neighborhood of Portsmouth, I continued unmolested about four years, being chiefly engaged in sawing boards and plank. On being advised to move Northward, I came with my wife to Philadelphia, where I have labored for a livelihood upwards of two years, in Summer mostly, along shore in vessels and stores, and sawing wood in the Winter. My mother was set free by Phineas Nickson, my sister by John Trueblood, and both taken up and sold into slavery, myself deprived of the consolation of seeing them, without being exposed to the like grievous oppression.

I, Thomas Pritchet, was set free by my master Thomas Pritchet, who furnished me with land to raise provisions for my use, where I built myself a house, cleared a sufficient spot of woodland to produce ten barrels of corn; the second year about fifteen, and the third, had as much planted as I suppose would have produced thirty barrels; this I was obliged to leave about one month before it was fit for gathering, being threatened by Holland Lockwood, who married my said master's widow, that if I would not come and serve him, he would apprehend me, and send me to the West Indies; Enoch Ralph also threatening to send me to jail, and sell me for the good of the country: being thus in jeopardy, I left my little farm, with my small stock and utensils, and my corn standing, and escaped by night into Virginia, where shipping myself for Boston, I was, through stress of weather landed in New York, where I served as a waiter for seventeen[13] months; but my mind being distressed on account of the situation of my wife and children, I returned to Norfolk in Virginia, with a hope of at least seeing them, if I could not obtain their freedom; but finding I was advertised in the newspaper, twenty dollars the reward for apprehending me, my dangerous situation obliged me to leave Virginia, disappointed of seeing my wife and children, coming to Philadelphia, where I resided in the employment of a waiter upwards of two years.

In addition to the hardship of our own case, as above set forth, we believe ourselves warranted, on the present occasion, in offering to your consideration the singular case of a fellow-black now confined in the jail of this city, under sanction of the act of General Government, called the Fugitive Law, as it appears to us a flagrant proof how far human beings, merely on account of color and complexion, are, through prevailing prejudice, out-lawed and excluded from common justice and common humanity, by the operation of such partial laws in support of habits and customs cruelly oppressive. This man, having been many years past manumitted by his master in North Carolina, was, under the authority of the aforementioned law of that State, sold again into slavery, and, after having served his purchaser upwards of six years, made his escape to Philadelphia, where he has resided eleven years, having a wife and {f}our children; and by an agent of the Carolina claimer, has been lately apprehended and committed to prison, his said claimer, soon after the man's escaping from him, having advertised him, offering a reward of ten silver dollars to any person that would bring him back, or five times that sum to any person that would make due proof of his being killed, and no questions asked by whom.

We beseech your impartial attention to our hard condition, not only with respect to our personal sufferings as freemen, but as a class of that people who, distinguished by colour, are therefore with a degrading partiality, considered by many, even of those in eminent stations, as unentitled to that public justice and protection which is the great object of Government. We indulge not a hope, or presume to ask for the interposition of your honorable body, beyond the extent of your constitutional power or influence, yet are willing to believe your serious, disinterested, and candid consideration of the premises, under the benign impressions of equity and mercy, producing upright exertion of what is in your power, may not be without some salutary effect, both for our relief as a people, and towards the removal of obstructions to public order and well-being.

If notwithstanding all that has been publicly avowed as essential principles respecting the extent of human right to freedom; notwithstanding we have had that right restored to us, so far as was in the power of those by whom we were held as slaves, we cannot claim the privilege of representation in your councils, yet we trust we may address you as fellow-men, who, under God, the sovereign Ruler of the Universe, are intrusted with the distribution of justice, for the terror of evil-doers, the encouragement and protection of the innocent, not doubting that you are men of liberal minds, susceptible of benevolent feelings and clear conception of rectitude to a catholic extent, who can admit that black people (servile as their condition generally is throughout this Continent) have natural affections, social and domestic attachments and sensibilities; and that, therefore, we may hope for a share in your sympathetic attention while we represent that the unconstitutional bondage in which multitudes of our fellows in complexion are held, is to us a subject sorrowfully affecting; for we cannot conceive their condition (more especially those who have been emancipated and tasted the sweets of liberty, and again reduced to slavery by kidnappers and man-stealers) to be less afflicting or deplorable than the situation of citizens of the United States, captured and enslaved through the unrighteous policy prevalent in Algiers.[14] We are far from considering all those who retain slaves as wilful oppressors, being well assured that numbers in the State from whence we are exiles, hold their slaves in bondage, not of choice, but possessing them by inheritance, feel their minds burdened under the slavish restraint of legal impediments to doing that justice which they are convinced is due to fellow-rationals. May we not be allowed to consider this stretch of power, morally and politically, a governmental defect, if not a direct violation of the declared fundamental principles of the Constitution; and finally, is not some remedy for an evil of such magnitude highly worthy of the deep inquiry and unfeigned zeal of the supreme Legislative body of a free and enlightened people? Submitting our cause to God, and humbly craving your best aid and influence, as you may be favored and directed by that wisdom which is from above, wherewith that you may be eminently dignified and rendered more conspicuously, in the view of nations, a blessing to the people you represent, is the sincere prayer of your petitioners.

    JACOB NICHOLSON.
    JUPITER NICHOLSON, his mark,
    JOB ALBERT, his mark,
    THOMAS PRITCHET, his mark.

PHILADELPHIA, *January* 23, 1797.

2

1797

Congress Debates the Freemen's Petition

On 30 January 1797, Pennsylvania congressman John Swanwick (1759?–1798) presented the freemen's petition to the House of Representatives. Swanwick, born in Liverpool, England, moved with his parents to Pennsylvania in 1770, when he was about eleven years of age. He educated himself and rose from an apprentice clerkship in Robert Morris's Philadelphia mercantile firm to full partnership in Willing, Morris, and Swanwick and from there to a position as one of Philadelphia's principal overseas merchants. In 1781, Morris made Swanwick his assistant in his post as acting superintendent of finances for the Continental Congress. Swanwick entered politics in the 1790s as a Republican, siding with James Madison on foreign policy issues but differing from the agrarian Republicans on economic issues. By 1797, the wars of the French Revolution had had a ruinous effect on his business affairs. His introducing of this petition was in character with his patronage of Philadelphia humanitarian associations.[15]

Many southern political leaders objected to any discussion in Congress that touched on slavery because they thought that such debates implied federal authority to legislate regarding slavery. In response to the Society of Friends' 1783 petition to end slave importations, some southern members of Congress even voted against a resolution recommending that each state address the issue individually, because the very act of referring to the issue set an unacceptable precedent.[16]

Given this background, it is not surprising that instead of discussing the merits of the freemen's petition, the members of the House disputed whether the petition should even be received.

The Annals of Congress

Source: Annals of Congress, 4th Cong., 2d sess., 23 January 1797, 2018–24.[17]

The petition being read—

Mr. SWANWICK said, he hoped it would be referred to a select committee.

Mr. BLOUNT[18] hoped it would not even be received by the House. Agreeably to a law of the State of North Carolina, he said they were slaves, and could, of course, be seized as such.

Mr. THATCHER[19] thought the petition ought to be referred to the Committee on the Fugitive Law. He conceived the gentleman much mistaken in asserting these petitioners to be absolute slaves. They state that they *were* slaves, but that their masters manumitted them, and that their manumissions were sanctioned by a law of that State, but that a subsequent law of the same State, subjected them to slavery; and if even there was a law that allowed them to be taken and sold into slavery again, he could not see any propriety in refusing their petition in that House—THEY CERTAINLY (said Mr. T.) ARE FREE PEOPLE. It appeared they were taken under the fugitive act, which he thought ought not to affect them; they now came and prayed the House so to model that fugitive act, as to prevent its affecting persons of their description. He therefore saw great propriety in referring their petition to the committee appointed to amend that act in another part; they could as well consider its relation to the present case. He could not see how there would be a propriety in rejecting their petition; they had an undoubted right to petition the House, and to be heard.

Mr. SWANWICK was surprised at the gentleman from North Carolina [Mr. BLOUNT] desiring to reject this petition; he could not have thought, nor could he indulge the suspicion now, that the gentleman was so far from acknowledging the rights of man, as to prevent any class of men from petitioning. If men were aggrieved, and conceive they have claim to attention, petitioning was their sacred right, and that right should never suffer innovation; whether the House ought to grant, was another question. The subject of their petition had a claim to the attention of the House. They state they were freed from slavery, but that they were much injured under a law of the United States. If a law was ever made that bore hard on any class of people, Mr. S. hoped that the door would never be shut to their complaints.

If the circumstance respecting these people was as they stated, their case was very hard. He animadverted on the atrocity of that reward of ten dollars offered for one of them if taken alive, but that fifty should be given if found dead, and no questions asked. Was not this, he said, encouragement to put a period to that man's existence? Horrid reward! Could gentlemen hear it and not shudder?

Mr. BLOUNT said, the gentleman last up was mistaken in calling the petitioners free men; the laws of North Carolina, as he observed before, did not suffer individuals to emancipate their slaves, and he should wish to know what evidence there was to prove these men free, and except that was proved, the House had no right to attend to the petition.

Mr. SITGREAVES,[20] in answer to the gentleman last up, said he would reverse his question, and ask what evidence he had to prove that these men are not freemen; can he prove that they are slaves? They have stated that a law has been made in North Carolina with a view to affect their case, and bring them again into a worse slavery than before; they want to know whether they cannot obtain relief by their application to the Government of the United States. Under these circumstances, Mr. S. wished to know why their petitions should not be taken into consideration? Was there anything in these men, he asked, that should prevent every kind of assistance being bestowed on them? Had they not an equal right to be heard with other petitioners? He hoped the House would not only give them a hearing, but afford them all the consolation of which their unfortunate case was susceptible. If the House were obliged, through a want of power to extend to the case, to object compliance with the prayers, yet, he hoped it would be done with all due tenderness; before hearing them, he thought it would be exceedingly unjust to decide. These people may produce documents sufficient to obtain favorable attention; therefore, it was impossible before they were heard to conceive whether the House could constitutionally grant relief or not. He could see no impropriety in referring it; the object of referring a case, was to inquire into facts; thus, the committee prepared the way for discussion in the House; and why the House should refuse to deliberate and discuss the case, he knew not.

Mr. HEATH[21] was clearly convinced these people were slaves, and therefore hoped their petition would lie on the table. He would remind the gentlemen that, if they undertook this business, they would soon have petitions enough of the same kind, and public business would be thereby prevented. It appeared to him to be more within the jurisdiction of the Legislature of that State; indeed, the United States had nothing to do with it.

Mr. MADISON[22] said, he should be sorry to reject any petition whatever, in which it became the business of the House to attend; but he thought this case had no claim on their attention. Yet, if it did not come within the purview of the Legislative body, he thought, it might be suffered to lie on the table. He thought it a Judicial case, and could obtain its due in a Court of Appeal in that State. If they are free by the laws of North Carolina, they ought to apply to those laws, and have their privilege established. If they are slaves, the Constitution gives them no hopes of being heard here. A law has been passed to prevent the owners of those slaves emancipating them; it is therefore impossible that any relief can be granted. The petitioners are under the laws of North Carolina, and those laws cannot be the interpreters of the laws of the United States.

Mr. SITGREAVES said, he was not prepared to deny that this petition is in the situation the gentleman from Virginia [Mr. MADISON] states; nor was he prepared to prove that it came under the power of the General Government, but he could see no kind of reason why it should not be sent to a committee who should examine the case and report whether it required Legislative interference, or whether it was a subject of Judicial authority in the country whence the petitioners came. Many petitions, he said, were sent to the House, who referred them for investigation to a committee, and many had been reported as being under Judicial power only, and as such been rejected here. If this underwent the same order, and should be found to be of a Judicial nature, the committee would report so, and the House would honorably refuse it. This he thought the only just method.

Mr. RUTHERFORD[23] concurred with the gentleman from Pennsylvania, that this memorial ought to be referred to a committee who would report whether these people had been emancipated, according to a law of the State of North Carolina, or not. The circumstances attending this case, he said, demanded a just and full investigation, and if a law did exist either to emancipate, or send these poor people into slavery, the House would then know. He doubted not, every thing just and proper would be done, but he hoped every due respect would be paid to the petition. In short, he was assured every member in the House would wish to act consistently. This case, from the great hardships represented in the petition, applied closely to the nicest feelings of the heart, and he hoped humanity would dictate a just decision.

Mr. GILBERT[24] hoped the petition would be referred to the committee proposed; he thought it laid claim to the humanity of the House. He thought every just satisfaction should be given, and attention paid, to every class of persons who appeal for decision to the House.

Mr. W. SMITH[25] said, the practice of a former time, in a similar case, was, that the petition was sealed up and sent back to the petitioners, not being allowed even to remain on the files of the office. This method, he said, ought to be pursued with respect to the present petition. It was not a matter that claimed the attention of the Legislature of the United States. He thought it of such an improper nature, as to be surprised any gentleman would present a petition of the kind. These men are slaves, and, he thought, not entitled to attention from that body; to encourage slaves to petition the House would have a tendency to invite continual applications. Indeed it would tend to spread an alarm throughout the Southern States; it would act as an "entering wedge," whose consequences could not be foreseen. This is a kind of property on which the House has no power to legislate. He hoped it would not be committed at all; it was not a proper subject for Legislative attention. He was not of the opinion of some gentlemen, that the House were bound to sit on every question recommended to their notice. He thought particular attention ought to be paid to the lateness of the session; if this subject were to be considered, too much time of the House would be devoured which was much wanted on important business.

Mr. THATCHER said, he was in favor of referring this petition. He could see no reason which had been adduced to prove the impropriety of receiving a petition from these people. The gentleman from North Carolina [Mr. BLOUNT] is of the opinion that these people being slaves, the House ought not to pay attention to their prayer. This, he said, was quite new language—a system of conduct which he never saw the House practise, and hoped he never should. That the House should not receive the petition without an evidence to prove it was from a free man. This was a language which opposed the Constitutional freedom of every State where the Declaration of Rights had been made; they all declare that every man is born equally free, and that each have an equal right to petition if aggrieved—this doctrine he never heard objected to.

The gentlemen from Virginia [Mr. MADISON and Mr. HEATH] had said, it was a Judicial and not a Legislative question; they say the petition proves it, and that it ought not to be attended to. Mr. T. said, he saw no proof whatever of the impropriety of the House receiving it. There might be some Judicial question growing out of the case; but that was no reason, because it might possibly undergo a Judicial course, that the General Government were not to be petitioned. The gentleman from South Carolina [Mr. SMITH] had said, "that this was a kind of property on which the House could not legislate;" but he would answer, this was a kind of property on which they were bound to legislate. The fugitive act could prove this authority; if petitions were not to be received they would have to legislate in the dark. It appeared plainly that these men were manumitted by their masters; and because a number of men who called themselves legislators should, after they had the actual enjoyment of their liberty, come forward and say that these men should not remain at liberty, and actually authorize their re-captivity, he thought it exceedingly unjust to deprive them of the right of petitioning to have their injuries redressed. These were a set of men on whom the fugitive law had no power, and he thought they claimed protection under the power of that House, which always ought to lean towards freedom. Though they could not give freedom to slaves, yet he hoped gentlemen would never refuse to lend their aid to secure freemen in their rights against tyrannical imposition.

Mr. CHRISTIE[26] thought no part of the fugitive act operated against freedom. He thought no good could be derived from sending the petition to a committee; they could not prove whether they were slaves or not. He was much surprised any gentleman in the House should present such a petition. Mr. C. said, he was of the same opinion with the gentleman from South Carolina [Mr. SMITH] that the petition ought to be sent back again. He hoped the gentleman from Pennsylvania [Mr. SWANWICK] would never hand such another petition into the House.

Mr. Holland[27] said, the gentleman from Massachusetts [Mr. THATCHER] said, "the House ought to lean towards freedom." Did he mean to set all slaves at liberty, or receive petitions from all? Sure he was that if this was received, it would not be long before the table would be filled with similar complaints, and the House might sit for no other purpose than to hear them. It was a Judicial question, and the House ought not to pretend to determine the point; why, then, should they take up time upon it? To put an end to it he hoped, it would be ordered to lie on the table.

Mr. MACON[28] said, he had hearkened very closely to the observations of gentlemen on the subject, and could see no reason to alter his desire that it would not be committed. No man, he said, wished to encourage petitions more than himself and no man had considered this subject more. These men could not receive any aid from the General Government; but by application to the State, justice would be done them. Trials of this kind had very frequently been brought on in all the different Courts of that State, and had very often ended in the freedom of slaves; the appeal was fair, and justice was done. Mr. M. thought it a very delicate subject for the General Government to act on; he hoped it would not be committed; but he should not be sorry if the proposition of a gentleman [Mr. SMITH] was to take place, that it was to be sent back again.

Mr. W. SMITH observed, that a gentleman [Mr. THATCHER] had uttered a wish to draw these people from their state of slavery to liberty. Mr. S. did not think they were sent there to take up the subject of emancipation. When subjects of this kind are brought up in the House they ought to be deprecated as dangerous. They tended to produce very uncomfortable circumstances.

Mr. VARNUM[29] said, the petitioners had received injury under a law of the United States, (the fugitive act) and not merely a law of North Carolina, and therefore, he thought, they had an undoubted right to the attention of the General Government if that act bore hard on them. They stated themselves to be freemen, and he did not see any opposition of force to convince the House they were not; surely it could not be said that color alone should designate them as slaves. If these people had been free, and yet were taken up under a law of the United States, and put into prison, then it appeared plainly the duty of the House to inquire whether that act had such an unjust tendency, and if it had, proper amendments should be made to it to prevent the like consequences in future. It required nothing more under that act than that the person suspected should be brought before a single magistrate, and evidence given that he is a slave, which evidence the magistrate could not know if distant from the State; the person may be a freeman, for it would not be easy to know whether the evidence was good, at a distance from the State; the poor man is then sent to his State in slavery. Mr. V. hoped the House would take all possible care that freemen should not be made slaves; to be deprived of liberty was more important than to be deprived of property. He could not think why gentlemen should be against having the fact examined; if it appears that they are slaves, the petition will of course be dismissed, but if it should appear they are free, and receive injury under the fugitive act, the United States ought to amend it, so that justice should be done.

Mr. BLOUNT said, admitting those persons who had been taken up were sent back to North Carolina, they would then have permission to apply to any of the Courts in the State for a fair trial of their plea; there are very few Courts in which some negroes have not tried this cause, and obtained their liberty. He agreed with the gentleman from Massachusetts, on the freedom of these men to procure their rights; it did not appear to him that they were free; true they had been set free, but that manumission was from their masters, who had not a right to set them free without permission of the Legislature.

Mr. KITCHELL[30] could not see what objection could obtain to prevent these people being heard. The question was not now, whether they are or are not slaves, but it is on a law of the United States. They assert that this law does act injuriously to them; the question is, therefore, whether a committee shall be appointed to inquire on the improper force of this law on the case of these men; if they are freemen, he said, they ought not to be sent back from the most distant part of the United States to North Carolina, to have justice done them, but they ought to receive it from the General Government who made the law they complain of.

Mr. K. said, he had not examined the force of the law on the subject, and was not prepared to decide; there could be no evil in referring it for examination, when the committee would report their opinion of the subject and gentlemen be prepared to act on it.

On the question for receiving the petition being put, it was negatived—ayes 33, noes 50.

3

1797

Pennsylvania Friends' Yearly Meeting Memorial to the Congress of the United States

The second petition to Congress touching on the situation in North Carolina was the following memorial by the Pennsylvania Yearly Meeting after their annual meeting, which was held in Philadelphia in September 1797.

The memorial recalls the Continental Association that was adopted by the First Continental Congress in 1774 in response to the British Coercive Acts. The Continental Association consisted of a system of committees from the provincial down to the town level that was charged with enforcing an embargo on all trade with Great Britain and with promoting frugality.

That the memorial should link condemnations of slavery, playhouses, and excesses in celebrations of national holidays was no anomaly. Rather, the linkage flowed logically from Friends' concern for public morality. Recognizing the crucial importance that the formative period of the new nation would have on shaping the people's character, Friends committed themselves to promoting public virtue. Convinced of the necessity of virtue for the happiness of a people, they sought to persuade the government to promote virtue and suppress vice, infidelity, and irreligion. The slave trade, attending plays, and public debauchery were all of a piece, national sins that needed to be suppressed.[31]

The maxim in the memorial that "national evils produce national judgments" encapsulates a traditional belief that God rewards and punishes communities of people according to their corporate behavior. In orations called jeremiads (after the Old Testament prophet Jeremiah), preachers of various denominations since at least the seventeenth century had warned governments of their duty to encourage virtue and suppress vice, for since nations could not be punished in the afterlife, they received the divinity's rewards and punishments in historical time. Communities experienced prosperity or natural calamities and peace or war according to their just deserts. God's judgment could be recognized in an earthquake, a famine, or pestilence. When the Philadelphia Society of Friends submitted their memorial to Congress, pestilence had just visited their city in the form of a yellow fever epidemic in 1796–1797. The petitioners point to that "awful calamity" as evidence of the need for moral reformation.[32]

To the Senate and House of Representatives of the United States, in Congress assembled

Source: Annals of Congress, 5th Cong., 2d sess., November 1797, 657–58.

To the Senate and House of Representatives of the

United States, in Congress assembled:

The memorial and address of the people called Quakers, from their yearly meeting held in Philadelphia, by adjournments, from the 25th of the 9th month, to the 29th of the same, inclusive, 1797, respectfully sheweth:

That, being convened, at this our annual solemnity, for the promotion of the cause of truth and righteousness, we have been favored to experience religious weight to attend our minds, and an anxious desire to follow after those things which make for peace; among other investigations the oppressed state of our brethren of the African race has been brought into view, and particularly the circumstances of one hundred and thirty-four in North Carolina, and many others whose cases have not so fully come to our knowledge, who were set free by members of our religious society, and again reduced into cruel bondage, under the authority of existing or retrospective laws; husbands and wives, and children, separated, one from another; which, we apprehend to be an abominable tragedy; and with other acts, of a similar nature, practiced in other States, has a tendency to bring down the judgments of a righteous God upon our land.

This city and neighborhood, and some other parts, have been visited with an awful calamity, which ought to excite an inquiry in the cause and endeavors to do away those things which occasion the heavy clouds that hang over us. It is easy with the Almighty to bring down the loftiness of men by diversified judgments, and to make them fear the rod, and Him that hath appointed it.

We wish to revive in your view the solemn engagement of Congress, made in the year one thousand seven hundred and seventy-four, as follows:

"And, therefore, we do for ourselves, and the inhabitants of the several colonies, whom we represent, firmly agree and associate, under the sacred ties of virtue, honor, and love of our country, as follows:

"Article 2. We will neither import nor purchase any slaves imported after the first day of December next; after which time we will wholly discontinue the slave trade, and will neither be concerned in it ourselves, nor will we hire our vessels, nor sell our commodities or manufactures to those who are concerned in it.

"Article 3. And will discountenance and discourage every species of extravagance and dissipation; especially horse-racing, and all kinds of gaming, cock fighting, exhibitions of shows, plays, and other expensive diversions and entertainments."

This was a solemn league and covenant, made with the Almighty in an hour of distress, and He is now calling upon you to perform and fulfil it; but how has this solemn covenant been contravened by the wrongs and cruelties practiced upon the poor African race, the increase of dissipation and luxury, the countenance and encouragement given to play-houses, and other vain amusements! And how grossly is the Almighty affronted on the day of the celebration of Independence! What rioting and drunkenness, chambering and wantonness! to the great grief of sober inhabitants, and the disgrace of our national character.

National evils produce national judgments; we therefore fervently pray the Governor of the Universe may enlighten your understandings and influence your minds, so as to engage you to use every exertion in your power, to have these things redressed.

With sincere desires for your happiness here and hereafter, and that, when you come to close this life, you may individually be able to appeal as a Ruler did formerly: "Remember now, O Lord, I beseech thee, how I have walked before thee, in truth and with a perfect heart, and have done that which is good in thy sight."³³

We remain your friends and fellow citizens.

Signed in and on behalf of the said Meeting, by

Jonathan Evans,

Clerk to the meeting this year.

4

1797–1798

Congress Debates the Pennsylvania Friends' Memorial

On 29 November 1797, when "The Memorial and Address of the People Called Quakers" (document 3, above) was laid before the Senate of the United States, it was read and immediately ordered to lie on the table.[34] In contrast, in the House of Representatives, the memorial engendered a heated argument. The passions the paper evoked brought to the surface sectional tensions over the issue of slavery and its future in the United States. Southern representatives suggested that debating the morality of slavery undermined the loyalty of southerners to the union of the states.

Pennsylvania congressman Albert Gallatin presented the Quaker memorial to the House of Representatives on 30 November 1797. The Swiss-born Gallatin moved to the United States as a young man during the War of Independence. In the late 1780s, by which time he was a rural Pennsylvania landowner, he made a name for himself in state politics as an authority on public finance. On the national scene he rose to prominence in the Republican Party in the 1790s as an opponent of the federalist policy of perpetuating the national debt. In 1801, President Thomas Jefferson appointed him secretary of the treasury.[35] "The memorial having been read by the Clerk," the following debate ensued.

The Annals of Congress

Source: Annals of Congress, 5th Cong., 2d sess., 27 November 1797, 29 January 1798, 13 February 1798, and 14 February 1798, 658–70, 945–46, 1030, and 1032–33 (respectively).

> Mr. GALLATIN moved that it be read a second time.
>
> Mr. HARPER[36] hoped not. This was not the first, second, or third

time, that the House had been troubled with similar applications, which had a tendency to stir up a class of persons to inflict calamities which would be of greater consequence than any evils which were at present suffered; and this, and every other Legislature, ought to set their faces against remonstrances complaining of what it was utterly impossible to alter.

Mr. THATCHER[37] hoped the petition would have a second reading, and be committed. It appeared to him that this would be the regular way of getting rid of the difficulty which was apprehended. The gentleman who had just sat down said, that this was not the first, second, or third time, that the House had been troubled with similar petitions. This, he said, was natural. If any number of persons considered themselves aggrieved, it was not likely they should leave off petitioning, until the House should act upon their petition. He thought this was what they ought to do. If the Quakers thought themselves aggrieved, it was their duty to present their petition, not only three, five, or seven times, but seventy times, until it was attended to. Gentlemen, therefore, who wished not to be troubled again, ought to be in favor of a second reading and reference. At present, they did not know what the particular grievance complained of was, nor whether it could or could not be remedied. He believed that one of the subjects of complaint had a reference to a matter complained of in a memorial presented at the last session, respecting some dark-complexioned citizens of North Carolina,[38] who were injured by the operation of an act of the United States called the Fugitive Act;[39] but as it was the wish of the House not to enter upon any business of a private nature at that time, the petition was ordered to lie on the table. It appeared, therefore, highly proper that this petition should be referred, as was customary, to a committee, that this grievance might be remedied.

Mr. LYON[40] said it appeared to him that the gentleman from South Carolina (Mr. HARPER) had not attended to the subject-matter of the petition, or he would not have objected to its being read a second time. There was a grievance complained of, which certainly ought to be remedied, viz: that a certain number of black persons who had been set at liberty by their masters, were now held in slavery, contrary to right. He thought this ought to be inquired into.

Mr. RUTLEDGE[41] should not be opposed to the second reading and reference of this memorial, if he thought the strong censure they deserved would be the report of a committee. This censure, he thought, this body of men ought to have; a set of men who attempt to seduce the servants of gentlemen travelling to the seat of Government, who were incessantly importuning Congress to interfere in a business with which the Constitution had said they had no concern. If he was sure this conduct would be reprobated, he would cheerfully vote for a reference of the present petition; but not believing this would be the case, he should be for its laying on the table, or under the table, that they might not only have done with the business for to-day, but finally. At a time when some nations were witnesses of the most barbarous and horrid scenes, these petitioners are endeavoring to incite a class of persons to the commission of similar enormities. He thought the matter of the greatest importance, and that the reference ought by no means to be made. A gentleman before him (Mr. LYON) had said that they had certainly something to do with the detention of freemen in slavery. If the fact were as stated, (which he doubted,) redress ought to be sought by means of a court of justice, and not by petitioning that House.

Mr. SWANWICK[42] was sorry to see so much heat produced by the introduction of this petition. He himself could see no reason why the petition should not be dealt with in the ordinary way. If the petitioners asked for any thing which it was not in the power of the House to grant, it would be of course refused; but this was no reason why their petition should not be treated with ordinary respect. In this memorial, he said, sundry things were complained of; not only slavery, but several other grievances. For instance, play-houses were complained of, whether justly or not, he was not about to decide. With respect to the grievance mentioned in North Carolina, something perhaps might be done to remedy it, without affecting the property which gentlemen seemed so much alarmed about. He could not suppose there was a disposition in the House to violate the property of any man; there was certainly as strong a disposition in the Middle States as in the Southern, to hold inviolable the right of property; nor could he see any reasonable ground for throwing this petition under the table. If these people were wrong in their understanding of this subject, it would be best to appoint a committee to set them right. He was sorry to hear gentlemen charge so respectable a body of men in that House with attempting to seduce and debauch their servants;

for, if this were the case, redress could doubtless be had in a court of justice. The uncommon warmth which was shown on the occasion would lead persons to believe that gentlemen were afraid of having the matter looked into, as this was generally the temper resorted to when argument was wanting. He hoped the memorial would be dealt with in the usual way.

Mr. GALLATIN said it was the practice of the House, whenever a memorial was presented, to have it read a first and a second time, and then to commit it, unless it were expressed in such indecent terms as to induce the House to reject it, or upon a subject upon which petitions had been lately rejected by a large majority of the House. In no other case were petitions rejected without examination and without discussion. He said without examination, and without discussion, because it was impossible, upon a single reading of a petition, to be able to form a sound judgment upon it. Indeed, seeing the way in which the gentleman from South Carolina (Mr. RUTLEDGE) had treated the subject, no cool examination could be expected at present; in the moment of passion it would be best not to decide, but to send the petition to a committee. What was the objection to this mode of proceeding? It was that the subject would shake a certain kind of property. How so? A petition that reminds us of the fate of certain blacks in this country, which did not refer to slaves, but to free men. This petition was to shake property! In the same manner it might be said that the law of Pennsylvania for the gradual abolition of slavery[43] had also a tendency to destroy that property; or that the legislative decision of the State of Massachusetts that there shall be no slaves under their Government,[44] would have that effect. But it was said the characters of the petitioners was such as they ought to brand with the mark of disapprobation.

In support of this charge, it was alleged that they were not satisfied with petitioning, but they attempted to debauch and seduce servants—to rob gentlemen of their property. He did not know to what the gentleman who made this assertion alluded; but he believed, if the matter was fairly stated, whatever may have been done in the State of Pennsylvania, has been no more than an endeavor to carry into full effect the laws of the State, which say, that "all men are free when they set their foot within the State," excepting only the servants of Members of Congress. As to the moral character of this body of people, though a number of their principles were different from those he professed, he believed it could not be said, with truth, that they were friends to any kind of disorder; and he was surprised to hear gentleman suppose that they could or would do any thing which would throw into disorder any part of the Union. On the contrary, he believed them to be good friends of order. Mr. G. said he wished to have avoided a discussion of the merits of the memorial; but when they were told it was improper to do any thing on the subject, it became necessary. He knew it was in their power to do something. They might lay a duty of ten dollars a head on the importation of slaves; he knew a memorial had been presented at a former session respecting the kidnapping of negroes, which had been favorably reported upon.[45] Finally, the present memorial did not apply only to the blacks, but to other objects. With respect to plays, they had a motion last session before them for laying a tax upon them, which had a reference to the subject. By committing this memorial, they should give no decision. If the committee reported they could do nothing in the business, and the House agreed to the report, the matter would be closed in a much more respectful way than by throwing the petition under the table.

Mr. SEWALL[46] said, the gentleman last up had stated two cases in which petitions had been received without a commitment. He might have added a third, more applicable to the present memorial. This was when a petition was upon matter over which this House had no cognizance, especially if it were of such a nature as to excite disagreeable sensations in one part of the House, who were concerned in property which was already held under circumstances sufficiently disagreeable. In such cases, they ought at once to reject the memorial, as it would be mispending time to commit it. If, for instance, a petition should be presented, complaining that a person had refused to discharge an obligation to another, it would be at once acknowledged that the House could not enforce the obligation; but application must be made to a court of justice. So in this case; the petitioners complain of a law of North Carolina. This House, he said, could not change that law. If any thing was done there contrary to right, the courts of that State, as well as those of the United States, were open to afford redress. It was their business, and not the business of that House. They did not come there to act upon subjects agreeable to their feelings, but upon such as the Constitution had placed in their hands.

The gentleman from Pennsylvania had said they might impose a tax of ten dollars upon the importation of every slave. Would this, he asked, relieve the petitioners? No. If they could prevent the kidnapping of negroes, it was well; but nothing was aimed at of this sort in this petition. He recollected a former instance of this kind, but the issue of the business showed that nothing could be done without injuring the public more than the individuals would be benefited. The petition alluded to stage plays. With what view? To revenue? No; but to a correction of them with respect to morals. It was not within their province to do this, but under the power of the State Governments. If they were taken up for the sake of revenue, they did not come within the purview of this petition, but of the Committee of Ways and Means. Upon the whole, as he considered this as a dangerous business, and that they could do noting to gratify the feelings of the petitioners, he would not wish to treat the application with contempt, but let it lie on the table.

Mr. MACON[47] said, there was not a gentleman in North Carolina who did not wish there were no blacks in the country. It was a misfortune—he considered it as a curse; but there was no way of getting rid of them. Instead of peace-makers, he looked upon the Quakers as war-makers, as they were continually endeavoring in the Southern States to stir up insurrections amongst the negroes. It was unconstitutional, he said, in these men to desire the House to do what they had no power to do; as well might they ask the President of the United States to come and take the Speaker's chair. There was a law in North Carolina, he said, which forbade any person from holding either a black or white person as a slave after he had been set at liberty.[48] The one hundred and thirty-four negroes alluded to in the petition, he knew nothing of. In the war, he said, the Quakers in their state were generally Tories. They began to set free their negroes, when the State passed a law that they should not set them free. If these people were dissatisfied with the law, they had nothing to do but transport their negroes into Pennsylvania, where, the gentleman from that State had told them, they would be immediately free. This subject had already been before the House, but they declined doing any thing in it. It was extraordinary that these people should come, session after session, with their petitions on this subject. They had put play-houses into their memorial; but they had nothing to do with them. In this State, he believed, the Legislature had passed a law authorizing them. It was altogether a matter of State policy. The whole petition was, indeed, unnecessary. The only object seemed to be to sow dissension. A petition could not come there touching any subject on which they had power to act, which he should not be in favor of committing; but this thing being wrong in itself, it was needless to commit it, as no single purpose could be answered by it.

Mr. ALLEN[49] was in favor of a second reading and committal. He did not know that no good could arise from such a proceeding. He wished time to consider the matter. He had another reason against getting rid of this business. When the debate upon this question came to be faithfully reported, it might be said that the society of Quakers had been found guilty of such foul conduct, that their petition to the House had been *thrown under the table*. Another reason. Last Summer, along with other strangers, he went to see the new jail of the city, where he was shown a man who had been a manumitted slave; but after being free twenty years, he was apprehended under the fugitive law, and was there imprisoned. If this were so, it was necessary that this law should be revised. He hoped, therefore, the petition might be committed, and that this evil might be remedied. At all events, he trusted the petition would not be rejected, as it would be highly disrespectful to a society of men revered by every man who set a value upon virtue and integrity.

Mr. LIVINGSTON[50] said, if he could believe that the persons who presented this petition were of the description which they had been represented; that they endeavored to raise insurrections in one part of the country, and practised robbery in another, he should not be inclined to pay much respect to them. But he did not believe these charges; he believed them indiscriminately made and unfounded. It was possible that a member of this community, as well as of any other, might be of this description; but, as against the body, he knew the charges were unworthily made. He was acquainted with many of these persons in those States where they were most numerous, and he was certain they did not deserve the character given them. Therefore, as the matter respected the petitioners, the petition ought not to be thrown under the table. Let us now, said he, examine the request, and see whether it be so improper and impracticable as to make us say, on its first reading, we have heard enough. What do they ask? They say a certain number of citizens are deprived of what belongs to them; and can we say we will not grant relief? No, said he, we cannot, before the business is inquired into, as it would be acting unlike the Legislature of a great nation. If they said this application was so improper as not to be committed, what did they say to their predecessors who sat in that House a few months ago, who not only received an application of a similar kind, but a committee reported in its favor.[51] They said universal emancipation is not in our power, but the evil is one for which a partial remedy may be provided. The want of time only prevented its being acted upon. This was a subject upon which they might at least debate; he could not say whether they could afford a remedy or not. His impressions were they could not, but he would not say they never could. He did not think they should do the duty which he was sent there to do, by saying so, which was to follow the dictates of a sober judgment, after facts were fairly and fully stated. He thought it best to follow the usual course, by appointing a committee, who would examine the matter and report what was best to be done, which the House could agree to or not, as they saw proper. He thought it would be for the advantage of those States most interested in the question, that it should be fully discussed and impassionately decided upon; for, so long as the petitions of these persons were neglected or treated with contempt, so long would they conceive they were unjustly treated, and continue their applications for redress.

Mr. L. said there were a number of general reflections contained in the memorial, upon the growth of vice and immorality, to the suppression of which he did not see that the power of Congress extended. They particularly pointed at the establishment of play-houses; but it might be remarked that these gentlemen, so averse to the establishment of play-houses, have not written their memorial without borrowing language from them, as they term the evil which they speak of "a terrible tragedy."

Mr. Isaac Parker[52] was of opinion with the gentleman from Pennsylvania, (Mr. Gallatin,) with respect to the disposal of petitions. But it appeared to him that the subject-matter of all petitions should be within the view and authority of the House; if not, to refer them would certainly be a waste of time. He had attended to the petition, and he did not think there was a single object upon which it was in their power to act. Nothing was prayed for. The petitioners speak of the slave trade, and, in general terms, of the immorality of the times, as injurious to the state of society; and wish some means may be taken to prevent the growth of them. To refer a petition of this sort, therefore, to a committee would answer no purpose. He did not think they were more obliged to take up the business than if they had read the address in a newspaper.

Mr. BAYARD[53] said it might be inferred, from the anxiety and warmth of gentlemen, that the question before them was, whether slavery should or should not be abolished. The present was, however, very remote from such a question, as it was merely whether a memorial should be read a second time. The contents of this memorial, he said, were right or wrong, reasonable or unreasonable; if right, it was proper it should go to a committee; and if wrong, if so clearly absurd as it had been represented, where would be the evil of a reference for a report thereon? He did not like things to be decided in the moment of passion, but from the fullest consideration. In some countries they knew persons accused of crimes were condemned without a hearing, but there could be but one sentiment as to the injustice of such a proceeding. There could be no objection, therefore, upon general principles, to the reference of this petition. But it was said it was not to be sent because of the general habits of this society. He believed there was no body of men more respectable; they were obedient, and contributed cheerfully to the support of Government; and, either politically or civilly speaking, as few crimes could be imputed to that body as to any other.

This memorial, he said, had been treated as coming from an Abolition Society—it was a memorial of the General Meeting of the people called Quakers; and if only out of respect to that body, it ought to be referred. But it was said it did not contain matter upon which the House could act. Gentlemen seemed not to have attended to the subject-matter of the petition. He did not believe that the House had the power to manumit slaves, but he believed there was not a word in the petition which had a reference to slavery. The petitioners state, indeed, that a number of negroes, not slaves, for negroes may be free, had been taken again into slavery, after they had been freed by their masters. He wished to know whether the House had not jurisdiction over this matter? He was warranted by the Constitution in saying they had, because that instrument says that no State shall make *ex post facto* laws. It belonged to that House, therefore, to see that the Constitution was respected, as it could not be expected from the justice of the individual States, that they would repeal such laws. It rested, therefore, with the Government of the United States to do it. Mr. B. read the clause of the Constitution touching this matter,[54] and concluded by reminding the House that this was not an ultimate decision, but merely a reference.

Mr. JOSIAH PARKER[55] said he was always inclined to lend a favorable ear to petitioners of every kind but when memorial was presented to the House contrary to the nature of the Government, he should consent to its lying on the table or under it. No one, he said, could say they had a right to legislate respecting the proceedings of any individual State; they, therefore, had no power to decide on the conduct of the citizens of North Carolina in the matter complained of. Petitions had frequently come from Quakers and others on this subject; whereas this Government had nothing to do with negro slavery, except that they might lay a tax upon the importation of slaves. He recollected, when the subject was brought before the House in the first Congress held at New York, wishing to put a stop to the slave trade as much as possible, being a friend of liberty, he took every step in his power, and brought forward a proposition for laying a tax of ten dollars upon every slave imported. It was not agreed to;[56] but there was only one State (Georgia) in which the importation of slaves was admitted. Since the establishment of this Government, Mr. P. said, the situation of slaves was much ameliorated, and any interference now might have the effect to make their masters more severe. He knew of no part of the Constitution which gave them power over horse-racing and cock-fighting, nor could they interfere with respect to play-houses; and where they had no right to legislate, they had no right to speak at all. As the session had begun harmoniously, he hoped that harmony would not be broken in upon by such applications as the present. Mr. P. produced a precedent from the Journals of 1792, where a memorial of Warner Mifflin, a Quaker, after being read, was ordered to lie on the table, and two days afterwards returned to the memorialist.[57]

Mr. NICHOLAS[58] felt as much as other gentlemen from the Southern States on the subject of the present petition, but his feelings did not produce the same effects. He was not afraid of an interference from the United States with their property, nor of any investigations or discussions respecting it. He believed it would be to the honor of people holding property in slaves, that the business should be looked into. He thought such an inquiry would rather secure than injure their property. He did not think it was the interest of slaveholders to cover improper practices. He was satisfied, that in the part of the country where he lived, there was no disposition to protect injuries—no disposition to reject an inquiry, or to refuse to understand a complaint. They had been told that the state of the negroes, whose cases were mentioned in the memorial, might be produced by the fugitive law; they had before heard that this law had operated mischievously. It ought, therefore, to be inquired into. On inquiry, Mr. N. said, it would not be found the fault of the Southern States that slavery was tolerated, but their misfortune; but to liberate their slaves at once, would be to act like madmen; it would be to injure all parts of the United States as well as those who possess slaves. It was their duty, however, to remedy evils; they were unfortunately placed in a situation which obliged them to hold slaves, but they did not wish to extend the mischief. He should, indeed, be sorry if his possessing property of this kind, obliged him to cover the violation of another man's right; if this were the case, he should think it necessary that his property should be taken from him. He did not think it necessary, and he doubted not, if a fair investigation took place, that this kind of property would be brought into the situation in which every man of sense would place it. He was firmly of an opinion, that to appear to be afraid of an inquiry would do more harm to this property than a fair investigation. He trusted, therefore, the petition would be committed.

Mr. BLOUNT[59] hoped this memorial would not be committed. As this was not the first time the society of Quakers had come forward with petitions to the House, seemingly with no other view than to fix an odium on the State of North Carolina, he thought it his duty positively to contradict a fact stated in this memorial. It was stated that 134 persons, set free from slavery in North Carolina, had been since enslaved by cruel retrospective, or *ex post facto* laws; they alleged that certain members of their society had done what no person was permitted to do. Mr. B. read part of a law of North Carolina, stating "that no negro or mulatto slave shall be set free, except for meritorious services, acknowledged by a license of the court; and when any person shall be set free contrary to this law, he may be seized and sold as a slave," &c.[60] He also read a clause from another law, passed afterwards, stating that several persons having set at liberty their slaves contrary to law, and persons having taken up and sold them, are doubtful of the validity of the sale, and that this law is passed to do away all doubts of such validity.[61] Mr. B. said these extracts proved the assertion untrue.

Mr. GORDON[62] lamented that this discussion had taken place, as it was certain that wherever interest is concerned, some degree of warmth will be produced; and when a petition was brought forward which might affect the property of many gentlemen in the House, and their constituents, it could not be expected they would hear it with the same calmness with persons wholly unconcerned about it. All that had been advanced in favor of the second reading of the petition was, the respectability of the persons presenting it, the opinion that would be entertained of the petitioners, if their petition were not referred, and the merits of the petition itself.

With respect to the persons of the petitioners, he felt inclined to do them every justice; but he did not think this any reason for acting upon their memorial, unless some good consequence could arise from it, any more than if they were the vilest persons on earth. As to the opinion that might be entertained out of doors, as the petition was not examined, he was not afraid that the citizens of the United States would believe that the House could be so far lost to its duty as not to look into a question of this kind, but that it would be conceived, if rejected, that they had nothing to do with it. The other reason, the only material one, was to the merits of the petition. The gentleman from Delaware, (Mr. BAYARD,) who had examined the business with much coolness and ability, had stated that a certain *ex post facto* law of North Carolina had occasioned grievances. Admitting there was such a law, what could the House do? Could they declare a law of North Carolina null and void? There would be no utility in this; but if there was a law in North Carolina that violated the Constitution, there was a clear remedy in the law which organizes the Judicial department of the United States, in which it is said, if any law of an individual State interferes with a law of the United States, a person has a right to take advantage of the law of the United States.[63] There was no necessity, therefore, to call upon Congress for a remedy against this law. Indeed, he saw nothing in this memorial which called for their interference, and he was therefore against a reference, as a further discussion of it would only produce uneasiness in certain parts of the United States, without producing any good.

Mr. RUTLEDGE observed, that notwithstanding all that had been said, considering the present extraordinary state of the West India Islands and of Europe, he should insist that "sufficient for the day is the evil thereof,"[64] and that they ought to shut their door against any thing which had a tendency to produce the like confusion in this country. If this were not done, the confidence of a great part of the Union in the General Government would be weakened. In the Southern States, where most of their property consisted of slaves, and where the rest was of no value without them, there was already a prejudice existing that the Northern and Eastern States were inimical to this kind of property, though they were bound by the Constitution from an interference with it; but when they heard of the House giving countenance to a petition like the present, it would increase their uneasiness. He referred to what had fallen from the gentleman from Delaware respecting *ex post facto* law, and thought a court of justice the proper tribunal to settle that business. Mr. R. said he was indisposed, notwithstanding the high panegyrics which had been passed upon the body of the Quakers, to withdraw the censures he had cast upon them. The gentleman from New York had doubted the charges which he had produced, and said such things could never be attempted by the body. It was true, they did not come in a body into his lodging to seduce his servant, but individuals did it. But why, he asked, do these men come here in a body? Because they believe that their presence will give more weight to their petition; so that they appeared in bodies, or as individuals, to answer their purposes. Gentlemen had charged the opposers of the petition with heat; he thought there was as much heat on one side as the other.

Mr. EDMOND[65] did not believe there was any real ground of irritation in the question; as no gentleman could suppose they were about to do any thing which was either unconstitutional, or which would affect their property. Whether the persons who presented the memorial are virtuous or vicious, was of no consequence, since justice was due to both classes of men. They had brought a petition before them, and they ought to consider it. It was addressed to their honesty or justice;

if the facts were claims upon their honesty or justice they should be attended to; and not only attended to, but, if possible, relief granted. It was stated that there were a number of persons held in bondage who were justly entitled to liberty.

This fact called for examination; and a question arose, if it were established, whether that House could afford redress. A gentleman from North Carolina (Mr. BLOUNT) had stated that the fact was not true; it was certainly, therefore, worth while to be inquired into. Another gentleman had said, if the fact were as stated, they had no power to act; and a third was of opinion that, by the Constitution, redress might be afforded. This diversity of opinion showed the necessity of an investigation of the subject, in order to determine the jurisdiction of the House. He wished it for another reason. It had been stated, that if the petition were attended to, it would open a door to faction and mischief. Can it have this effect? These people bring forward a petition stating a number of facts; they certainly do not come forward for the mere design of exciting disorder in any quarter. If the House say they will throw their petition under the table, would not such treatment give the factious some ground of clamor by which to sow dissension? But if, on the contrary, they coolly looked into the petition, and reported thereon, would it not stop the mouths of these people? It certainly would; since they could not then say common justice was refused to the petitioners. Again: having once investigated the subject fully, if petitions of a similar kind should hereafter come forward, it would be reasonably said, this matter has already been taken up and fully decided upon; and, therefore, we will not again go into it. Until this was done, the factious would doubtless have cause of complaint.

Mr. BLOUNT said, several gentlemen who had spoken on this subject seemed to express themselves as if they believed there was no punishment for individuals reducing to slavery persons who had been manumitted. He read an extract from a law, passed in 1779, in North Carolina, by which the punishment of death is awarded against such an offence.[66]

Mr. MACON read the proceedings of the House on the petition respecting the kidnapping of negroes, in order to show that the gentleman from New York (Mr. LIVINGSTON) had misstated the issue of that business. The last report on the subject was that it would be best to leave the regulation of the subject to the Legislatures of the several States.[67] Mr. M. allowed that his reflections upon the whole body of Quakers were too general and he had no hesitation in retracting them; but he believed a number of them were guilty of the charges brought against them by the gentleman from South Carolina.

Mr. Thatcher said, if, when the motion was first made, he had been against it, from what had fallen from gentlemen on the subject, he should now be in favor of it; for, notwithstanding they opposed the second reading of the petition, they were filing off in squads to read it, and ready to fight for a sight of it. He believed, therefore, they had some reasons for opposing the second reading which did not appear. He referred to what had been said by the gentleman from North Carolina, as to the fact stated in the petition, and said that notwithstanding the laws which he had read, the fact might be true; but that this very doubt about the fact was an additional reason for going into the inquiry.

Gentlemen had said, however good and virtuous the petitioners might be, it ought to have no effect upon the petition; if this were true, he hoped when they were represented as the worst of men, that representation was not meant to influence their decision on the question. Mr. T. could not conceive for what purpose they were carried to Europe, to witness scenes which had taken place there for the last ten years. Was this, he asked, the state of society? If he thought so, if it had the faintest resemblance of what was taking place there, he would fly from it to the uttermost parts of the earth, and there make his habitation. Mr. T. wished an inquiry to take place; there was a part of the United States in which slavery was tolerated—some of the members from those parts thought it not right; there were other parts of the Union which disclaimed it. These two opposing principles were like two opposite powers in mechanism, which produced rest; but, the more frequently the subject was looked into, the more mitigated would be its effects.

Mr. BAYARD went into a justification of what he had before advanced with respect to its being within the jurisdiction of the House to afford a remedy with respect to the *ex post facto* law complained of, and insisted that, without some such interference, persons might be in a situation in which they could get no redress. Mr. B. concluded by saying, that gentlemen knew little of human nature, who thought to silence these petitioners by contemptuous treatment, and alluded to the indulgence which had been shown them with respect to taking of oaths.[68]

Mr. S. SMITH[69] wished for an explanation on the subject of *ex post facto* law. He thought the Constitution of the United States could have no power over laws passed before it existed. He was of opinion this petition ought to be referred, as it was presented in a respectful form, and by a respectable body of men—a body of men so respectable that their word was equal to the oath of other men. He thought, also, that a fair and candid decision would prevent future similar applications. Because some few men had attempted to delude the servants of gentlemen, it ought not to be the ground of a reflection upon the whole body.

The gentleman from Pennsylvania had said that the manumission law of that State had done no harm to property of this kind; that he denied; he believed it had made many of the slaves in the neighboring States unhappy in their situations, and had given their masters considerable uneasiness.

Mr. VENABLE[70] would not have risen, had it not been that he wished to correct a mistaken notion of the disrespect that was attached to ordering a petition to lie upon the table. When a petition was received and read, and no matter found in it upon which the House could act, the proper mode of disposing of it was to order it to lie on the table, where every member could have recourse to it, and could call it up whenever he pleased. This was not disrespectful, and it would give members a better opportunity of becoming acquainted with it than a general second reading, which the gentleman from Massachusetts (notwithstanding his attempt at wit on the subject) knew was merely a matter of form, the first words only being repeated. With respect to the society from whence the petition came, he respected them as much as any other society in the United States; but, if they presented a petition upon which the House could not act, he should be for its lying upon the table.

Mr. GORDON defended what he had before asserted with respect to the law organizing the Judiciary system being equal to the redress of any grievance arising from a State law, in opposition to the gentleman from Delaware. He read the law at length.

The question was taken for the second reading of the petition, and carried—53 votes being in the affirmative.

Mr. GALLATIN moved that it be referred to a select committee.

Mr. COIT[71] wished it to be referred to the Committee of the Whole, to whom was referred the petition on the subject of kidnapping negroes, &c.

Mr. RUTLEDGE thought a select committee would be best, as stage-plays, cock-fighting, horse-racing, and other evils, would, of course, be considered.

The question for reference to a select committee was put and carried—59 members being in the affirmative.

Five members being agreed upon to form the committee, the SPEAKER names Messrs. SITGREAVES,[72] NICHOLAS, DANA,[73] SCHUREMAN,[74] and S. SMITH, for the purpose.

The House adjourned. . . .

MONDAY, January 29{, 1798}.

MEMORIAL OF THE QUAKERS.

Mr. SITGREAVES, from the committee to whom was referred the memorial and address of the people called Quakers, from their yearly meeting held in Philadelphia, in November last, made a report, stating, that as the above memorial was expressed only in general terms, the committee applied to the memorialists, desiring them to exhibit the precise grievances which they wished to have redressed; that, in consequence of this request, the committee received certain documents from them;[75] after which the memorialists were invited to a conference, in order to suggest a remedy to the evils which they complained of; and, after several consultations, the committee state it to be clearly their opinion, that the facts referred to are exclusively of judicial cognizance, that therefore it is not competent for the Legislature to do anything in the business, and recommended that the memorialists have leave to withdraw their memorial.

Mr. S. moved that the report be read a second time, for the purpose of being concurred in.

Mr. THATCHER hoped the report would be committed. As several applications had been made to the Legislature by this body of people for redress of a similar kind prayed for in this memorial, in order, therefore, to give them full satisfaction, and thereby prevent future applications, he hoped the determination made upon it might be done in the most solemn manner.

Mr. SITGREAVES hoped this course would be taken. He wished the memorialists to be fully satisfied with the proceedings taken on their application.

Mr. T. CLAIBORNE[76] was also of this opinion.

Mr. MCDOWELL[77] could not conceive the object of the gentleman who moved this report to be committed, except it were to pay a compliment to the memorialists. He was opposed to paying this compliment. He thought the manner in which they had so frequently come forward to attempt to disturb the peace of society, and to arraign the conduct of State Governments, was not entitled to it. He hoped, therefore, the report would not be referred.

The question was put, and there appeared to be 35 for the committing the report, and 35 against it; the Speaker determined in the affirmative, and the question was carried. . . .

TUESDAY, February 13{, 1798}.

Mr. SITGREAVES hoped the House would go into a Committee of the Whole on a report of a select committee on the memorial of the people called Quakers.

Mr. RUTLEDGE wished this subject might be deferred till to-morrow, as he thought it might be proper to introduce an amendment into the report, which he was not at this time prepared to make.

Mr. SITGREAVES consented. . . .

WEDNESDAY, February 14{, 1798}.

Mr. SITGREAVES moved the order of the day on the report of a select committee on the memorial of the people called Quakers; which motion being agreed to, the House went into a Committee of the Whole on the subject, Mr. DENT[78] in the Chair. The report having been read as follows:

"That, inasmuch as the said memorial and address presents, in general terms only, certain subjects to the consideration of the Legislature, without containing any definite state of facts, or any specific application for its interposition, the memorialists were desired to exhibit a particular view of the grievances of which they complained, in order that the attention of the House might be directed to precise objects, and that it might be better discerned whether the complaints of the memorialists were of a nature to justify Legislative interference:

"That, in consequence of this request, the memorialists laid before the committee the representation and documents which accompany this report:

"That, on the subject of this representation, the memorialists were invited to confer with the committee, and were solicited to suggest the remedy which they conceived it to be in the power of Congress to apply to the case, as stated by them:

"That the committee, after several conferences with the memorialists, and an attentive consideration of the subject, are very clearly of opinion that the facts disclosed in the said representation are exclusively of judicial cognizance; and that it is not competent to the Legislative authority of Congress to do any act in relation to the matter thereof:

"Wherefore the committee recommend the following resolution:

"*Resolved,* That the memorialists have leave to withdraw the said memorial and address."

Mr. THATCHER could not say that he was perfectly satisfied with the report of the committee in all its parts. He wished the business disposed of without coming to any decisive resolution upon it, so as either to approve or disapprove of it. He was not ready to say that the facts disclosed in that memorial were exclusively of judicial cognizance, and that the Legislature of the Union was incompetent to do anything in it. It might, however, be true, but it was not clear to him. He would rather that the subject should not now be acted upon: he would, therefore, propose an amendment to the report, which might conclude the business without coming to any resolution upon it, which had been the course heretofore taken with similar applications. He moved, therefore, to strike out the resolution giving the petitioners leave to withdraw their petition; and if his motion was agreed to, he should wish the committee to rise, and that the House would not act further upon it at present.

Mr. RUTLEDGE said, he, as well as the gentleman from Massachusetts, was dissatisfied with the report of the select committee.

He thought the report ought to have stated that the peace of certain States of the Union had been much disturbed by applications of this kind. He had prepared a resolution to this effect, which he would read in his place. It was as follows:

"*Resolved*, That part of the memorial of the people called Quakers has a tendency to disturb the tranquility of some of the States of the Union; that this House is not competent to act upon it, and therefore they have leave to withdraw their memorial."

There could be little difference of opinion on the assertion that the internal tranquility of several States had been disturbed by these applications; and he believed there would be no difficulty in obtaining a majority of the House to declare it; as if the Representatives of three or four States were to rise and declare the fact, it must have sufficient weight to carry a declaration of this kind. He had, however, mentioned the matter to some of his friends, and found it was not very agreeable to them, as they wished to get rid of the business without debate. But if the present motion were to obtain, he should afterwards bring forward this resolution.

The CHAIRMAN declared the motion of the gentleman from Massachusetts out of order.

The question on the resolution, as reported, was put and carried, there being 74 votes in the affirmative. The committee then rose, and the House concurred in the report.

5

1798

The Society of Friends Reacts to the House's Rejection of Its Memorial

Source: Minutes for 16 February 1798, Records of the Pennsylvania Yearly Meeting for Sufferings, Friends Historical Library of Swarthmore College, Swarthmore, Pennsylvania.

The minutes of the Meeting for Sufferings for 16 February 1798 report the fate of the memorial in the halls of Congress with these words:

> It appears by Account now given that the Concern of our Yearly Meeting respecting the Oppression of the freed black People in No. Carolina as set forth in the Memorial to Congress, has been carefully attended to; and issued in a Conclusion of the united States Representatives, that a Remedy for the Grievance complained of is not within their Department; but belongs to the judicial Branch of the State Government wherein the Evil prevails—What further may be expedient to do, under the religious pressure of this affecting Case, it is desired may be kept under continued weighty Attention.

Epilogue

About 1783, things began to go wrong for George Walton. In that year the Perquimans Monthly Meeting heard complaints against him for frequent inebriation. George confessed his fault and promised to try to conquer his weakness, and the monthly meeting passed by his offense. In 1788, reports of George's excessive drinking revived, along with similar complaints against his wife, Mary. After having the cases under care for several months, the meeting expelled husband and wife from unity because of their incorrigible alcoholism, Mary in December 1788 and George in February 1789.[1] The Walton couple's later alcoholism suggests a new and ironic meaning for George's 1773 dream of a grape arbor, in his relating of which he notes that he came to love grapes through marrying his wife. George died in December of the year of his disownment, and in 1792 Mary followed him to the grave.

Like George Walton's story, the story of North Carolina Quaker manumission has no happy ending. Year after year, the yearly meeting petitioned the state assembly to change the law so that those who wanted to could free their slaves, and year after year, the assembly refused to alter the law. County courts continued to take up and re-enslave blacks that Quakers set free. In fact, the North Carolina assembly passed legislation in 1795 that made manumission even more difficult by requiring all freed slaves to post bonds of £200 to ensure their good behavior. The general emancipation law that North Carolina finally adopted in 1830 still made manumission difficult. According to the 1830 act, six weeks before freeing slaves, a master had to file a petition and post a bond of $1,000 for each slave, and the freedmen had to leave the state within three months.[2]

The Yearly Meeting Becomes a Slaveholder

In 1796, the legislature adopted another law that inadvertently opened a new avenue individual Quakers could use to relieve their consciences of the burden of slaveholding. The 1796 act allowed religious societies to name trustees who could accept gifts of property on their behalf. Slaves, as property, fell under this regulation. After considerable hesitation, in 1808 the North Carolina Yearly Meeting appointed trustees and empowered them to accept slaves as gifts from Friends who wished to transfer their ownership. The trustees received the wages due for the slaves' labor and used the moneys for the slaves' benefit. In other ways, the trustees treated the slaves virtually as free.[3]

In 1814, the society's agents held some 350 slaves in trust. By then Friends in North Carolina's Eastern Quarter had transferred to the society's ownership nearly all the slaves they still owned in 1808. The number of slaves under the trustees' administration gradually increased until it peaked at more than 700 in about 1826. From that point on, the number began to decrease.[4]

The number of society-owned slaves dropped as a result of an effort begun in 1824 to move them to free states, especially Ohio and Indiana, where the Northwest Ordinance had banned slavery. In addition, some slaves were set free and transported overseas to Haiti and Liberia. Despite obstacles, which included cases where the Quakers' slaves were mates of slaves owned by non-Quakers, laws adopted in the northern states that were designed to discourage immigration of free blacks, and the reluctance of many blacks to travel across the ocean, the effort succeeded in transporting to freedom more than 1,100 former slaves. By the eve of the Civil War, the yearly meeting had reduced the number of slaves it owned to eighteen.[5]

Emigration

Around the year 1800, North Carolina Quakers began taking another avenue of escape from the burdens of slaveholding. Rather than send their slaves to free states north of the Ohio River, they themselves began emigrating to those states, eventually in great numbers.

Westward emigration of North Carolinians, both Friends and non-Friends, began in the 1780s with movement into Tennessee. Like the non-

Quaker North Carolinians who moved there, Friends who settled in Tennessee, which had been admitted into the union in 1796 as a slave state, were motivated by the lure of cheap land and opportunity to improve their lot, not by antipathy to slavery. By 1800, the North Carolinians emigrating west became a stream whose flow continued down to the Civil War. Wealthy planters joined the flow of emigrants, transplanting their slaves and the plantation system to new areas of settlement south of the Ohio River. But the emigrants whose numbers swelled the stream were mainly middling sorts, typically small farmers from the piedmont and the mountains. Most of these North Carolinians were not opposed to slavery, but many resented having to compete with unpaid workers and nursed grievances against the planter aristocracy whose wealth rested on their ability to mobilize a bound labor force. The territories of the Old Northwest, Ohio, Indiana, and Illinois, from which slavery was banned, proved congenial to a number of these North Carolinian emigrants.[6]

Members of the Society of Friends amplified the number of North Carolinians who moved to the Old Northwest in the period 1800 to 1860. Of 1,826 members of the Society of Friends whose certificates of removal to Ohio and Indiana were recorded for the years from 1803 to 1807, 1,418, or seven-ninths of the total, were from North Carolina. For the first decade or so of the nineteenth century, Friends from the Albemarle region tended to move into central North Carolina first before moving out of state, but after 1812, they began moving directly to the territories of the Old Northwest. This outmigration drained the Quaker population of North Carolina and of the Albemarle region especially. As a result, the Albemarle region's diminished meetings began to merge, gradually reducing the number of meetings from a total of eleven in Pasquotank and Perquimans counties in 1800 to only two at the end of the nineteenth century. After 1815, North Carolina Quakers tended to settle in Indiana in particular, and a large percentage of Indiana Quakers were transplanted North Carolinians. In 1843, although North Carolina still led the southern states as a center of Quakerism (the state had 4,500 members compared to a mere 500 in Virginia), North Carolina's Quaker numbers paled in comparison with Indiana's 30,000 and Ohio's 18,000.[7]

For North Carolina Friends who moved to the Old Northwest, motives of conscience as well as economics lay behind the decision to emigrate, but both sets of motives related directly to slavery. As Charles F. McKiever, the chief historian of the Quaker exodus, explains: "To many the only answer was to emigrate—to remove themselves from that section of the country where slavery was tolerated and where their own beliefs made competition within the slave economy virtually impossible."[8] This combination of concerns operated similarly in the cases of non-Quaker opponents of slavery in southern states, such as antislavery evangelicals. David Barrow, an outspoken antislavery Baptist preacher of Portsmouth, Virginia, made the connections between antislavery, economics, and emigration explicit. In identifying what drove his decision in 1797 to leave his native state, he stated that in Virginia he could not support his family without owning slaves and that he could not own slaves and remain true to his beliefs.[9]

Most often, Friends departed North Carolina for the west without leaving a record of their reasons for moving. When Friends did explain why they emigrated, however, the desire to get away from slavery appeared prominently. Borden Stanton, a leader of one of the earliest of the North Carolina Quaker emigrations, one that involved the move of practically an entire meeting to Ohio, explained the exodus as the product of a longing to move "out of that oppressive part of the land ... to a place where there were no slaves held."[10] Levi Coffin, an antislavery activist who emigrated from his native North Carolina to Indiana in the mid-1820s, believed that the fact that "slavery and Quakerism could not prosper together" lay behind the exodus of North Carolina Quakers.[11] Addison Coffin, a mid-nineteenth-century Quaker North Carolina expatriate, observed, "If the question is asked, why did Friends emigrate from North Carolina? It can be answered with one dark, fearful word SLAVERY." Coffin quoted one of the North Carolina Friends who remained behind as saying, "The first cause of emigration was to get away from slavery."[12]

That some emigrating Friends were more concerned about removing themselves from a society dominated by slavery and freeing their consciences from the burden of slaveholding than they were about rendering justice to the enslaved is evident in complaints against Quakers who moved out of state after freeing their slaves. These individuals left destitute blacks behind without making any provision for their future.[13] The genuine concern of many Quakers for the welfare of enslaved blacks, however, is evident in the membership and leadership rolls of manumission societies of North Carolina and the states of the Old Northwest as well as in the names of participants and managers of the Underground Railroad. The biographies of three North Carolina Friends in three sequential generations—Charles Osborn, 1776–1850, Levi Coffin, 1798–1877, and Addison Coffin, 1822–1897—illustrate the depth and continuity of the North Carolina Quaker tradition of antislavery action.

Charles Osborn

William Lloyd Garrison, one of America's best-known abolitionists, called Charles Osborn "the father of all us Abolitionists." Born in central North Carolina as the War of Independence was commencing, Osborn moved with his Quaker parents to Tennessee in 1794 at the age of nineteen. By 1807, he was active in the ministry and the next year was recognized as a public minister. In 1814 or 1815, he formed a manumission society but found only a half-dozen others who were willing to join him in promoting the freedom of slaves.[14]

In 1816, Osborn moved to Mount Pleasant, Ohio. That same year, the American Colonization Society was founded in Washington, D.C., to organize the transportation of free blacks to Haiti and West Africa. The society's founders had mixed motives for promoting black colonization. Some believed that free blacks would have better opportunities where they did not face the prejudices of the dominant white race. Some hoped that slaveholders would be more willing to manumit their slaves if freedmen could be carried somewhere distant. And some saw a resident American population of free blacks as a threat to the system of racial slavery and embraced colonization as a tool to protect that system. Although North Carolina's Friends cooperated with the colonizationists and in 1816 even petitioned Congress in their favor, Osborn would have nothing to do with a movement he viewed as intended to strengthen slavery and denounced the American Colonization Society and its adherents.[15]

In Mount Pleasant, Osborn established *The Philanthropist,* a newspaper in which he called for immediate and unconditional emancipation. After working with Osborn at *The Philanthropist,* Benjamin Lundy later founded his own abolitionist paper, *The Genius of Universal Emancipation,* in 1821. William Lloyd Garrison became co-editor of the latter paper in 1829 and two years later established his famous radical abolitionist organ, *The Liberator.* Thus one can trace a direct line from the North Carolina Quaker antislavery activism of the revolutionary era to the radical abolitionism of antebellum America.[16]

Like John Woolman of the colonial era, and in imitation of the British abolitionists' sugar boycotts, Osborn disavowed the use of the products of slavery, even to the extent of ensuring that his burial clothes would not be of cotton. Disagreements between advocates of gradual emancipation and champions of immediate abolitionism split Ohio Quakers into rival organizations in the early 1840s. Osborn escaped the rancor by moving to the state of Michigan in 1842. Eight years later he moved once more, this time to Indiana, where he died in 1850.[17]

Levi Coffin

Friends who remained in North Carolina through the antebellum years maintained their interest in aiding blacks, bond and free. They filed suit as occasion required to sustain and enforce manumissions made in wills, sometimes purchased slaves and moved them to free states, opened schools for blacks until forced by threats to close them, and petitioned the state legislature on the behalf of blacks. They assisted manumitted slaves to escape re-enslavement by spiriting them out of the state and participated in the Underground Railroad, hiding runaway slaves and transporting them to freedom.[18]

"Since slavery had been one of the chief causes for the Quaker movement to the Northwest," observes a twentieth-century historian of the Society of Friends in Indiana, "it was only to be expected that Friends would maintain their interest in that subject." Friends in antebellum Indiana established committees on "concerns of people of color," petitioned the territorial and state governments for amelioration of the black code, memorialized Congress on slavery, and opposed the admission of Texas to the Union as a slave state. The Underground Railroad in Indiana, largely managed by Quakers, helped some three thousand blacks move northward before the issuance of the Emancipation Proclamation.[19] Levi Coffin was prominent among the transplanted Friends who carried their antislavery passion with them from North Carolina to Indiana. In fact, Coffin was known by his contemporaries as the president of the Underground Railroad.

Born in New Garden, North Carolina, in 1798, Levi Coffin was a descendant of a family of the first English settlers of Nantucket, Massachusetts. His parents were among the Nantucket Quakers who migrated to central North Carolina before the War of Independence. Levi developed a strong aversion to slavery at an early age and when he was fifteen began a lifelong involvement in helping runaway blacks escape capture. He established a Sunday school in 1818 and in 1821 started a school for slaves with his cousin

Vestal Coffin in which, with the masters' approval, they taught Christianity and Bible reading. White opposition soon forced the closing of the black Sunday school.[20]

Coffin married Catherine White in 1824 and in 1826 the couple moved to Newport (now Fountain City), Indiana, where they opened a store. Newport was a major route used by slaves escaping to the north. A community of free blacks descended from North Carolinian slaves who had been manumitted by their Quaker owners had settled around Newport and was active in hiding the runaways. But Levi and Catherine soon recognized that the vulnerability of members of this community of free blacks because of their poverty and race inhibited their effectiveness as conductors on the Underground Railroad and joined in the work of moving escapees from hiding place to hiding place. Although the Coffins's involvement in the Underground Railroad became an open secret, Levi's economic position as a prosperous merchant, linseed oil manufacturer, and board member of the local bank protected him from retaliation by aggrieved whites. In the course of two decades in Newport, the Coffins helped as many as two thousand individuals live freely in the North or in Canada. Moving to Cincinnati, Ohio, in 1847, Levi Coffin operated a wholesale mercantile house dealing in merchandise produced exclusively by free labor. In Cincinnati, the Coffins helped another 1,300 fugitive slaves.[21]

Today the Levi Coffin home in Fountain City, "Grand Central Station" of the Underground Railroad, is a state historic site and National Historic Landmark. It is believed that in her 1852 antislavery novel *Uncle Tom's Cabin* Harriet Beecher Stowe based the story of Eliza Harris, an escaped slave who carries her infant child across the frozen Ohio River pursued by bloodhounds, on an actual event in which the Coffins were involved and that she modeled the Hallidays, who aid Eliza, on Levi and Catherine Coffin.

Addison Coffin

Addison and Levi Coffin's common ancestors were among the earliest Quakers of Nantucket and settled in central North Carolina in the mid-eighteenth century. Addison's father, Vestal Coffin, was Levi's cousin. Vestal was born near New Garden in 1792 and died in 1826 in the house where he was born. Vestal joined the North Carolina Manumission Society in 1816, and later he and his cousin Levi operated a Sunday school for slaves. Vestal became active in the Underground Railroad in 1819, principally protecting slaves who had been freed by Friends from being re-enslaved by heirs and helping escaped blacks move to Ohio. Addison was born in 1822. Although he was only four years old when his father died in 1826 and when Levi left the area for Indiana, Addison from an early age embraced the Coffin family's antislavery convictions. At the age of thirteen, he and his older brother Alfred began following in their father's footsteps by assisting on the Underground Railroad.[22]

Events of the 1820s and 1830s dissuaded North Carolina Friends from looking for the manumission movement to succeed. The Missouri Compromise of 1820 ended any expectation that slavery would be abolished by law in the southern states. The Nullification Crisis of 1830 made it clear that the South would take extreme measures to protect its peculiar institution. In 1831, the Nat Turner slave uprising in Virginia sent a wave of anxiety throughout the white South that led to stricter regulation of slaves. North Carolina disenfranchised free blacks in 1835, made it illegal for free blacks to teach or preach, disarmed slaves and free blacks, and imposed heavy penalties for teaching slaves to read. The rise of militant abolitionism in the 1830s pushed southern public opinion to the right, and open discussion of the immorality of slavery was no longer tolerated. During the same period, the argument that slavery was a positive good gained currency in the slave states. In these circumstances, despair of ending slavery spurred many of the Quakers still remaining in North Carolina to emigrate.[23]

In 1833, when Addison was eleven, his mother, Alethea Coffin, planned to move the family to Indiana. But when she was appointed to a committee to plan the New Garden Boarding School, which later became Guilford College, she delayed the move. Ten years later, Addison, by then twenty-one, traveled to Indiana, visited Levi Coffin, and even considered emigrating to Oregon, where he thought he "would be forever beyond the influence of slavery." Instead he remained in Indiana, accepted a position as a schoolteacher, and soon married and took up farming. Alethea Coffin did not join him in Indiana until 1852. In that year, Addison's brother, Alfred, now a physician who had managed the Underground Railroad in North Carolina since 1836, was forced to flee the state because of threats against his life. From the time Addison settled in Indiana until the Civil War, he took an active part in abolition organizations.[24]

At the end of the Civil War, a number of refugees from the South that included Confederate soldiers and deserters as well as a black man, engaged Addison to go to North Carolina and arrange for the transportation of their families to the North and West. His success in this commission led him to establish a business that arranged for the transportation of emigrants from North Carolina and Virginia by steamship and railroad. In the first year of this business, 1866, Addison arranged ten such trips that settled some 5,000 emigrants, including about 150 blacks, in Ohio, Indiana, Illinois, Iowa, Missouri, and Kansas.[25]

A Burden Unshed

Like George Walton and Thomas Nicholson in the 1770s, Friends in antebellum North Carolina viewed slavery as a burden for both slaveowner and slave. They sought an end to slavery not only for the self-centered motive of freeing themselves of sin but also for the sake of the slaves. In 1865, ratification of the Thirteenth Amendment to the Constitution finally ended slavery wherever it was still legal in the United States. With slavery's final demise, some former abolitionists realized that the struggle for racial equality would have to continue. Among these clear-seeing individuals was Quaker abolitionist Levi Coffin.

During the Civil War, even before the Emancipation Proclamation, Levi traveled from Cincinnati to Cairo, Illinois, to help establish schools for destitute blacks who had fled behind Union lines. Returning to Cincinnati, he devoted all his energies to organizing aid for the blacks displaced by the war. After Lincoln issued the Emancipation Proclamation, he helped organize and then was appointed general agent of the nonsectarian Western Freedman's Aid Commission, which established schools and collected and sent supplies and money for the benefit of freed blacks. Levi persuaded the quarterly meetings of Ohio and Indiana to act on behalf of the freedmen. In May he made another visit to the freedmen's camps, visiting Cairo and Memphis, Tennessee, and venturing as far south as Corinth, Mississippi. He then traveled to Washington, D.C., as a member of a delegation from freedmen's aid associations to lobby in favor of creation of the federal Freedmen's Bureau. After the war and until his death in 1877 he continued to work to improve the plight of blacks, traveling in America, Great Britain, and France to raise funds and form aid societies for freedpeople. In Cincinnati he was recognized for the help he offered blacks who wanted to start a business or get an education.[26]

In 1774, nine decades before the Thirteenth Amendment, George Walton had a dream that led him to contemplate the end of slavery. He dreamed of a slave newly imported from Africa, hardly able to speak English, who admonished Quaker leaders to stay out of the conflicts that would come to be known as the American Revolutionary War. This dream, Walton wrote, "brought me under deep thought concerning the workings of divine providence, and my firm belief [that the] Blacks will become a people in which God will be glorified, and show forth his power." A host of circumstances and a mixture of motivations brought about the eventual end of slavery in the United States. Not the least among the forces that produced that end were the convictions of North Carolina Friends who, like Walton, recognized the dignity of all people and, having the courage of their convictions, strove to make their dreams reality.

Notes

Introduction

1. "George Walton's Accounts of Two Dreams," document 1, Part I, this volume.

2. Although the Society of Friends lacked a clerical hierarchy and distributed authority widely, it had a definite organizational structure. The lowest business unit was the preparative meeting, consisting of one or more meetings for worship. The preparative meetings prepared business to be concluded by the monthly meeting, which was formed from two or more preparative meetings. Members of several monthly meetings in a neighborhood gathered four times a year in quarterly meetings for worship and business. The highest level of organization was the yearly meeting, to which all monthly meetings under its care sent delegates. Yearly meetings covered extensive geographical areas. In the colonial era, the Philadelphia yearly meeting, for instance, included monthly meetings in Pennsylvania, New Jersey, Delaware, and, for a time, parts of Maryland. Yearly meetings exercised moral oversight of monthly meetings, issuing spiritual advice and queries regarding standards of behavior. At each level, committees made up of elders, financial officers, and a clerk administered society affairs and reported up the organizational ladder.

3. Hugh Barbour and J. William Frost, *The Quakers* (New York: Greenwood Press, 1988), 3–7; H. Larry Ingle, *First among Friends: George Fox and the Creation of Quakerism* (New York: Oxford University Press, 1994), 107–17, and passim.

4. Ibid.

5. Ingle, *First among Friends*, 256–61; Frederick B. Tolles, *Meetinghouse and Counting House: The Quaker Merchants of Colonial Philadelphia 1682–1763* (1948; repr., New York: W. W. Norton, 1963), 7.

6. Barbour and Frost, *The Quakers*, 4–6.

7. Marvin L. Michael Kay and Lorin Lee Cary, *Slavery in North Carolina, 1748–1775* (Chapel Hill: University of North Carolina Press, 1995), 202.

8. Jean R. Soderlund, *Quakers & Slavery: A Divided Spirit* (Princeton, N.J.: Princeton University Press, 1985), 54–86.

9. Thomas E. Drake, *Quakers and Slavery in America* (1950; repr., Gloucester, Mass.: Peter Smith, 1965), 1–47; Sydney V. James, *A People among Peoples: Quaker Benevo-*

lence in Eighteenth-Century America (Cambridge, Mass.: Harvard University Press, 1963), 103–40.

10. Soderlund, *Quakers & Slavery*, 15–49.

11. Ibid., 49–53.

12. Ralph L. Ketcham, "Conscience, War, and Politics in Pennsylvania, 1755–1757," *William and Mary Quarterly*, 3d ser., 20 (1963): 416–39.

13. Jack D. Marietta, *The Reformation of American Quakerism, 1748–1783* (Philadelphia: University of Pennsylvania Press, 1985); Tolles, *Meetinghouse and Counting House*, 231–43. For pressure on Friends in political office to support war measures and the ways many white Pennsylvanians viewed Quakers as holding values alien to those of the majority, see Peter Silver, *Our Savage Neighbors: How Indian War Transformed Early America* (New York: W. W. Norton, 2008), esp. 191–226.

14. Richard Bauman, *For the Reputation of Truth: Politics, Religion, and Conflict among the Pennsylvania Quakers, 1750–1800* (Baltimore, Md.: Johns Hopkins Press, 1971), 35–46.

15. James, *A People among Peoples*, 117–19.

16. Woolman's tract is reprinted in Roger Bruns, ed., *Am I Not a Man and a Brother: The Antislavery Crusade of Revolutionary America 1688–1788* (New York: Chelsea House, 1977), 68–78, and in J. William Frost, ed., *The Quaker Origins of Antislavery* (Norwood, Pa.: Norwood Editions, 1980), 138–66.

17. Reprinted in Frost, *Quaker Origins of Antislavery*, 167–70.

18. Bauman, *For the Reputation of Truth*, 27–31.

19. Soderlund, *Quakers & Slavery*, 87–111.

20. Christopher Clark, *Social Change in America: From the Revolution through the Civil War* (Chicago: Ivan R. Dee, 2006), 15–16. The decrease in the number of slaves was not steady throughout the period: The years of the French and Indian War (the late 1750s and early 1760s) witnessed a brief resurgence of slaveholding in Philadelphia, when employers were reluctant to bear the expense of importing indentured laborers from Europe only to see their servants inducted into the British army. Gary B. Nash, "Slaves and Slave Owners in Colonial Philadelphia," *William and Mary Quarterly*, 3d ser., 30 (1973): 223–56.

21. Maurice Jackson, *Let This Voice Be Heard: Anthony Benezet, Father of Atlantic Abolitionism* (Philadelphia: University of Pennsylvania Press, 2009), 16–17, 217–19; Gary B. Nash and Jean R. Soderlund, *Freedom by Degrees: Emancipation in Pennsylvania and Its Aftermath* (New York: Oxford University Press, 1991), 91; Soderlund, *Quakers & Slavery*, 104.

22. Drake, *Quakers and Slavery in America*, 68–84; Arthur Zilversmit, *The First Emancipation: The Abolition of Slavery in the North* (Chicago: University of Chicago Press, 1967), 55–83.

23. For the distinction between societies with slaves and slave societies, see Clark, *Social Change in America*, 7, 15.

24. U.S. Bureau of the Census, comp., *Historical Statistics of the United States: Colonial Times to 1970* (Washington, D.C.: U.S. Dept. of Commerce, Bureau of the Census, 1975), 1168.

25. Kay and Cary, *Slavery in North Carolina*, 22.

26. 1772 Tax List, Perquimans County, North Carolina, North Carolina State Archives, Record Series G.A. 11.1, available at http://perqtax.homestead.com/files/perq1772.html. The tax list gives a total of 1,793 taxables, which included white males and male and female slaves. Indecipherable entries caused by damage to the record excluded from this analysis forty-two of the taxables in about a dozen out of a total of some 540 households. According to the 1790 U.S. census, slightly more than a third of the county's inhabitants in 1790 were slaves. This group was held in 46 percent of the households. Sixty percent of slave-owning families owned fewer than five slaves. Alan D. Watson, *Perquimans County: A Brief History* (Raleigh: Division of Archives and History, North Carolina Department of Cultural Resources, 1987), 18, 43.

27. Kay and Cary, *Slavery in North Carolina*, 31.

28. J. William Frost proposed this distinction in "The Origins of the Quaker Crusade against Slavery: A Review of Recent Literature," *Quaker History* 67 (1978), 56–58. Jean Soderlund confirmed its validity in a close examination of four regional components of the Philadelphia Yearly Meeting; see *Quakers & Slavery*, especially 140–47. For a similar distinction, see Christopher L. Brown, *Moral Capital: Foundations of British Abolitionism* (Chapel Hill: North Carolina University Press, 2006), 26.

29. Tolles, *Meeting House and Counting House*, 232.

30. Soderlund, *Quakers & Slavery*, 140–47.

31. Marietta, *Reformation of American Quakerism*, 3–72.

32. Ibid., 121–27, 272–79.

33. Soderlund, *Quakers & Slavery*, 140–47.

34. Thomas Nicholson, "Considerations on Slavery," document 5, Part II, this volume.

35. Thomas Nicholson, *An Epistle to Friends in Great Britain; Also a Testimony Concerning Thomas Nicholson of N.C.* (Carthage, Ind.: David Marshall, 1888), 6–7.

36. Robin Blackburn, *The Overthrow of Colonial Slavery 1776–1848* (London: Verso, 1988), 35.

37. David Brion Davis, *The Problem of Slavery in the Age of Revolution, 1770–1823* (Ithaca, N.Y.: Cornell University Press, 1975), 80; Adam Hochschild, *Bury the Chains: Prophets and Rebels in the Fight to Free an Empire's Slaves* (Boston: Houghton Mifflin, 2005), 2–3.

38. Davis, *The Problem of Slavery in the Age of Revolution*, 325–27.

39. Bureau of Democracy, Human Rights and Labor, U.S. Department of State, "Mauritania: Country Reports on Human Rights Practices, 2002," March 31, 2003, available at www.state.gov/g/drl/rls/hrrpt/2002/18215.htm.

40. Blackburn, *The Overthrow of Colonial Slavery*, 36–38.

41. Davis, *The Problem of Slavery in the Age of Revolution*, 11, 41, 44–45.

42. Ibid., 45–48, 213–14.

43. Ibid., 213–14.

44. Brown, *Moral Capital*, 19, 460.

45. Ibid., 88–91.

46. Ibid., 396, 399; Jackson, *Let This Voice Be Heard*, 55, 64–65; Thomas P. Slaughter,

The Beautiful Soul of John Woolman, Apostle of Abolition (New York: Hill and Wang, 2008), 243–44.

47. Brown, *Moral Capital*, 105.

48. Ibid., 115.

49. Brown, *Moral Capital*; Davis, *The Problem of Slavery in the Age of Revolution*; Hochschild, *Bury the Chains*; Simon Schama, *Rough Crossings: Britain, the Slaves and the American Revolution* (New York: Harper Collins, 2006).

50. Davis, *The Problem of Slavery in the Age of Revolution*, 213–14.

51. The London Meeting for Sufferings was a standing committee of the London Yearly Meeting of the Society of Friends. It was established in 1675 to document, publicize, and lessen the persecution of Friends. In the eighteenth century, it took on additional responsibilities that included campaigning to end the slave trade.

52. Brown, *Moral Capital*, 391. For the post–Revolutionary War antislavery activities of English Quakers, see Jackson, *Let This Voice Be Heard*, 164–65.

53. Michael Craton, *Testing the Chains: Resistance to Slavery in the British West Indies* (Ithaca, N.Y.: Cornell University Press, 1982), 125–58; Andrew J. O'Shaughnessy, *An Empire Divided: The America Revolution and the British Caribbean* (Philadelphia: University of Pennsylvania Press, 2000), 38–40, 151–54.

54. Jeffrey J. Crow, "Slave Rebelliousness and Social Conflict in North Carolina, 1775 to 1802," *William and Mary Quarterly*, 3d ser., 37 (1980): 79–102; Douglas R. Egerton, *Death or Liberty: African Americans and Revolutionary America* (New York: Oxford University Press, 2009), 41–64; O'Shaughnessy, *An Empire Divided*, 153; Schama, *Rough Crossings*, 16–17.

55. Sylvia R. Frey, *Water from the Rock: Black Resistance in a Revolutionary Age* (Princeton, N.J.: Princeton University Press, 1991), 45–171; Schama, *Rough Crossings*, 18, 66.

56. Egerton, *Death or Liberty*, 65–73; Frey, *Water from the Rock*, 58, 86, 148–69; Cassandra Pybus, "Jefferson's Faulty Math: The Question of Slave Defections in the American Revolution," *William and Mary Quarterly*, 3d ser., 62 (2005): 243–64; Pybus, *Epic Journeys of Freedom: Runaway Slaves of the American Revolution and Their Global Search for Liberty* (Boston: Beacon Press, 2006), 3–72; Schama, *Rough Crossings*, 93–126.

57. Egerton, *Death or Liberty*, 73, 84–88; Frey, *Water from the Rock*, 118–19, 141–42, 155–56.

58. Brown, *Moral Capital*, 108–9, 283, 289–90; Egerton, *Death or Liberty*, 95.

59. Crow, "Slave Rebelliousness," 90.

60. Douglas R. Egerton, *Gabriel's Rebellion: The Virginia Slave Conspiracies of 1800 and 1802* (Chapel Hill: University of North Carolina Press, 1993), 163–68.

61. Charles Rappleye, *Sons of Providence: The Brown Brothers, the Slave Trade, and the American Revolution* (New York: Simon & Schuster, 2006), 76–79, 129–30, 133–34, 140, 146.

62. Ibid., 140, 143–46; Jackson, *Let This Voice Be Heard*, 142, 248.

63. Slaughter, *The Beautiful Soul of John Woolman*, 3–12.

64. Although the Society of Friends had no paid clergy and anyone was eligible to speak during worship, monthly meetings formally recognized as public Friends members who had a special calling to preach.

65. Rebecca Larson, *Daughters of Light: Quaker Women Preaching and Prophesying in the Colonies and Abroad, 1700–1775* (Chapel Hill: University of North Carolina Press, 1999), 9–11, 64, 108–13, and passim.

66. John Woolman, *The Journal and Major Essays of John Woolman* (New York: Oxford University Press, 1971), 17, 18, 37, 70–71; Slaughter, *The Beautiful Soul of John Woolman*, 194–96.

Part I. An Individual: George Walton Confronts Slavery

1. Alan D. Watson, *Perquimans County: A Brief History* (Raleigh: Division of Archives and History, North Carolina Department of Cultural Resources, 1987), 9–13, 18, 43.

2. For George Walton's admission to the Society of Friends and Walton's and Mary Newby Winslow's request for permission to marry, see Perquimans Monthly Meeting Minutes, 3rd of 4th Month 1773, 2nd of 6th Month 1773, and 4th of 8th Month 1773, North Carolina Yearly Meeting Archives, Friends Historical Collection, Guilford College, Greensboro, North Carolina (hereafter cited as Perquimans Monthly Meeting Minutes). For the marriage of George Walton and Sarah Earls, see *North Carolina Marriage Bonds, 1741–1868*, online database at www.ancestry.com; and Jordan Dodd, *North Carolina Marriages to 1825*, online database formerly at www.ancestry.com. In the FamilySearch Ancestral File, an online database at www.familysearch.org, the "Family Group Record" for George Walton provides birth dates (approximate for George), marriage and death dates for George and Mary Newby, and the "Individual Record" for Mary Newby, which provides dates of her marriages to Timothy Winslow and George Walton. For George Walton's children by both his marriages, see Mrs. Watson Winslow (Ellen Good Rawlings), *History of Perquimans County* (Raleigh, N.C., 1931; repr., Baltimore: Regional Publishing Co., 1974), 310.

3. Mechal Sobel, *Teach Me Dreams: The Search for Self in the Revolutionary Era* (Princeton, N.J.: Princeton University Press, 2000), 62–86.

4. Josiah White was a member of the Perquimans Monthly Meeting. In 1776, he served with Walton and others on a committee appointed to provide assistance to Friends who were preparing manumission papers. With Walton and others, he signed a petition to the North Carolina General Assembly, dated 25th of the 10th Mo. 1779, explaining the Friends' motives for freeing their slaves. "Memorial from Friends Who Manumitted Slaves to the North Carolina General Assembly," Document 7, Part III, this volume. White freed at least four of his slaves.

5. Carla Gerona, *Night Journeys: The Power of Dreams in Transatlantic Quaker Culture* (Charlottesville: University of Virginia Press, 2004), 128.

6. Thomas Nicholson, "A Copy of a Letter to R. J. of Newbegun Creek in Pasquotank County," 21st of the 7th Mo. 1769, in Simon Garriques, Commonplace Book, 1757–1814, MSS, Quaker Collection, Haverford College, Haverford, Pennsylvania.

7. Sobel, *Teach Me Dreams*, 62–86

8. Gerona, *Night Journeys*, 125–72, quotation on 128.

9. The most useful investigations of the manumission movement among revolutionary-era North Carolina Friends are Meeting for Sufferings of the North Carolina

Yearly Meeting, *A Narrative of Some of the Proceedings of North Carolina Yearly Meeting on the Subject of Slavery within Its Limits* (Greensborough, N.C.: Meeting for Sufferings of North Carolina Yearly Meeting, 1848); Stephen B. Weeks, *Southern Quakers and Slavery: A Study in Institutional History* (1896; repr., N.Y.: Bergman, 1968), 199–244; John M. Shay, "The Antislavery Movement in North Carolina" (Ph.D. diss., Princeton University, 1971); Hiram H. Hilty, *Toward Freedom for All: North Carolina Quakers and Slavery* (Richmond, Ind.: Friends United Press, 1984); Hiram H. Hilty, *By Land and by Sea: Quakers Confront Slavery and Its Aftermath in North Carolina* (Greensboro, N.C.: North Carolina Yearly Meeting of Friends, 1993); and Katherine Dungy, "A Friend in Deed: Quakers and Manumission in Perquimans County, North Carolina, 1775–1800," *The Southern Friend* 24 (2002): 3–36.

10. Minutes of North Carolina Friends Yearly Meeting, 1768, 97–98; Minutes of North Carolina Friends Yearly Meeting, 1772, 117–18; and Minutes of North Carolina Friends Yearly Meeting, 1773, 127–28. All in North Carolina Yearly Meeting Archives, Friends Historical Collection, Guilford College, Greensboro, North Carolina, hereafter cited as Minutes of North Carolina Friends Yearly Meeting.

11. Sydney V. James, *A People among People: Quaker Benevolence in Eighteenth-Century America* (Cambridge, Mass.: Harvard University Press, 1963), 129–30.

12. Minutes of North Carolina Friends Yearly Meeting, 1772, 97–98.

13. For the text of the request and the reply, see document 3, Part II, this volume.

14. Perquimans Monthly Meeting Minutes, 6th of 4th Month 1774, 4th of 5th Month 1774, and 3rd of 8th Month 1774; Minutes of the Standing Committee, Eastern Quarter, 14th of 4th Month 1774, North Carolina Yearly Meeting Archives, Friends Historical Collection, Guilford College, Greensboro, North Carolina, hereafter cited as Minutes of the Standing Committee.

15. The Perquimans Monthly Meeting recommended Francis Jones as a minister with whom it had unity on 3 April 1773. In 1780 it declared Jones out of unity because he had courted and married a widow without waiting a decent interval after the death of his wife. See Perquimans Monthly Meeting Minutes, 3d of 4th Month 1773, 1st of 11th Month 1780. As evidenced by Walton's journal, Jones and Walton were frequent companions, visiting the Yearly Meeting in Virginia together in 1775 and 1777 and attending in company burials of children on two separate occasions in 1777.

16. Marvin L. Michael Kay and Lorin Lee Cary, *Slavery in North Carolina, 1748–1775* (Chapel Hill: University of North Carolina Press, 1995), 26.

17. Exodus 3:7.
18. Isaiah 30:1.
19. Matthew 6:33.
20. Matthew 10:37.
21. Matthew 7:12.
22. Genesis 3:19.
23. Galatians 3:28.
24. Isaiah 61:1.
25. Matthew 5:14.

26. Proverbs 16:5.
27. Habakkuk 1:13.
28. 1 John 2:15.
29. Matthew 16:26; Mark 8:36.
30. Matthew 6:20.
31. John 16:22.
32. John 8:21.
33. James 5:4.
34. Romans 2:11.
35. Daniel 6.
36. Daniel 3.
37. 2 Corinthians 4:18.
38. John 15:20.
39. 1 Corinthians 15:58.
40. Isaiah 4:4.

41. Connecticut-born David Ferris (1707–1779) moved to Philadelphia and joined the Society of Friends in 1733. In 1737, he moved again to Wilmington, Delaware. In 1758, he was recorded as a public Friend and began a series of travels in the ministry. During the 1760s and 1770s he wrote a number of letters on the subject of slaveholding. In September 1774, the same year that Thomas Newby wrote to Ferris for his advice, Ferris wrote a letter to Robert Pleasants, a Virginia Quaker who owned eighty slaves, urging him to free his slaves. Within three years Pleasants had freed all but a half dozen who were minors. Regarding a visit among North Carolina Friends in early 1773, Ferris noted in his memoirs, "Although they were generally in the practice of keeping slaves, yet they had begun to see the error of it, and were desirous to be relieved of the burden, but saw no way to effect it, to the satisfaction of themselves and their slaves, because of the cruel laws in force in these colonies; by which, if a man set his slaves free, they would be liable to be seized and sold to the highest bidder; which appears grievous, both to themselves and their owners." David Ferris, *Resistance and Obedience to God: Memoirs of the Life of David Ferris (1707–1779)*, ed. Martha Paxson Grundy (Philadelphia: Friends General Conference, 2001), 61.

42. Isaiah 42:8.
43. Matthew 25:30.
44. Jeremiah 2:13. A separate copy of the account of this dream in Walton's hand includes the word *not* that Walton omitted from the quotation here.
45. Romans 1:28.
46. Hebrews 10:29.
47. Matthew 3:7; Luke 3:7.
48. "An Additional Act to an Act Concerning Servants and Slaves," in *The State Records of North Carolina*, ed. and comp. Walter Clark (1905; repr., Wilmington, N.C.: Broadfoot Publishing, 1994), 23:388.
49. Sally E. Hadden, *Slave Patrols: Law and Violence in Virginia and the Carolinas* (Cambridge, Mass.: Harvard University Press, 2001), 32–35.

50. Ibid., 36, 72, 106.

51. Ibid., 36–37, 86; Laws of North Carolina for 1779, Chapter VII, in Clark, *The State Records of North Carolina*, 24:276–77.

52. Jon F. Sensbach, *A Separate Canaan: The Making of an Afro-Moravian World in North Carolina, 1763–1840* (Chapel Hill: University of North Carolina Press, 1998), 88, 208.

53. Philadelphian Samuel Hopkins appears to have traveled frequently on religious visits. For instance, he was in Maryland in 1760 and in North Carolina twenty years later. "A Journal of the Life, Travels & Gospel Labours of a Faithful Minister of Jesus Christ, Daniel Stanton, Late of Philadelphia, in the Province of Pennsylvania," in *The Friends' Library: Comprising Journals, Doctrinal Treatises, and Other Writings of Members of the Religious Society of Friends*, ed. William Evans and Thomas Evans (Philadelphia, 1848), 12:172; and "The Life and Travels of John Pemberton, a Minister of the Gospel of Christ," in *The Friends' Library: Comprising Journals, Doctrinal Treatises, and Other Writings of Members of the Religious Society of Friends*, ed. William Evans and Thomas Evans (Philadelphia, 1842), 6:299.

54. Joshua Thompson, "a worthy experienced elder," lived near Salem, New Jersey, and traveled some two thousand miles in the cause of the Society of Friends in 1771. His companion, Joseph Oxley, found him "a choice companion, and very serviceable in the discipline of the church." "Joseph Oxley's Journal of His Life, Travels, and Labours of Love, in the Faith and Fellowship of Our Lord Jesus Christ," in *The Friends' Library: Comprising Journals, Doctrinal Treatises, and Other Writings of Members of the Religious Society of Friends*, ed. William Evans and Thomas Evans (Philadelphia, 1838), 2:464, 472.

55. Matthew 7:12.

56. Isaiah 2:4; Micah 4:3.

57. Romans 8:39.

58. Minutes of North Carolina Friends Yearly Meeting, 1775, 136–37.

59. Perquimans Monthly Meeting Minutes, 6th of 3rd Month 1776. See the manumission paper in document 6, Part II, this volume.

60. On the coming of the Revolution to North Carolina, see the introductory section to Part III, this volume.

61. This was the Friends' meeting on the western branch of the Nansemond River, in Isle of Wight County, Virginia.

62. Summerton, Nansemond County, Virginia.

63. John 14:6.

64. Minutes of North Carolina Friends Yearly Meeting, 1776, 149; Perquimans Monthly Meeting Minutes, 4th of 12th Month 1776.

65. Some secondary accounts state that eleven Friends manumitted their slaves, basing the number on the names listed in the Minutes of North Carolina Friends Yearly Meeting, 1779, 182–84. But the minutes for the Standing Committee, from which the text in the yearly meeting minutes is drawn, list the names of four additional men. Before the end of the eighteenth century, at least fifty-eight Friends in Chowan, Pasquotank, and Perquimans counties emancipated their slaves, according

to a list printed in *Memorial and Address of the People Called Quakers, from Their Yearly Meeting Held in Philadelphia, by Adjournments, from the 25th of the 9th Month, to the 29th of the Same Inclusive, 1797* (Philadelphia: Philadelphia Meeting of the Religious Society of Friends, 1797). This list is reproduced in document 9, Part II, this volume.

66. Samuel Emlen (1730–1799) of Philadelphia, nearsighted and slight, possessed a gift for languages, including Latin, Greek, Hebrew, French, and German. Born to wealth, he became a public Friend and traveled widely in service to the Society of Friends, including travels to Ireland and England. "Samuel Emlen," in *Quaker Biographies: A Series of Sketches, Chiefly Biographical, Concerning Members of the Society of Friends, from the Seventeenth Century to More Recent Times* (Philadelphia, 1912), 3:143–56.

67. Joseph Oxley mentions the attendance of Mark Reeves, of Salem, New Jersey, at the 1771 yearly meeting at Shrewsbury, New Jersey. See "Joseph Oxley's Journal of His Life, Travels, and Labours of Love, in the Faith and Fellowship of Our Lord Jesus Christ," in *The Friends' Library: Comprising Journals, Doctrinal Treatises, and Other Writings of Members of the Religious Society of Friends*, ed. William Evans and Thomas Evans (Philadelphia, 1838), 2:470. John Churchman stayed with Reeves at Cohansey, New Jersey, in 1772. See "An Account of the Gospel Labours and Christian Experiences, of that Faithful Minister of Christ, John Churchman, Late of Nottingham, in Pennsylvania," in *The Friends' Library: Comprising Journals, Doctrinal Treatises, and Other Writings of Members of the Religious Society of Friends*, ed. William Evans and Thomas Evans (Philadelphia, 1842), 6:259.

68. George Dilwyn (1738–1830) of Burlington, New Jersey, was a frequent traveling companion of Samuel Emlen, including during his travels England, Ireland, France, and the Netherlands. "Samuel Emlen," 147.

69. Edward Stabler occasionally gave lodging in his home to Friends traveling on religious visits. "A Short Account of the Life and Some of the Religious Labours of Patience Brayton," in *The Friends' Library: Comprising Journals, Doctrinal Treatises, and Other Writings of Members of the Religious Society of Friends*, ed. William Evans and Thomas Evans (Philadelphia, 1846), 10:451; and "A Journal of the Life, Travels & Gospel Labours of a Faithful Minister of Jesus Christ, Daniel Stanton, Late of Philadelphia, in the Province of Pennsylvania," in *The Friends' Library: Comprising Journals, Doctrinal Treatises, and Other Writings of Members of the Religious Society of Friends*, ed. William Evans and Thomas Evans (Philadelphia, 1848), 12:171.

70. See map and caption in Part I.

71. See "An Act to Prevent Domestic Insurrections," document 1, Part III, this volume.

72. See "The Trial of Several Negroes Manumitted by Friends," document 2, Part III, this volume.

73. See ibid. and "Accounts of Sales of Blacks Emancipated by Friends," document 3, Part III, this volume.

74. "An Act to Prevent Domestic Insurrections."

75. John Pemberton (1727–1795), "one of the most influential Quaker ministers in the Philadelphia yearly meeting," played a leading role in the Quaker reform move-

ment that promoted moral discipline and separation from the world. He served the Society of Friends in many capacities, including as clerk of the Philadelphia Yearly Meeting, overseer of the press, and member of the Friendly Association for Regaining and Preserving Peace with the Indians by Pacific Measures. His religious visit to Maryland and Virginia in 1776 that Walton mentions here was one of several he made to American colonies outside Pennsylvania. With other suspected Loyalists, Pemberton spent a period of exile in Virginia from September 1777 to April 1778. In the 1790s he took an active part in the Pennsylvania Abolition Society. He died in Germany during a religious visit to the continent. Jessica Kross, "Pemberton, John," in *American National Biography*, ed. by John A. Garraty and Mark C. Carnes (New York: Oxford University Press, 1999), 17:269–71.

76. Rev. Daniel Earl (d. 1790), youngest son of an Irish nobleman, entered holy orders in 1746 and emigrated to the Albemarle region in 1757. He accepted appointment as rector of St. Paul's, Edenton, in 1759. Earl was criticized for giving too much attention to his investments in fisheries, to the neglect of his clerical duties. After his resignation from St. Paul's in 1778, he established a classical school for boys at his plantation, Blandon, fifteen miles above Edenton on the Chowan River. He is known to have owned slaves. George Troxler, "Earl, Daniel," *Dictionary of North Carolina Biography*, ed. William S. Powell (Chapel Hill: University of North Carolina Press, 1986) 2:128; *The Herald and Norfolk and Portsmouth Advertiser* (Norfolk, Va.), 27 June 1795.

77. Matthew 7:12.

78. Matthew 5:32.

79. Romans 3:8.

80. This was the Friends meeting on the western branch of the Nansemond River in Isle of Wight County, Virginia.

81. This was the Friends meeting at Chuckatuck, in Nansemond County, Virginia, just south of the James River.

82. This was the Friends meeting at Summerton, Virginia.

83. Article 34 of the North Carolina constitution of 18 December 1776 declared that "there shall be no establishment of any one religious church or denomination in this State," thus disestablishing the Church of England. *The Federal and State Constitutions, Colonial Charters, and Other Organic Laws of the States*, comp. Benjamin P. Poore, 2 vols. (Washington, D.C.: Government Printing Office, 1909), 2:1409–14.

84. William Skinner, one of North Carolina's revolutionary leaders, served as state treasurer and held the rank of brigadier general in the militia. He participated in the Battle of Great Bridge in 1775. Alan D. Watson, *Perquimans County: A Brief History* (Raleigh: Division of Archives and History, North Carolina Department of Cultural Resources, 1987), 31, 42. He was among the larger slaveowners of the county, owning forty-seven in 1790.

85. Sarem, North Carolina, in modern Gates County.

86. Jeffrey J. Crow, *The Black Experience in Revolutionary North Carolina* (Raleigh: Division of Archives and History, North Carolina Department of Cultural Resources, 1977), 62–63; Hilty, *Toward Freedom for All*, 26; "An Act for Apprehending and Selling

Certain Slaves Set Free Contrary to Law and for Confirming the Sales of Others, and for Other Purposes," document 6, Part III, this volume.

87. Minutes of the Standing Committee, 25th of 10th Month 1779.

88. For more about Nicholson, see "Thomas Nicholson Urges Gradual Emancipation," document 1, Part II, this volume.

89. Minutes of the Standing Committee, 26th of 10th Month 1778, 25th of 10th Month 1779, 25th of 2nd Month 1781, 4th of 1st Month 1783, 31st of 12th Month 1785; and Perquimans Monthly Meeting Minutes, 5th of 2d Month 1777, 6th of 8th Month 1778, 5th of 5th Month 1778, 1st of 12th Month 1779, 5th of 12th Month 1781, 3rd of 7th Month 1782.

Part II. The Community: The Society of Friends in North Carolina Chooses Manumission

1. Robert M. Calhoon, *Religion and the American Revolution in North Carolina* (Raleigh: North Carolina Department of Cultural Resources, Division of Archives and History, 1976), 41.

2. John Woolman, *The Journal and Major Essays of John Woolman*, ed. Phillips P. Moulton (New York: Oxford University Press, 1971), 70–71.

3. Roger Bruns, ed., *Am I Not a Man and a Brother: The Antislavery Crusade of Revolutionary America 1688–1788* (New York: Chelsea House, 1977), 141.

4. Woolman, *The Journal and Major Essays of John Woolman*, 70–71.

5. The text of the memorial, which was drafted by the Standing Committee on the Slave Trade and was presented to the North Carolina Yearly Meeting, is published in Calhoon, *Religion and the American Revolution in North Carolina*, 45.

6. Eva Sheppard Wolf, *Race and Liberty in the New Nation: Emancipation in Virginia from the Revolution to Nat Turner's Rebellion* (Baton Rouge: Louisiana State University Press, 2006), 3, 9, 31–35, 59.

7. Nicholson's *An Epistle to Friends in Great Britain*, written from "Little River in North Carolina," was published in Newbern, North Carolina, in 1762. In 1774, the Standing Committee permitted him to disseminate *Liberty and Property*, a pamphlet about the law of emancipation. See *Perquimans County Historical Society Year Book* (Hertford, N.C., 1970), 47; and John S. Bassett, *Slavery and Servitude in the Colony of North Carolina* (Baltimore: Johns Hopkins University Press, 1896), 54.

8. Matthew 6:22; Luke 11:34.

9. Stephen B. Weeks, *Southern Quakers and Slavery: A Study in Institutional History* (1896; repr., N.Y.: Bergman, 1968), 208.

10. The 1775 date for this essay is speculative. A piece on Nicholson in *The Friend* dates "Considerations on Slavery" to "about 1770." See "Thomas Nicholson to B. H.," *The Friend* 18 (1844): 13.

11. Isaiah 1.

12. Luke 11:52: "Woe unto you, lawyers! for ye have taken away the key of knowledge: Ye entered not in yourselves, and them that were entering in ye hindered."

13. Perquimans County taxed Newby for thirteen slaves in 1772, fourteen in 1775, and four (after he had freed ten) in 1779. The 1779 evaluation gives his worth as £4,644. Tax List, 1772, Perquimans County, North Carolina, North Carolina State Archives, Record Series G.A. 11.1; Tax List, 1775, Perquimans County, North Carolina, North Carolina Archives, Perquimans County, Tax Records, Taxables, 1773–1776; Property Tax List, 1779, Perquimans County, North Carolina, North Carolina State Archives, Perquimans County, Lists of Taxables, CR.077.701.1; all available at http://perqtax.homestead.com/.

14. For the background to the document, see Part I, this volume.

15. Tax List, 1772, Perquimans County, North Carolina; and Tax List, 1775, Perquimans County, North Carolina.

16. *The Memorial and Address of the People Called Quakers, from Their Yearly Meeting held in Philadelphia, by Adjournments, from the 25th of the 9th Month, to the 29th of the Same Inclusive, 1797* (Philadelphia: Philadelphia Meeting of the Religious Society of Friends, 1797), reprinted below, document 9.

17. Wolf, *Race and Liberty*, 58.

18. "An Act to Prevent Domestic Insurrections, and for Other Purposes," reproduced in document 1, Part III, this volume.

19. *Memorial and Address of the People Called Quakers*, 2.

20. Standing Committee for the Western Quarter in North Carolina to the Meeting for Sufferings in Philadelphia, 7th 29th 1797, in the Records of the Pennsylvania Yearly Meeting, Meeting for Sufferings, Friends Historical Library of Swarthmore College, Swarthmore, Pennsylvania.

21. Standing Committee of the Eastern Quarter of the Yearly Meeting in North Carolina to the Meeting for Sufferings in Philadelphia, 9th day, 1st month, 1797, in the Minutes of the Pennsylvania Yearly Meeting, Meeting for Sufferings, 16th day, 2nd month, 1797, Friends Historical Library of Swarthmore College, Swarthmore, Pennsylvania; *Memorial and Address of the People Called Quakers*, 4.

22. Reproduced in "Accounts of Sales of Blacks Emancipated by Friends," document 3, Part III, this volume.

23. Reproduced in "New State Legislation Annuls the Superior Court's Judgment," document 6, Part III, this volume.

24. Reproduced in "The Trial of Several Negroes Manumitted by Friends," document 2, Part III, this volume; and "Accounts of Sales of Blacks Emancipated by Friends."

25. Mark Newby's attempt to posthumously free his slaves when they turned twenty-one was also thwarted when the General Assembly disallowed his will in 1790. Jeffrey J. Crow, "Slave Rebelliousness and Social Conflict in North Carolina, 1775 to 1802," *William and Mary Quarterly*, 3d ser., 37 (1980): 92.

Part III. The State: North Carolina Thwarts Quaker Manumission

1. This and the next six paragraphs are based primarily on Hugh F. Rankin, *The North Carolina Continentals* (Chapel Hill: University of North Carolina Press, 1971), 3–27.

2. Quoted in Jeffrey J. Crow, *The Black Experience in Revolutionary North Carolina* (Raleigh: Division of Archives and History, North Carolina Department of Cultural Resources, 1977), 58.

3. Crow, *The Black Experience in Revolutionary North Carolina*, 55–61; Jeffrey J. Crow, "Slave Rebelliousness and Social Conflict in North Carolina, 1775 to 1802," *William and Mary Quarterly*, 3d ser., 37 (1980): 83–86.

4. The text of Newby's petition is reproduced in "Thomas Newby's Petition to Free His Slave Hannah," document 7, Part II, this volume.

5. Laws of North Carolina for 1777, Chapter VI, in *The State Records of North Carolina*, collected and edited by Walter Clark, vol. 24, *Laws 1777–1788* (1905; repr., Wilmington, N.C.: Broadfoot Publishing, 1994), 14–15.

6. Natalie Wexler, "Iredell, James," in *American National Biography*, ed. by John A. Garraty and Mark C. Carnes (New York: Oxford University Press, 1999), 11:674–75; Lindley S. Butler, "Johnston, Samuel," in ibid., 12:164–65.

7. The North Carolina Yearly Meeting sent this account to the Philadelphia Yearly Meeting in 1797. See "An Account of the Substance of the Trial of Several Negroes That Had Been Manumitted by Friends Subsequent to an Act of the General Assembly of the State of North-Carolina, Passed at Newbern in the month of April or May Last," 22d. of the 7th month, 1777, Records of the Meeting for Sufferings in Philadelphia, Friends Historical Library of Swarthmore College, Swarthmore, Pennsylvania. The Philadelphia Yearly Meeting published the account. The text reprinted here is transcribed from the published version.

8. For Section 24 of the North Carolina Bill of Rights and Section 44 of the North Carolina Constitution, see *The Federal and State Constitutions, Colonial Charters, and Other Organic Laws of the States*, 2 vols., Benjamin P. Poore, comp. (Washington, D.C.: Government Printing Office, 1909), 2:1410 and 1414.

9. A congress elected for the particular purpose framed the North Carolina constitution of 1776. The constitution went into effect without being submitted to the people for ratification. Ibid., 1409n.

10. The appendix to the *Memorial and Address of the People Called Quakers* includes a similar order issued in Pasquotank County, which reads:

> Pasquotank County, Sept. County Court, &c. &c. 1777.
>
> Present the Worshipful *Thomas Boyd, Timothy Hixon, John Pailin, Edmund Chancy, Joseph Reding,* and *Thomas Reese,* Esquires, Justices.
>
> It was then and there ordered, that *Thomas Reding,* Esq. take the free Negroes taken up under an act to prevent domestic insurrection and other purposes, and expose the same to the best bidder at public vendue, for ready money, and be accountable for the same, agreeable to the aforesaid act, and make return to this or the next succeeding court, of his proceedings.
>
> *A Copy.* ENOCH REEFE. *C.C.*

11. "Deposition Concerning the Enslavement of Free Negroes," in *The Papers of James Iredell*, ed. Don Higginbotham (Raleigh: Division of Archives and History, Department of Cultural Resources, 1976), 2:83.

12. The words in brackets, which, as the note at the end of this document states, were "by mistake omitted in the transcript," are inserted here as quoted in "Memorial of Friends Who Manumitted Slaves to the North Carolina General Assembly," 1779, document 7, Part III, this volume.

13. Crow, *The Black Experience in Revolutionary North Carolina*, 62–63; Hiram H. Hilty, *Toward Freedom for All: North Carolina Quakers and Slavery* (Richmond, Ind.: Friends United Press, 1984), 26.

14. "Address to the People of Great-Britain," 21 October 1774, in *Journals of the Continental Congress, 1774–1779*, vol. 1, ed. Worthington C. Ford, Gaillard Hunt, John Clement Fitzpatrick, Roscoe R. Hill, Kenneth E. Harris, and Steven D. Tilley (Washington, D.C., 1904), 82–90.

15. That Nicholson addressed the man as "Friend" suggests that "B. H." may have been a fellow Quaker. Although there is no evidence of a Benjamin Hawkins who was a North Carolina Quaker at the time, a Benjamin Hawkins was a member of the Bush River Monthly Meeting in Newberry County, South Carolina, in the 1770s. William Wade Hinshaw, *Encyclopedia of American Quaker Genealogy*, vol. 1 (1936; reprint, Baltimore: Genealogical Publishing Co., 1978), 1020, 1031.

16. Jordan's note to Elliott is handwritten at the foot of the printed bill.

17. See document 10, Part III, this volume.

Part IV. The Nation: African-American Freedom and the Manumission Debate in Congress

1. John M. Shay, "The Antislavery Movement in North Carolina" (Ph.D. diss., Princeton University, 1971), 203–13. Benjamin Quarles discusses the influence of enlightenment ideas on the manumission movement and the response of enslaved blacks to those ideas in *The Negro in the American Revolution*, (Chapel Hill: University of North Carolina Press, 1961), 33–51. On Bannaker and Wheately, see Sidney Kaplan and Emma Nogrady Kaplan, *The Black Presence in the Era of the American Revolution* (Amherst: University of Massachusetts Press, 1989), 132–51 and 170–91, respectively. Most commentators agree that Quaker antislavery arose primarily from the Friends' religious ideas, yet several argue that the emergence of the Enlightenment's natural rights argument bolstered the Quaker commitment to antislavery. See, for instance, J. William Frost's introduction to *The Quaker Origins of Antislavery* (Norwood, Pa.: Norwood Editions, 1980), 1–30; and Sydney V. James, *A People among People: Quaker Benevolence in Eighteenth-Century America* (Cambridge, Mass.: Harvard University Press, 1963), 216–39.

2. Arthur Zilversmit, *The First Emancipation: The Abolition of Slavery in the North* (Chicago: University of Chicago Press, 1967); Jackson Turner Main, *The Sovereign States, 1775–1783* (New York: New Viewpoints, 1973), 333–45; "An Act for the Gradual Abolition of Slavery," 1 March 1780, Record Group 26, Records of the Department of State, Engrossed Laws, Pennsylvania State Archives. A transcription of this document is available at www.docheritage.state.pa.us/documents/slaveryabolition.asp.

3. Eva Sheppard Wolf, *Race and Liberty in the New Nation: Emancipation in Virginia from the Revolution to Nat Turner's Rebellion* (Baton Rouge: Louisiana State University Press, 2006): 39–84.

4. Shay, "The Antislavery Movement in North Carolina," 115–16.

5. Matthew Mason, *Slavery and Politics in the Early American Republic* (Chapel Hill: University of North Carolina Press, 2006), 1–31.

6. "An Act Respecting Fugitives from Justice, and Persons Escaping from the Service of Their Masters," 12 February 1793, in *The Public Statutes at Large of the United States of America*, ed. Richard Peters, vol. 1 (Boston: Charles C. Little and James Brown, 1845), 302–5.

7. Mason, *Slavery and Politics in the Early American Republic*, 31–41.

8. The text of the address to Congress is reprinted in Frost, ed., *The Quaker Origins of Antislavery*, 262, and a facsimile of the original, including all the signatures, is in Roger Bruns, ed., *Am I Not a Man and a Brother: The Antislavery Crusade of Revolutionary America 1688–1788* (New York: Chelsea House, 1977), 494–501.

9. Richard Bauman, *For the Reputation of the Truth: Politics, Religion, and Conflict among the Pennsylvania Quakers 1750–1800* (Baltimore: Johns Hopkins Press, 1971), 191–99.

10. See Kaplan and Kaplan, *The Black Presence in the Era of the American Revolution*, 265–72, for Jones's role in drafting the petition.

11. See document 5, Part III, this volume.

12. The version of this petition that was printed as part of *The Memorial and Address of the People Called Quakers, from their Yearly Meeting Held in Philadelphia, by Adjournments, from the 25th of the 9th Month, to the 29th of the Same Inclusive, 1797* (Philadelphia: Philadelphia Meeting of the Religious Society of Friends, 1797) reads "Zachary Nickson"; see page 7.

13. The version of this petition printed as part of ibid. reads "seven."

14. In 1785, the corsairs of Algiers, one of the Barbary powers on the north coast of Africa, began seizing American merchant vessels sailing to the Mediterranean. The dey of Algiers demanded ransom for the captured American passengers and crews, whom he treated as slaves. By the time the United States and Algiers agreed to a peace treaty in 1795, the Algerian corsairs had captured 122 Americans. By the time the ransom was paid and the prisoners were released in 1796, thirty-seven of the captured Americans had died in captivity.

15. Roland M. Bauman, "Swanwick, John," in *American National Biography*, ed. John A. Garraty and Mark C. Carnes (New York: Oxford University Press, 1999), 21:193–94.

16. Mason, *Slavery and Politics in the Early American Republic*, 28.

17. This source is also available online as part of the Library of Congress's "A Century of Lawmaking for a New Nation" project as "Proceedings of the Senate of the United States, at the Second Session of the Fourth Congress, Begun at the City of Philadelphia, December 5, 1796," in *The Debates and Proceedings of the Congress of the United States* (Washington, D.C.: Gales and Seaton, 1849), available online at http://memory.loc.gov/ammem/amlaw/lwaclink.html.

18. Thomas Blount (1759–1812) of North Carolina.
19. George Thacher (1754–1824) of Massachusetts.
20. Samuel Sitgreaves (1764–1827) of Pennsylvania.
21. John Heath (1758–1810) of Virginia.
22. James Madison (1751–1836) of Virginia. In 1791, when asked by a Virginia Quaker to present an antislavery petition to the House of Representatives, Madison refused, stating that it would be wrong for him to betray the economic interests of his constituents. Madison to Robert Pleasants, 30 October 1791, in *The Papers of James Madison*, ed. Robert A. Rutland, Thomas A. Mason, Robert J. Brugger, Jeanne K. Sisson, and Frederika J. Teuta (Charlottesville: University Press of Virginia, 1983), 14:91–92.
23. Robert Rutherford (1728–1803) of Virginia.
24. Ezekiel Gilbert (1756–1841) of New York.
25. William Smith (1751–1837) of South Carolina.
26. Gabriel Christie (1755–1808) of Maryland.
27. James Holland (1754–1823) of North Carolina.
28. Nathaniel Macon (1757–1837) of North Carolina.
29. Joseph Bradley Varnum (1750–1821) of Massachusetts.
30. Aaron Kitchell (1744–1820) of New Jersey.
31. Bauman, *For the Reputation of Truth*, 185–90.
32. Philadelphia endured an even deadlier yellow fever epidemic in 1798.
33. 2 Kings 20:3. Spoken by Hezekiah, a king of Judah, eighth to seventh century B.C.
34. *Annals of Congress*, 5th Cong., 2d sess., December 1797, 475.
35. Edwin G. Burrows, "Gallatin, Albert," in *American National Biography*, ed. by John A. Garraty and Mark C. Carnes (New York: Oxford University Press, 1999), 8:839–42.
36. Robert Goodloe Harper (1765–1825) of South Carolina.
37. George Thacher (1754–1824) of Massachusetts.
38. "Petition of Freemen," document 1, Part IV, this volume.
39. Thatcher was referring to "An Act Respecting Fugitives from Justice, and Persons Escaping from the Service of Their Masters," 12 February 1793, in *The Public Statutes at Large of the United States of America*, ed. Richard Peters, vol. 1 (Boston: Charles C. Little and James Brown, 1845), 302–5.
40. Matthew Lyon (1746–1822) of Vermont.
41. John Rutledge, Jr. (1766–1819) of South Carolina.
42. John Swanwick (1759?–1798) of Pennsylvania.
43. "An Act for the Gradual Abolition of Slavery," 1 March 1780, Pennsylvania State Archives, Record Group 26, Records of the Department of State, Engrossed Laws.
44. Slavery ended in Massachusetts as the result of a judicial interpretation of the state's constitution of 1780, which stated that all are born free and equal.
45. Early in 1796 the state of Delaware petitioned Congress for a national remedy to the problem of ship masters carrying off free negroes and mulattoes from ports in the United States and selling them into slavery abroad. In January 1797, a House committee proposed that it was "not expedient . . . to interfere with existing laws of the States on this subject." For the journey of the petition through the Committee of

Commerce and Manufactures, see *House Journal*, 4th Cong., 2d sess., 18 April, 5 May, and 29 December 1796, 516, 540, 632, respectively, available at http://memory.loc.gov/ammem/amlaw/lwhjlink.html. For the debate in the House about the committee's report, see *Annals of Congress*, 4th Cong., 2d sess., December 1796, 1729–38, available at http://memory.loc.gov/ammem/amlaw/lwaclink.html#anchor4. For the House vote on the committee's report, see Walter Lowrie and Walter S. Franklin, eds., *American State Papers*, class 10, *Miscellaneous*, vol. 1 (Washington, D.C.: Gales and Seaton, 1834), 155.

46. Samuel Sewall (1757–1814) of Massachusetts.

47. Nathaniel Macon (1757–1837) of North Carolina.

48. "An Act to Prevent the Stealing of Slaves" prescribed death for anyone conveying a free Negro or mulatto out of the state with an intention to sell. Laws of North Carolina for 1778, Chapter XI, in *The State Records of North Carolina*, collected and edited by Walter Clark, vol. 24, *Laws 1777–1788* (1905; repr., Wilmington, N.C.: Broadfoot Publishing, 1994), 220–21.

49. John Allen (1763–1812) of Connecticut.

50. Edward Livingston (1764–1836) of New York.

51. See "Petition of Freemen," document 1, Part IV, this volume.

52. Isaac Parker (1768–1830) of Massachusetts.

53. James Asheton Bayard, Sr. (1767–1815) of Delaware.

54. Art. I, sec. 10, U.S. Constitution.

55. Josiah Parker (1751–1810) of Virginia.

56. On 12 February 1790, a petition from the Pennsylvania Society for Promoting the Abolition of Slavery was introduced into the House and referred to a committee; *House Journal*, 1st Cong., 2d sess., 12 February 1790, 157–58. The House debated the committee's report of 5 March from 16 to 23 March; *Annals of Congress*, 1st cong., 2d sess., 1500–25.

57. Warner Mifflin's petition against the slave trade was introduced to the House on 26 November and the decision to return it was taken on 28 November 1792; *Annals of Congress*, 2d Cong., 2d sess., 730–31. Mifflin (1745–1798) was a leading Quaker abolitionist from Delaware. He had freed his own slaves in 1774–1775.

58. John Nicholas (ca. 1757–1819) of Virginia.

59. Thomas Blount (1759–1812) of North Carolina.

60. "An Act to Prevent Domestic Insurrections," document 1, Part III, this volume.

61. "An Act for Apprehending and Selling Certain Slaves Set Free Contrary to Law and for Confirming the Sale of Others," document 6, Part III, this volume.

62. William Gordon (1763–1802) of New Hampshire.

63. "An Act to Establish the Judicial Courts of the United States," 24 September 1789, in *The Public Statutes at Large of the United States of America*, ed. Richard Peters, vol. 1 (Boston: Charles C. Little and James Brown, 1845), 73–93, available at http://memory.loc.gov/ammem/amlaw/lwsllink.html. Section 25 allows the Supreme Court to review, on a writ of error, decisions of state courts wherein there is a claim of incompatibility of state law with federal law; see 85–86.

64. Matthew 5:34.

65. William Edmond (1755–1838) of Connecticut.
66. See note 48, above.
67. See note 45, above.
68. Because of Quakers' scruples against swearing oaths, many states allowed individuals to substitute statements of affirmation. The U.S. Constitution also provides for either oaths or affirmations.
69. Samuel Smith (1752–1839) of Maryland.
70. Abraham Bedford Venable (1758–1811) of Virginia.
71. Joshua Coit (1758–1798) of Connecticut.
72. Samuel Sitgreaves (1764–1827) of Pennsylvania.
73. Samuel Whittlesey Dana (1763–1830) of Connecticut.
74. James Schureman (1756–1824) of New Jersey.
75. In 1797, the Philadelphia Meeting for Sufferings published the memorial with several supporting documents. Presumably these were the documents the meeting's representatives presented to the House select committee: Philadelphia Meeting for Sufferings to the Standing Committee of the Yearly Meeting for the Western Quarter in North Carolina, 15th day, 3d month, 1792; Philadelphia Meeting for Sufferings to the Standing Committee of the Yearly Meeting in North Carolina, 17th day, 5th month, 1796; Standing Committee for the Eastern Quarter of the Yearly Meeting in North Carolina to the Philadelphia Meeting for Sufferings, 9th day, 1st month, 1797 (reprinted in document 9, Part II, this volume); "List of Sundry Emancipated Blacks" (reprinted at ibid.); order of Perquimans County Court for the sale of emancipated blacks, July 1777 (reprinted in document 3, Part III); order of Pasquotank County Court for the sale of emancipated blacks, September 1777 (reproduced above at note 10 of Part III); the second sentence of the Declaration of Independence ("We Hold these truths to be self-evident—that all men are created equal; that they are endowed by their Creator with certain unalienable rights; that among these are Life, Liberty, and the Pursuit of Happiness"); "An account of the substance of the trial of several Negroes, 22 July 1777" (reprinted in document 2, Part III); the superior court's reversal of the condemnation of the manumitted Negroes, 1 May 1778 (reprinted in document 5, Part III); and "Petition of Freemen to the Senate and House of Representatives of the United States, 25 January 1797" (reprinted in document 1, Part IV).
76. Thomas Claiborne (1749–1812) of Virginia.
77. Joseph McDowell (1756–1801) of North Carolina.
78. George Dent (1756–1813) of Maryland.

Epilogue

1. Perquimans Monthly Meeting Minutes, 5th day of 11th Month 1783, 7th of first Month 1784, 7th of 5th Month 1788, 4th of 2d Month 1789, and Perquimans Monthly Meeting Women's Minutes, 5th of 11th Month 1788, 3rd of 12th Month 1788, both in North Carolina Yearly Meeting Archives, Friends Historical Collection, Guilford College, Greensboro, North Carolina.

2. Charles Fitzgerald McKiever, *Slavery and the Emigration of North Carolina Friends* (Murfreesboro, N.C.: Johnson Publishing, 1970), 27, 37.

3. Ibid., 28; Peter Kent Opper, "North Carolina Quakers: Reluctant Slaveholders," *North Carolina Historical Review* 52 (1975), 38–39.

4. McKiever, *Slavery and the Emigration of North Carolina Friends*, 29; Opper, "Reluctant Slaveholders," 39.

5. McKiever, *Slavery and the Emigration of North Carolina Friends*, 29–43; Opper, "Reluctant Slaveholders," 39–58.

6. Archibald Henderson, *North Carolina: The Old State and the New*, 5 vols. (Chicago: Lewis Publishing Co., 1941), 2:13–14; McKiever, *Slavery and the Emigration of North Carolina Friends*, 45; Stephen B. Weeks, *Southern Quakers and Slavery: A Study in Institutional History* (1896; repr., N.Y.: Bergman, 1968), 284–85.

7. Henderson, *North Carolina: The Old State and the New*, 2:13–14; Harold Lindley, "A Century of Indiana Yearly Meeting," *Bulletin of Friends' Historical Society of Philadelphia* 12, no. 1 (1923): 3–21; McKiever, *Slavery and the Emigration of North Carolina Friends*, 52; Weeks, *Southern Quakers and Slavery*, 261–62, 284.

8. McKiever, *Slavery and the Emigration of North Carolina Friends*, 43–44.

9. David Barrow, *Circular Letter* (Norfolk, Va., 1798), cited in Donald G. Mathews, "Religion and Slavery—The Case of the American South," in *Anti-Slavery, Religion, and Reform: Essays in Memory of Roger Anstey*, ed. Christine Bolt and Seymour Drescher (Folkstone, Kent, England, and Hamden, Conn.: Dawson/Anchor, 1980), 215.

10. Quoted in Weeks, *Southern Quakers and Slavery*, 256–57.

11. Levi Coffin, *The Reminiscences of Levi Coffin, the Reputed President of the Underground Railroad* (1876; 2nd ed., Cincinnati, Ohio: Robert Clark & Co., 1880), 76.

12. Quoted in McKiever, *Slavery and the Emigration of North Carolina Friends*, 66.

13. Weeks, *Southern Quakers and Slavery*, 229.

14. "Testimony of Clear Lake Monthly Meeting of Anti-Slavery Friends Concerning Charles Osborn, Deceased," in Charles Osborn, *Journal of That Faithful Servant of Christ, Charles Osborn* (Cincinnati, 1854), xi.

15. "Testimony of Clear Lake Monthly Meeting," xi–xii; Eric Burin, *Slavery and the Peculiar Institution: A History of the American Colonization Society* (Gainesville, Fla.: University Press of Florida, 2005), 13–19, 35–45; Weeks, *Southern Quakers and Slavery*, 229.

16. "Testimony of Clear Lake Monthly Meeting," xii.

17. Ibid., xii–xiv.

18. Weeks, *Southern Quakers and Slavery*, 229–42.

19. Lindley, "A Century of Indiana Yearly Meeting," 14–15.

20. Mary Katherine Hoskins, "Coffin, Levi," in *Dictionary of North Carolina Biography*, vol. 1, ed. William S. Powell (Chapel Hill: University of North Carolina Press, 1979), 394.

21. Ibid.; Levi Coffin, *Reminiscences of Levi Coffin*, 107, 674.

22. Addison Coffin, *Life and Travels of Addison Coffin* (Cleveland, Ohio: W. G. Hubbard, 1897), 13–22.

23. Weeks, *Southern Quakers and Slavery*, 231–32.
24. Coffin, *Life and Travels of Addison Coffin*, 14, 26, 48–49, 55–56, 95, and passim.
25. Ibid., 133–43.
26. Coffin, *Reminiscences of Levi Coffin*, 619–712, passim.

Bibliography of Works Cited

ARCHIVAL COLLECTIONS

Friends Historical Collection, Guilford College, Greensboro, North Carolina

Correspondence of the London Meeting for Sufferings
Minutes of North Carolina Friends Yearly Meeting
Minutes of the Standing Committee, Eastern Quarter
North Carolina Yearly Meeting Archives
Perquimans Monthly Meeting Minutes
Perquimans Monthly Meeting Women's Minutes

Friends Historical Library of Swarthmore College, Swarthmore, Pennsylvania

Journal of Thomas Nicholson
Minutes of the Pennsylvania Yearly Meeting, Meeting for Sufferings
Records of the Pennsylvania Yearly Meeting, Meeting for Sufferings
Standing Committee of the Eastern Quarter of the Yearly Meeting in North Carolina
Standing Committee for the Western Quarter in North Carolina to the Meeting for Sufferings in Philadelphia

Haverford College, Haverford, Pennsylvania

Simon Garriques, Commonplace Book, 1757–1814, MSS, Quaker Collection

Historical Society of Pennsylvania, Philadelphia, Pennsylvania

Society Miscellaneous Collection

National Society Daughters of the American Revolution, Washington, D.C.

Papers of George Walton

ONLINE DATABASES

North Carolina Marriage Bonds, 1741–1868. Available at Ancestry.com. Original data: State of North Carolina, *An Index to Marriage Bonds Filed in the North Carolina State Archives.* Raleigh: North Carolina Division of Archives and History, 1977.

Dodd, Jordan. *North Carolina Marriages to 1825.* Available at Ancestry.com.

GOVERNMENT DOCUMENTS

Poore, Benjamin P., comp. *The Federal and State Constitutions, Colonial Charters, and Other Organic Laws of the States*, 2 vols. Washington, D.C.: Government Printing Office, 1909.

North Carolina

Clark, Walter, comp. and ed. *The State Records of North Carolina.* 1905; repr., Wilmington, N.C., Broadfoot Publishing, 1994.

Perquimans County Court. "Minutes of Perquimans County Court, July Term 1777." In *Perquimans County Historical Society Year Book 1975*, ed. Raymond A. Winslow, Jr. Ahoakie, N.C.: Perquimans County Historical Society, 1976.

Perquimans County Tax List, 1772, North Carolina State Archives, Record Series G.A. 11.1, available at http://perqtax.homestead.com/.

Perquimans County Tax List, 1775, available at http://perqtax.homestead.com/.

Perquimans County Property Tax List, 1779, Lists of Taxables, North Carolina State Archives, Record Series CR.077.701.1, available at http://perqtax.homestead.com/.

Pennsylvania

"An Act for the Gradual Abolition of Slavery, 1 March 1780," Record Group 26, Records of the Department of State, Engrossed Laws, Pennsylvania State Archives, available at http://www.portal.state.pa.us/portal/server.pt/community/1776-1865_revolution_to_civil_war/8644/abolition_of_slavery/527024.

United States

Annals of Congress, 1st Congress, 2d session, 4 January 1790–16 February 1790.
———. 2nd Congress, 2d session, 5 November 1792–2 March 1793.
———. 4th Congress, 2d session, 5 December 1796–3 March 1797.
———. 5th Congress, 2d session, 13 November 1797–5 March 1798.

Bureau of Democracy, Human Rights and Labor, Department of State. "Mauritania: Country Reports on Human Rights Practices, 2002." March 31, 2003. Available at www.state.gov/g/drl/rls/hrrpt/2002/18215.htm.

Ford, Worthington Chauncey, Gaillard Hunt, John Clement Fitzpatrick, Roscoe R. Hill, Kenneth E. Harris, and Steven D. Tilley, eds. *Journals of the Continental Congress, 1774–1779.* Vol. 1. Washington, D.C.: Government Printing Office, 1904.

House Journal, 1st Cong., 2d sess., 4 March 1789–29 September 1791.
———. 4th Cong., 2d sess., 5 December 1796–3 March 1797.

Lowry, Walter, and Walter S. Franklin. *American State Papers*. Class 10, *Miscellaneous*, Vol. 1. Washington, D.C.: Gales and Seaton, 1834.
Peters, Richard, ed. *The Public Statutes at Large of the United States of America*. Vol. 1. Boston: Charles C. Little and James Brown, 1845.
U.S. Bureau of the Census. *Historical Statistics of the United States: Colonial Times to 1970*. Washington, D.C.: U.S. Dept. of Commerce, Bureau of the Census, 1975.

ARTICLES, DICTIONARY AND ENCYCLOPEDIA ENTRIES, AND NEWSPAPERS

"An Account of the Gospel Labours and Christian Experiences, of that Faithful Minister of Christ, John Churchman, Late of Nottingham, in Pennsylvania." In *The Friends' Library: Comprising Journals, Doctrinal Treatises, and Other Writings of Members of the Religious Society of Friends*, vol. 6, ed. William Evans and Thomas Evans. Philadelphia: 1842.
Bauman, Roland M. "Swanwick, John." *American National Biography*, vol. 21, ed. by John A. Garraty and Mark C. Carnes. New York: Oxford University Press, 1999.
Burrows, Edwin G. "Gallatin, Albert." In *American National Biography*, vol. 8, ed. John A. Garraty and Mark C. Carnes. New York: Oxford University Press, 1999.
Butler, Lindley S. "Johnston, Samuel." In *American National Biography*, vol. 12, ed. John A. Garraty and Mark C. Carnes. New York: Oxford University Press, 1999.
Crow, Jeffrey J. "Slave Rebelliousness and Social Conflict in North Carolina, 1775 to 1802." *William and Mary Quarterly*, 3d ser., 37 (1980): 79–102.
Dungy, Katherine. "A Friend in Deed: Quakers and Manumission in Perquimans County, North Carolina, 1775–1800." *The Southern Friend* 24 (2002): 3–36.
Frost, J. William. "The Origins of the Quaker Crusade against Slavery: A Review of Recent Literature." *Quaker History* 67 (1978): 42–58.
The Herald and Norfolk and Portsmouth Advertiser. Norfolk, Va. 1795.
Hoskins, Mary Katherine. "Coffin, Levi." In *Dictionary of North Carolina Biography*, vol. 1, ed. William S. Powell. Chapel Hill: University of North Carolina Press, 1979.
"Joseph Oxley's Journal of His Life, Travels, and Labours of Love, in the Faith and Fellowship of Our Lord Jesus Christ." In *The Friends' Library: Comprising Journals, Doctrinal Treatises, and Other Writings of Members of the Religious Society of Friends*, vol. 2, ed. William Evans and Thomas Evans. Philadelphia: 1838.
"A Journal of the Life, Travels & Gospel Labours of a Faithful Minister of Jesus Christ, Daniel Stanton, Late of Philadelphia, in the Province of Pennsylvania." In *The Friends' Library: Comprising Journals, Doctrinal Treatises, and Other Writings of Members of the Religious Society of Friends*, vol. 12, ed. William Evans and Thomas Evans. Philadelphia: 1848.
Ketcham, Ralph L. "Conscience, War, and Politics in Pennsylvania, 1755–1757." *William and Mary Quarterly*, 3d ser., 20 (1963): 416–39.
Kross, Jessica. "Pemberton, John." In *American National Biography*, vol. 17, ed. John A. Garraty and Mark C. Carnes. New York: Oxford University Press, 1999.
"The Life and Travels of John Pemberton, a Minister of the Gospel of Christ." In *The*

Friends' Library: Comprising Journals, Doctrinal Treatises, and Other Writings of Members of the Religious Society of Friends, vol. 6, ed. William Evans and Thomas Evans. Philadelphia: 1842.

Lindley, Harold. "A Century of Indiana Yearly Meeting." *Bulletin of Friends' Historical Society of Philadelphia* 12, no. 1 (1923): 3–21.

Mathews, Donald G. "Religion and Slavery—The Case of the American South." In *Anti-Slavery, Religion, and Reform: Essays in Memory of Roger Anstey*, ed. Christine Bolt and Seymour Drescher, 207–32. Folkstone, Kent, England, and Hamden, Conn.: Dawson/Anchor, 1980.

Nash, Gary B. "Slaves and Slave Owners in Colonial Philadelphia." *William and Mary Quarterly*, 3d ser., 30 (1973): 223–56.

Opper, Peter Kent. "North Carolina Quakers: Reluctant Slaveholders." *North Carolina Historical Review* 52 (1975): 37–58.

Pybus, Cassandra. "Jefferson's Faulty Math: The Question of Slave Defections in the American Revolution." *William and Mary Quarterly*, 3d ser., 62 (2005): 243–64.

"Samuel Emlen." In *Quaker Biographies: A Series of Sketches, Chiefly Biographical, Concerning Members of the Society of Friends, from the Seventeenth Century to More Recent Times*, vol. 3 (Philadelphia, 1912).

"A Short Account of the Life and Some of the Religious Labours of Patience Brayton." In *The Friends' Library: Comprising Journals, Doctrinal Treatises, and Other Writings of Members of the Religious Society of Friends*, vol. 10, ed. William Evans and Thomas Evans. Philadelphia: 1846.

"Thomas Nicholson to B. H." *The Friend* 18 (October 1844): 13–14.

Troxler, George. "Earl, Daniel." In *Dictionary of North Carolina Biography*, vol. 2, ed. William S. Powell. Chapel Hill: University of North Carolina Press, 1986.

Wexler, Natalie. "Iredell, James." In *American National Biography*, vol. 11, ed. John A. Garraty and Mark C. Carnes. New York: Oxford University Press, 1999.

BOOKS AND DISSERTATIONS

Barbour, Hugh and J. William Frost. *The Quakers*. New York: Greenwood Press, 1988.

Bassett, John S. *Slavery and Servitude in the Colony of North Carolina*. Ed. Herbert B. Adams. Baltimore, Md.: Johns Hopkins University Press, 1896.

Bauman, Richard. *For the Reputation of Truth: Politics, Religion, and Conflict among the Pennsylvania Quakers, 1750–1800*. Baltimore: The Johns Hopkins Press, 1971.

Blackburn, Robin. *The Overthrow of Colonial Slavery 1776–1848*. London: Verso, 1988.

Brown, Christopher L. *Moral Capital: Foundations of British Abolitionism*. Chapel Hill: North Carolina University Press, 2006.

Bruns, Roger, ed. *Am I Not a Man and a Brother: The Antislavery Crusade of Revolutionary America 1688–1788*. New York: Chelsea House, 1977.

Burin, Eric. *Slavery and the Peculiar Institution: A History of the American Colonization Society*. Gainesville: University Press of Florida, 2005.

Calhoon, Robert M. *Religion and the American Revolution in North Carolina*. Raleigh:

North Carolina Department of Cultural Resources, Division of Archives and History, 1976.
Clark, Christopher. *Social Change in America: From the Revolution through the Civil War*. Chicago: Ivan R. Dee, 2006.
Coffin, Addison. *Life and Travels of Addison Coffin*. Cleveland, Ohio: W. G. Hubbard, 1897.
Coffin, Levi. *The Reminiscences of Levi Coffin, the Reputed President of the Underground Railroad*. 1876; 2d ed., Cincinnati, Ohio: Robert Clark & Co., 1880.
Craton, Michael. *Testing the Chains: Resistance to Slavery in the British West Indies*. Ithaca, N.Y.: Cornell University Press, 1982.
Crow, Jeffrey J. *The Black Experience in Revolutionary North Carolina*. Raleigh: Division of Archives and History, North Carolina Department of Cultural Resources, 1977.
Davis, David Brion. *The Problem of Slavery in the Age of Revolution, 1770–1823*. Ithaca, N.Y.: Cornell University Press, 1975.
Drake, Thomas E. *Quakers and Slavery in America*. 1950; repr., Gloucester, Mass.: Peter Smith, 1965.
Egerton, Douglas R. *Death or Liberty: African Americans and Revolutionary America*. New York: Oxford University Press, 2009.
———. *Gabriel's Rebellion: The Virginia Slave Conspiracies of 1800 and 1802*. Chapel Hill: University of North Carolina Press, 1993.
Ferris, David. *Resistance and Obedience to God: Memoirs of the Life of David Ferris (1707–1779)*. Ed. Martha Paxson Grundy. Philadelphia: Friends General Conference, 2001.
Frey, Sylvia R. *Water from the Rock: Black Resistance in a Revolutionary Age*. Princeton, N.J.: Princeton University Press, 1991.
Frost, J. William, ed. *The Quaker Origins of Antislavery*. Norwood, Pa.: Norwood Editions, 1980.
Gerona, Carla. *Night Journeys: The Power of Dreams in Transatlantic Quaker Culture*. Charlottesville: University of Virginia Press, 2004.
Hadden, Sally E. *Slave Patrols: Law and Violence in Virginia and the Carolinas*. Cambridge, Mass.: Harvard University Press, 2001.
Henderson, Archibald. *North Carolina: The Old State and the New*. 5 vols. Chicago: Lewis Publishing Co., 1941.
Hilty, Hiram H. *By Land and by Sea: Quakers Confront Slavery and Its Aftermath in North Carolina*. Greensboro, N.C.: North Carolina Yearly Meeting of Friends, 1993.
———. *Toward Freedom for All: North Carolina Quakers and Slavery*. Richmond, Ind.: Friends United Press, 1984.
Hinshaw, William Wade. *Encyclopedia of American Quaker Genealogy*. Vol. 1. 1936; repr., Baltimore, Md.: Genealogical Publishing Co., 1978.
Hochschild, Adam. *Bury the Chains: Prophets and Rebels in the Fight to Free an Empire's Slaves*. Boston: Houghton Mifflin, 2005.
Ingle, H. Larry. *First among Friends: George Fox and the Creation of Quakerism*. New York: Oxford University Press, 1994.

Iredell, James. *The Papers of James Iredell*. Vol. 2. Ed. Don Higginbotham. Raleigh: Division of Archives and History, Department of Cultural Resources, 1976.
Jackson, Maurice. *Let This Voice Be Heard: Anthony Benezet, Father of Atlantic Abolitionism*. Philadelphia: University of Pennsylvania Press, 2009.
James, Sydney V. *A People among Peoples: Quaker Benevolence in Eighteenth-Century America*. Cambridge, Mass: Harvard University Press, 1963.
Kaplan, Sidney, and Emma Nogrady Kaplan. *The Black Presence in the Era of the American Revolution*. Amherst: University of Massachusetts Press, 1989.
Kay, Marvin L. Michael, and Lorin Lee Cary. *Slavery in North Carolina, 1748–1775*. Chapel Hill: University of North Carolina Press, 1995.
Larson, Rebecca. *Daughters of Light: Quaker Women Preaching and Prophesying in the Colonies and Abroad, 1700–1775*. Chapel Hill: University of North Carolina Press, 1999.
Main, Jackson Turner. *The Sovereign States, 1775–1783*. New York: New Viewpoints, 1973.
Marietta, Jack D. *The Reformation of American Quakerism, 1748–1783*. Philadelphia: University of Pennsylvania Press, 1985.
Mason, Matthew. *Slavery and Politics in the Early American Republic*. Chapel Hill: University of North Carolina Press, 2006.
McKiever, Charles Fitzgerald McKiever. *Slavery and the Emigration of North Carolina Friends*. Murfreesboro, N.C.: Johnson Publishing, 1970.
Meetings for Sufferings of the North Carolina Yearly Meeting. *A Narrative of Some of the Proceedings of North Carolina Yearly Meeting on the Subject of Slavery within Its Limits*. Greensborough, N.C., 1848.
Nash, Gary B., and Jean R. Soderlund. *Freedom by Degrees: Emancipation in Pennsylvania and Its Aftermath*. New York: Oxford University Press, 1991.
Nicholson, Thomas. *An Epistle to Friends in Great Britain*. Newbern, N.C., 1762.
———. *An Epistle to Friends in Great Britain; Also a Testimony Concerning Thomas Nicholson of N.C.* Carthage, Ind.: David Marshall, 1888.
O'Shaughnessy, Andrew J. *An Empire Divided: The America Revolution and the British Caribbean*. Philadelphia: University of Pennsylvania Press, 2000.
Osborn, Charles, *Journal of That Faithful Servant of Christ, Charles Osborn*. Cincinnati: A. Pugh, 1854.
Perquimans County Historical Society Year Book. Hertford, N.C.: Perquimans County Historical Society, 1970.
Pybus, Cassandra. *Epic Journeys of Freedom: Runaway Slaves of the American Revolution and Their Global Search for Liberty*. Boston: Beacon Press, 2006.
Quarles, Benjamin. *The Negro in the American Revolution*. Chapel Hill: University of North Carolina Press, 1961.
Rankin, Hugh F. *The North Carolina Continentals*. Chapel Hill: University of North Carolina Press, 1971.
Rappleye, Charles. *Sons of Providence: The Brown Brothers, the Slave Trade, and the American Revolution*. New York: Simon & Schuster, 2006.

Rutland, Robert A. et al., eds. *The Papers of James Madison*. Vol. 14. Charlottesville: University Press of Virginia, 1983.
Schama, Simon. *Rough Crossings: Britain, the Slaves and the American Revolution*. New York: Harper Collins, 2006.
Sensbach, Jon F. *A Separate Canaan: The Making of an Afro-Moravian World in North Carolina, 1763–1840*. Chapel Hill: University of North Carolina Press, 1998.
Shay, John M. "The Antislavery Movement in North Carolina." Ph.D. diss., Princeton University, 1971.
Silver, Peter. *Our Savage Neighbors: How Indian War Transformed Early America*. New York: W. W. Norton, 2008.
Slaughter, Thomas P. *The Beautiful Soul of John Woolman, Apostle of Abolition*. New York: Hill and Wang, 2008.
Sobel, Mechal. *Teach Me Dreams: The Search for Self in the Revolutionary Era*. Princeton, N.J.: Princeton University Press, 2000.
Society of Friends, Philadelphia Yearly Meeting. *Memorial and Address of the People Called Quakers, from Their Yearly Meeting Held in Philadelphia, by Adjournments, from the 25th of the 9th Month, to the 29th of the Same Inclusive, 1797*. Philadelphia, Pa., 1797.
Soderlund, Jean R. *Quakers & Slavery: A Divided Spirit*. Princeton, N.J.: Princeton University Press, 1985.
Tolles, Frederick B. *Meetinghouse and Counting House: The Quaker Merchants of Colonial Philadelphia 1682–1763*. 1948; repr., New York: W. W. Norton, 1963.
Watson, Alan D. *Perquimans County: A Brief History*. Raleigh: Division of Archives and History, North Carolina Department of Cultural Resources, 1987.
Weeks, Stephen B. *Southern Quakers and Slavery: A Study in Institutional History*. 1896; repr., N.Y.: Bergman, 1968.
Winslow, Watson, Mrs. (Ellen Good Rawlings). *History of Perquimans County*. Raleigh, N.C., 1931; repr., Baltimore: Regional Publishing Co., 1974.
Wolf, Eva Sheppard. *Race and Liberty in the New Nation: Emancipation in Virginia from the Revolution to Nat Turner's Rebellion*. Baton Rouge: Louisiana State University Press, 2006.
Woolman, John. *The Journal and Major Essays of John Woolman*. New York: Oxford University Press, 1971.
Zilversmit, Arthur. *The First Emancipation: The Abolition of Slavery in the North*. Chicago: University of Chicago Press, 1967.

Index

Aaron (biblical Jewish leader), 41
Aaron (Joseph Thornton's manumitted slave), 104, 119
Abolition, 31–34, 187–88, 190, 191. *See also* Emancipation
Abolition Societies, 170
Abraham (manumitted slave): ordered hired out, 64
Abraham/Abram (Josiah White's manumitted slave), 119, 123
Abram (Benjamin and Chalkly Albertson's manumitted slave), 102
Africa and Africans, 5, 12–13, 15, 19, 40, 70, 78, 120, 143, 159, 160, 192
African Methodist Episcopal Church, 143
Albemarle region, N.C., 9, 49, 70, 185, 202n76
Albert, Job: biography, 2, 144–45; petitions Congress, 2–3, 143–48
Albertson, Benjamin, 2, 98, 102, 130, 144–45
Albertson, Benjamin, Jr., 99
Albertson, Chalkly, 83, 102, 130
Albertson, William, 58, 78, 97, 99, 102, 118, 124, 130
Alexander II, Tsar, 13
Algiers, 147, 207n14
Allen, John, 168
American Colonization Society, 187
American Revolution, 129, 133, 192; and antislavery, 16–17, 18, 139; in North Carolina, 107–9; and Society of Friends, 54; stimulates black resistance to slavery, 19
Anderson, Elihu, 102
Anderson, John, 78, 102
Angola, 13
Ann (Mary Nixon's manumitted slave), 104, 123, 124
Anna (Samuel Moore's manumitted slave), 103
Antichrist, 51, 52
Antigua, 19
Antislavery: black activism in, 18–21; in British Empire, 22; in England, 21; and evangelicals, 186; in Indiana, 188; in the Middle Ages, 14; as motivation for Quaker emigration from North Carolina, 185–86, 190; motivations for, 2, 10–12, 15–16, 17–18, 24, 35, 91, 120–21, 139–40; as movement, 2; in North Carolina, 17, 70, 140; and North Carolina Friends, 11–12, 24, 35–36, 191; origins of, among Pennsylvania Quakers, 11; prerequisites for activism in, 15–16; Quaker leadership in, 22; and Quakers, 2, 3, 206n1; strategies, 16; in United States, 174; in Western thought, 14–15
Apostles, 44
Army, British, 20–21, 108, 194n20

Army, Continental, 20, 108
Ashe, Samuel, 123
Askill, William, 119

Baker, Widow, 65–66
Baker, Capt. William, 65–66
Baker, Mrs. William, 65–66
Ballard, Jethro, 64, 114, 116
Banneker, Benjamin, 139
Baptists, 63, 91, 139, 186
Barbados, 5, 19
Barbary powers, 207n14
Barrow, David, 186
Bayard, James Asheton, Sr.: debates Friends' memorial, 170–71, 176–77; referenced in debate, 173, 174, 177
Beaufort County, N.C., 109
Beeson, Isaac, 83
Bell, Lancelot, 79
Ben (Zachariah Newby's manumitted slave), 103
Benevolence, 5, 15
Benezet, Anthony, 16, 18
Benjamin (Caleb Trueblood's manumitted slave), 105
Bible, references to: 1 Corinthians 15:58, 43; 2 Corinthians 4:18, 43; Exodus 3:7, 40; Galatians 3:28, 41; Habakkuk 1:13, 41; Hebrews 10:29, 46; James 5:4, 42; 1 John 2, 15, 41; 2 Kings 20:3, 160–61; Mark 8:36, 41–42; Proverbs 16:5, 41
—Daniel: 3, 43; 6, 42–43
—Isaiah: 11:15–17, 85; 2:4, 51–52; 2:8, 45; 26:21, 121, 130; 30:1, 41; 4:4, 43; 61:1, 41
—Jeremiah: 2:13, 46; 34:15–17, 42
—John: 14:4, 55; 15:20, 43; 16:22, 42; 8:21, 42
—Luke: 11:52, 85–86, 203n12; 3:7, 47
—Matthew: 10:37, 41; 16:26, 42, 85; 25:30, 45; 3:7, 47; 5:14, 41; 5:32, 60; 6:20, 42; 6:33, 41; 7:12, 41–42, 51, 60, 85. See also Golden Rule
—Micah: 4:3, 51–52; 6:8, 85
—Psalms 116, 5:3, 84
—Revelations: 18:2, 85; 5:13, 85; 5:24, 85; 5:4, 85
—Romans: 1:28, 46; 2:11, 42; 3:8, 60; 8:39, 52
Bindham, Turner, 118
Black, the color, 1, 35, 41
Black codes: in Indiana, 188; in Virginia, 21

Blacks: aid to, during and after Civil War, 191; army enlistment of, 127; and aspirations of freedom, 108; as occasions of sin, 35; compared to Israelites, 41; disenfranchised in North Carolina, 190; education of, 188–89, 191; in George Walton's dreams, 1, 47; hiring of, 94; and George Walton, 40; in Indiana, 188, 189; in North Carolina, 100; justify resistance to slavery, 42; kidnapping of, 166, 167, 175, 178, 208n45; legal assistance for, 59, 93; legal restrictions on, in North Carolina, 138; North Carolina Friends assist, 60, 188–89; North Carolina Friends petition General Assembly on behalf of, 67, 133–34; North Carolina Friends organize meeting for, 59; from North Carolina jailed in Virginia, 67; and North Carolina slave rebellions, 109; northern states discourage immigration of, 184; numbers of, owned by North Carolina yearly meeting, 184; oppression of, 182; petition Congress, 2–3; re-enslavement of, 2–3, 59, 60–61, 64, 80, 86, 90, 93, 94, 100–105, 111, 122–25, 123–24, 126–27, 128–30, 131, 134, 135, 138, 143, 145, 146, 159, 163, 168, 170, 188, 190, 199n41, 205n10; re-enslavement trial of, 63–64, 113–16; and resistance to slavery, 2, 18–21; rights of, 42, 73–75, 78, 128, 129, 139, 143, 147; treatment of, in North Carolina, 190. *See also* Slaves
Blair, William, 125
Blandon, N.C., 202n76
Blount, John G., 118
Blount, Thomas: debates freemen's petition, 150, 151, 156; debates Friends' memorial, 172–73, 175; referenced in debate, 150, 153, 175, 176
Bofor (Charles Overman's manumitted slave), 104
Boston, Mass., 47, 54, 107–8, 108, 139, 145
Boston Tea Party, 107
Boyd, Thomas, 205n10
Brazil, 13
Brown, Christopher Leslie, 16–17
Brown, John, 22
Brown, Moses, 21
Bufkin, Samuel, 61
Bundy, Moses, 50, 56, 58, 83

Burlington, N.J., 56, 201n68
Burton, Colonel, 118
Bush River, S.C., monthly meeting, 206n15

Caesar (Albertson's manumitted slave), 119
Cairo, Ill., 191
Canada, 189
Cancer (Margaret White's manumitted slave), 105
Candace (George and Sarah Metcalfe's manumitted slave), 103
Candace (Samuel Charles's manumitted slave), 10
Candace (Thomas White's manumitted slave), 105
Cannon, Jeremiah, 103
Cape Fear River, 108
Carter, John, 83
A Caution and a Warning to Great Britain and Her Colonies (Anthony Benezet), 16
Ceasar (Elihu Anderson's manumitted slave), 102
Central America, 13
Chancy, Edmund, 205n10
Charity (Thomas Nicholson's manumitted slave), 104
Charles (Caleb Trueblood's manumitted slave), 105, 124
Charles, Samuel, 103
Charlton, Jasper, 114
Chesterfield, N.J., monthly meeting, 10–11, 12
China, 12
Chowan County, N.C., 200n65; Court of Pleas and Quarter Sessions, 102
Chowan River, 202n76
Christ, 1, 32, 34, 35, 42, 43, 44, 45, 46, 51, 52, 56, 61, 85, 121, 129
Christie, Gabriel, 154
Chuckatuck, Va., 62; monthly meeting, 202n81
Churchman, John, 201n67
Church of England, 64; disestablished in North Carolina, 114, 202n83, 205n8; Evangelicals in, 17–18
Cincinnati, Ohio, 189, 191
Civil War, 184, 185, 190
Claiborne, Thomas, 179
Clarkson, Thomas, 17

Coercive Acts, 107–8, 158
Coffin, Addison: biography, 189–91; on Quaker motivations for emigrating from North Carolina, 186
Coffin, Alethea, 190
Coffin, Dr. Alfred, 190
Coffin, Catherine White, 189
Coffin, Levi: aids blacks during and after Civil War, 191; biography, 188–89; mentioned, 190; on Quaker motivations for emigrating from North Carolina, 186
Coffin, Vestal, 188–89, 189
Coffin, William, Jr., 93
Cohansey, N.J., 201n67
Coit, Joshua, 178
Concord, Mass., Battle of, 108
Confederation Congress, 142
Congregationalists, 139
Connecticut, 13
Continental Association, 158, 160
Continental Congress: adopts Continental Association, 158, 160; declaration on rights of mankind, 129; North Carolina delegates to, 108, 122
Continental Congress, Second, 108
Copeland, Elisha, 56, 62
Copeland, Sarah, 65
Copeland, Zachariah, 65
Corinth, Miss., 191
Cornwallis, William, 20
Cosand, Gabriel, 83, 134
Craven County, N.C., 109
Creecy, Nathan, 119
Creecy/Creesy, Thomas, 119, 145
Cuba, 13
Cudger/Cudgo (Thomas Newby's [of Perquimans] manumitted slave), 88, 103, 118, 123
Cuffee (Jeremiah Cannon's manumitted slave), 103
Cuffee/Cuff (Thomas White's manumitted slave), 105, 118, 123

Dana, Samuel Whittlesey, 178
Daniel, biblical prophet, 43
Darius, King, 43
David (Charles Morgan's manumitted slave), 103
David (manumitted slave), 124

David (Robert Newby's manumitted slave), 103
David (William Albertson's manumitted slave), 102, 118, 123
Davis, David Brion, 14–15, 18
Declaration of Independence, 64, 122, 133, 139, 210n75
Delaware, 5, 21, 208n45
Denson, John, 62
Dent, George, 179, 181
Devil (Satan), 1–2, 19, 32, 33, 34, 35
Dick (Isaac Lamb's manumitted slave), 103
Dick (John Smith's manumitted slave), 104
Dick (Josiah White's manumitted slave), 119, 123
Dick (Lydia White's manumitted slave), 105, 118, 123
Dick (Rachel Williams' manumitted slave), 105
Dick/Dicks, Zachariah, 83, 93
Dick/Richard (Samuel Smith's manumitted slave), 104, 119
Dickson, Zachary, 144
Dill (Nicholas Nicholson's manumitted slave), 104
Dillon, Peter, 83
Dilwyn, George, 56; biography, 201n68
Dinah (George Walton's manumitted slave), 101, 105
Dinah (Jacob Wilson's manumitted slave), 105, 124
Dol (Caleb Winslow's manumitted slave), 105
Dorcas (John Smith's manumitted slave), 104
Draper, Joseph, 98
Draper, Silas, 98
Dreams: George Walton's, 1, 29–34, 36, 40, 47, 54, 67–68, 183, 191–92; interpretation of, 1–2, 29, 32–33, 34–35; in Quaker culture, 29, 34–35; Thomas Nicholson's, 35
Dublin (Jeremiah Cannon's manumitted slave), 103
Dunmore, Lord (John Murray, 4th Earl of Dunmore), 20, 109

Earl, Rev. Daniel, 61, 202n76
Earls, Sarah (Sarah Earls Walton), 27, 31
Eason, Jesse, 64, 114, 116
Easter (Jesse Symons's manumitted slave), 104
East India Company, 107
Edenton, N.C., 59, 60, 113, 202n76
Edenton District, N.C., 122, 123, 125, 129, 137

Edmond, William, 174–75
Edwards, Benjamin, 118
Egypt and Egyptians, 41
Elliot, James, 103
Elliot, Mrs. James, 103
Elliott, Isaac, 103
Elliott, John, 137
Emancipation: and Congress, 155, 169, 170; dangers from, 172; in Massachusetts, 165, 208n44; in the North, 139–40; in North Carolina, 183, 203n7; in Pennsylvania, 165; in the South, 140. *See also* Abolition; Manumission
Emancipation, gradual, 13; in Cuba, 13; opposed to immediate abolitionism, 188; in Pennsylvania, 17, 140, 165; in Rhode Island, 21; Thomas Nicholson endorses, 70, 73–75, 84; in United States, 21
Emancipation Manifesto, Russian, 13
Emancipation Proclamation, 188, 191
Emlen, Samuel, 57, 201n66, 201n68
England: American public Friends in, 201n66, 201n68; antislavery in, 17–18, 21; John Woolman in, 21; and War of Independence, 54–55
Enlightenment, the, 15, 16, 91, 139, 206n1
Ephraim (Elizabeth Symons's manumitted slave), 104
Epistle of Caution and Advice Concerning the Buying and Keeping of Slaves (Friends Yearly Meeting in Philadelphia), 7
Epistle to Friends in Great Britain, An (Thomas Nicholson), 203n7
Esther (Aaron Morris Jr.'s manumitted slave), 103
Europe, 174, 176
Evangelicalism, 15
Evans, Jonathan, 161
Ex post facto laws, 113–15, 170–71, 172, 173, 174, 176, 177

Fanny (Josiah White's manumitted slave), 105, 119, 123
Fanny (William Robinson's manumitted slave), 104, 119
Fayetteville, N.C., 133
Federalist Party, 162
Ferris, David, 44, 199n41
Fletcher, Ralph, 78

Fort Johnston, N.C., 108
Fountain City, Ind., 189
Fox, George, 3, 4
France, 191, 201n68
Francis (Thomas Nicholson's manumitted slave), 104
Francis (Zachariah Nixon's manumitted slave), 104
Frank (John Smith's manumitted slave), 104
Freedmen's Bureau, 191
French and Indian War, 6, 7, 194n20
Friendly Association for Regaining and Preserving Peace with the Indians, 202n75
Friends' Meeting for Sufferings in London, 18, 78, 80, 81, 196n51
Friends' Meeting for Sufferings in Philadelphia, Pa., 100–101, 182, 210n75
Friends' meetings: at Bush River, S.C., 206n15; at Chuckatuck, Va., 62, 202n81; at Little River, N.C., 38, 56; at Newbegun Creek, N.C., 38, 58; at Pasquotank, N.C., 92; at Perquimans, N.C. (See Perquimans, N.C., monthly meeting); at Piney Woods, N.C., 38, 70; at Sarem, N.C., 65; at Shrewsbury, N.J., 201n67; at Summerton, Va., 62; at Symons Creek, N.C., 69–70; at Trueblood's, N.C., 38, 58; at Vix, Va., 63; at Western Branch, Va., 55, 62
Friends' preparative meeting at Piney Woods, N.C., 58
Friends' preparative meetings, North Carolina, 97–98, 99
Friends' Quarterly Meeting at Western Branch, Va., 55
Friends' Quarterly Meeting, Eastern Quarter, North Carolina: aids manumitted blacks, 67; appoints committees, 67, 96, 97; disturbed by soldiers, 57; extracts from minutes, 98; George Walton attends, 67; at Little River, 58; at Old Neck, 56–57, 60; at Pasquotank, 55; and Philadelphia Friends meeting, 137; on re-enslavements, 101–5; and slave trading among Quakers, 92; Standing Committee, 101; at Symons Creek, 64; transfers slaves to yearly meeting, 184; urges manumissions, 96, 97, 98–99; at Wells, 56
Friends' quarterly meeting, Indiana, 191
Friends' quarterly meeting, Ohio, 191

Friends' quarterly meeting, Western Quarter, North Carolina, 70, 73, 76, 77, 83, 100
Friends' yearly meeting in London, 18, 36, 69, 193n51
Friends' yearly meeting in Maryland, 9
Friends' yearly meeting in New England, 8–9
Friends' yearly meeting in New York, 9
Friends' yearly meeting in North Carolina: accepts slaves in trust, 184; adopts antislavery discipline, 9; appoints committee to aid blacks, 60; appoints committee to aid manumissions, 57, 58, 93; approves antislavery tract, 11; approves eulogy on Thomas Nicholson, 11; approves Thomas Nicholson's essay, 84, 203n7; authorizes disownment of slaveholders, 95–96; authorizes manumissions, 37, 82, 89; committee reports on slave trading by members, 92; committee reports progress of manumission, 93; condemns slave trading, 78, 92–93; considers morality of slavery, 35–36, 37, 70; consults London yearly meeting, 36, 78, 80; discourages binding freed slaves during life, 94; elects George Walton clerk, 128; employs lawyers on behalf of blacks, 59, 61, 63–64, 93, 113; encourages manumission, 54, 57–58, 91, 92; explains motives for freeing slaves, 67, 128–30; extracts of minutes, 92–97; George Walton as member and clerk, 67, 128; instructs meetings to protect freed slaves, 57; and law on re-enslavements, 60; and legal restrictions on manumission, 71; and manumission, 91; on motives for manumission, 120–21, 128–30; number of slaves owned by, 184; organization of, 69; petitions General Assembly on slavery, 70, 73, 102, 128–30, 133–34, 183, 197n4; policy on slaveholding, 36, 82–83; policy on slave trade, 36, 57, 70, 76–79; queries on slavery, 77, 79, 83; renounces hiring slaves, 94; rotation of venue of, 57; on sales of manumitted slaves, 117, 205n7; on treatment of slaves, 94; sends slaves to freedom in Haiti and Liberia, 184; sends slaves to free states, 184; Standing Committee, 203n7; Standing Committee on the Slave Trade, 203n5. *See also* Society of Friends: in North Carolina

Friends' yearly meeting in Philadelphia: and antislavery movement, 5–6; approves John Woolman's antislavery tract, 7, 8; Committee on Publications, 6; committee reports to House of Representatives on Friends' memorial, 178; condemns slaveholding, 7–8; disciplines slave traders and importers, 7–8; disowns slave owners, 8; leadership of, 6, 201–2n75; memorial of, debated in Congress, 162–81; memorial of, in House Committee of the Whole, 179–81; and North Carolina report on re-enslavements, 205n7; and North Carolina yearly meeting, 69; petitions Congress, 3, 142, 158–61, 170, 178; petitions Continental Congress, 142; policy of, on slave holding, 7; policy of, on slave trading, 7; publishes antislavery tract, 7

Friends' yearly meeting in Virginia, 9, 50–51, 70, 198n15

Fugitive Slave Law (1793), 143; and congressional authority over slavery, 154; enactment of, 142; extent of, 154; House of Representatives committee on, 150; operation of, 24, 155–56, 156–57, 163, 168, 172; petitions regarding, 2, 146, 150

Gabriel's Rebellion, 21
Gallatin, Albert: biography, 162; debates Friends' memorial, 162, 165–66; moves to refer Friends' memorial to a select committee, 178; presents Friends' memorial to House of Representatives, 162; referenced in debate, 166, 167, 169, 177
Garrison, William Lloyd, 187
Gates County, N.C., 202n85
The Genius of Universal Emancipation, 187
Georgia, 20, 171
Germans, 6
Gerona, Carla, 34, 35
Gilbert, Ezekiel, 153
Glasgow (Thomas Newby's [of Perquimans] manumitted slave), 88, 103, 118, 123
Glorious Revolution, 4
Golden Rule, 5, 73, 85, 121, 129. *See also* Bible, references to: Matthew, 7:12
Gordon, William, 173–74, 177
Granberry, Josiah, 118

Great Awakening, 7
Great Bridge, Battle of, 202n84
Great Britain: and aid to freedmen, 191; civil liberties of Quakers in, 7; conflict of, with American colonies, 129; Parliament, 13, 16, 18, 107; policy of, on slavery during War of Independence, 20–21; slavery in, 19
Griffin, William, 103
Guilford College, 190

Hagar (Benjamin White's manumitted slave), 105
Hagar (Charles Overman's manumitted slave), 104
Hagar (Elizabeth Symons's manumitted slave), 104
Hagar (Mary Nixon's manumitted slave), 104, 123, 124
Hagar (Thomas Newby's [of Perquimans] manumitted slave), 88
Hagar (William Robinson's manumitted slave), 104, 119
Haiti, 13, 140, 184, 187
Halifax, N.C., 129
Halliday, Mr. and Mrs., 189
Hannah (Kezia Nixon's manumitted slave), 103, 124
Hannah (Thomas Newby's [of Perquimans] manumitted slave), 89–90, 103, 111, 118, 123
Hannah (Thomas White's manumitted slave), 105, 118, 123
Harper, Robert Goodloe, 162–63
Harris, Eliza, 189
Harry (John Anderson's manumitted slave), 102
Harry (Thomas Newby's [of Perquimans] manumitted slave), 88
Hartford, N.C., 2
Harvey, J., 117
Haskitt, John, 103, 118, 119
Hawey, Thomas, Jr., 118
Hawkins, Benjamin, 118, 131, 206n15
Heath, John, 151–52, 154
Hendley/Henley, Joseph, 93, 97, 130
Hertford, N.C., 59, 63, 90, 113, 114, 117–18, 131, 145
Hertford County, N.C., 60
Hixon, Timothy, 205n10

Holland, James, 155
Holliday, Samuel, 83
Hollowell, William, 119
Holy Spirit, 1, 3, 32, 34, 80
Hooper, William, 122–23
Hopkins, Samuel, 51, 57, 200n53
Hugh/Hughes, Widow, 62
Hunt, Eleazer, 93
Hunt, Jacob, 83

Illinois, 185, 191
Indentured servants, 8
Independence Day, 160
India, 12, 13
Indiana: black code in, 188; black immigration to, 184, 191; North Carolinian immigration to, 185; Quaker antislavery in, 188; Quaker immigration to, 185, 186, 188, 190; Underground Railroad in, 188
Inner light, 3, 6
Iowa, 191
Iredell, James, 113, 114, 115, 122, 123
Ireland, 201n66, 201n68
Ishmaelites, 41
Isle of Wight County, Va., 62, 202n80
Israelites, 41. *See also* Jews

Jack (Isaac Elliott's manumitted slave), 103
Jack (Thomas Newby's [of Perquimans] manumitted slave), 88, 103, 118, 123
Jacob (Benjamin White's manumitted slave), 105, 118, 123
Jacob (John Anderson's manumitted slave), 102
Jamaica, 19
James (Thomas Newby's [of Perquimans] manumitted slave), 88
James/Jem (Mark Newby's manumitted slave), 103, 118, 123
James River, 202n81
Jane (Lydia White's manumitted slave), 118, 123
Jane (Matthew White's manumitted slave), 105
Jane (Nicholas Nicholson's manumitted slave), 118, 123
Jane (Thomas White's manumitted slave), 105
Jane/Joan (William Albertson's manumitted slave), 102, 123, 124

Jaob (Aaron Morris Jr.'s manumitted slave), 103
Jefferson, Thomas, 162
Jem (John Anderson's manumitted slave), 102
Jem/James (Mark Newby's manumitted slave), 103, 118, 123
Jenney/Jenny (Robert Newby's manumitted slave), 103, 119
Jenny (Matthew White's manumitted slave), 105
Jenny (Nicholas Nicholson's manumitted slave), 104
Jenny (William Townshend's manumitted slave), 104, 119
Jenny, Joseph, 51
Jeremiads, 158–59
Jeremiah, Old Testament prophet, 158
Jessep, Thomas, 83
Jews, 43, 46. *See also* Israelites
Joan/Jane (William Albertson's manumitted slave), 102, 123, 124
Job (Charles Overman's manumitted slave), 104
Job (William Robinson's manumitted slave), 104
Johnston, Samuel, 113, 114, 115
Jonas (Christopher Nicholson's manumitted slave), 104
Jones, Rev. Absalom, 143
Jones, Francis: attends burials, 60, 65; attends Friends' meeting at Newbegun Creek, N.C., 58; attends yearly meeting in Virginia, 50; falls sick, 65; and George Walton, 40; identified, 198n15; letter to, from George Walton, 45–46, 46–48; visits Virginia, 61–63
Jones, Joseph, 103
Jordan, Ann, 56
Jordan, Josiah, 103
Jordan, Robert, 56, 62
Jordan, Thomas, 102, 137
Juda (John Trueblood's manumitted slave), 104
Juda/Judah (John Haskitt's manumitted slave), 103, 118
Judah (Lydia White's manumitted slave), 162
Judah (Thomas Newby's [of Perquimans] manumitted slave), 88
Judiciary Act, 209n63

Judith (manumitted slave), 123, 124
Judy (manumitted slave), 123
Jupiter (Elihu Anderson's manumitted slave), 102

Kansas, 191
Kitchell, Aaron, 156–57
Knowles, William, 119
Knox, Ambrose, 118
Knox, John, 83
Knox, Thomas, 83, 93

Labrador, 12
Lamb, Isaac, 103
Langa/Zango (Mark Newby's manumitted slave), 103, 118, 123
Lemuel (John Smith's manumitted slave), 104
Lexington, Mass., Battle of, 108
The Liberator, 187
Liberia, 184
"Liberty and Property" (essay by Thomas Nicholson), 84, 203n7
Libya, 13
Little River, 38
Little River, N.C., 203n7; Friends' meeting at, 56; Friends' quarterly meeting at, 58; Quaker meetinghouse at, 38
Liverpool, England, 149
Livingston, Edward, 168–69, 175
Locke, John, 12, 19
Lockwood, Holland, 145
Lower Cape Fear, N.C., 9
Loyalists, 108, 111, 202n75
Luke (Caleb White's manumitted slave), 105, 124
Lundy, Benjamin, 187
Lyddai (William White's manumitted slave), 105
Lyon, Matthew, 163, 164

Macay, Spruce, 125
Macon, Nathaniel, 155, 167–68, 175–76
Madison, James, 152, 154, 208n22
Manumission: and American Colonization Society, 187; bill on, in North Carolina General Assembly, 137–38; black participation in movement, 2–3; discouragements to, 190; effects of, on blacks, 18–19; George Walton advises Thomas Newby on, 37–40; George Walton promotes, 68; in Maryland, 130; motivation for, in Virginia, 140; motivation for, of North Carolina Quakers, 61, 67, 197n4; in New England, 130; in New Jersey, 130; in New York, 130; in North Carolina, 143, 150, 167, 172, 188; in North Carolina Friends' Western Quarter, 100; North Carolina General Assembly denounces, 59, 66–67, 111; North Carolina government resists, 120; North Carolina laws restrict, 21, 36, 71, 74, 80, 84, 126–27, 133–34, 135–36; by North Carolina Quakers, 2–3, 11, 24, 57–58, 58–59, 142, 183; North Carolina yearly meeting considers policy on, 36, 82; North Carolina yearly meeting endorses, 37, 54, 57; in Pennsylvania, 130; by Pennsylvania Quakers, 8; Perquimans monthly meeting draws up papers for, 54; petition for permission to manumit slave, 89–90, 111; progress of, among North Carolina Friends, 91–99, 95–96, 96–97; progress of, in Perquimans monthly meeting, 98, 99; Quaker resistance to, 45; Quakers' motivations for, 128–30; in Rhode Island, 21, 130; societies, 186, 187, 189; Thomas Newby frees slaves, 54; Thomas Newby's manumission paper, 87–88; trial regarding, 113–16; in Virginia, 21, 91, 130; Virginia laws restrict, 21, 71. *See also* Emancipation
Maroons, 20
Martin, Josiah, 108–9
Maryland, 5, 130, 200n53, 202n75
Massachusetts, 21, 139–40, 165, 208n44
Massachusetts Bay Colony, 107
Massachusetts Constitution, 208n44
Mauritania, 13–14
McAdam, Joseph, 79
McDowell, Joseph, 179
McKiever, Charles F., 185–86
McLane, Alexander, 119
Mediterranean Sea, 207n14
Memphis, Tenn., 191
Metcalfe, George, 103
Metcalfe, Sarah, 58, 103
Methodists, 21, 91, 139, 140
Mexico, 13
Michigan, 188

Middle Ages, 14
Mifflin, Warner, 171, 209n57
Military service, 3
Mingo (Caleb White's manumitted slave), 105
Mingo (John Haskitt's manumitted slave), 103, 119
Missouri, 191
Missouri Compromise, 190
Montserrat, 19
Moore, Charles, 119
Moravians, 50
More, Hannah, 17
Morgan, Charles, 103
Morris, John, 79
Morris, Joshua, 78
Morris, Robert, 149
Morris/Morriss, Aaron, Jr., 97, 103
Moses (Caleb Trueblood's manumitted slave), 105
Moses, biblical prophet, 41
Mount Pleasant, Ohio, 187
Munden, Levi, 134

Nancy (Caleb White's manumitted slave), 105, 124
Nancy (Jacob Winslow's manumitted slave), 105
Nansemond County, Va., 202n81
Nansemond River, 62, 202n76
Nantucket, Mass., 188, 189
Navy, British, 13, 108
Navy, United States, 13
Nebuchadnezzar, 44
Ned (Josiah White's manumitted slave), 105
Ned (Mark Newby's manumitted slave), 103, 118, 123
Nero (Josiah Trueblood's manumitted slave), 104, 124
The Netherlands, 13, 201n68
Nevis, 19
Newbern, N.C., 94, 114, 203n7
Newby, Exum, 58
Newby, Gabriel, 98
Newby, Joseph, 50
Newby, Mark: attends re-enslavement trial, 59, 60–61; debates slavery with Rev. Daniel Earl, 61; frees slaves, 103, 118, 204n25; as member of committee to assist manumissions, 58, 97, 99; petitions against importation of slaves, 78; to present petition to General Assembly, 130; recommends prohibiting slave trading, 83; signs petition defending manumissions, 130
Newby, Mary. See Walton, Mary Newby Winslow
Newby, Robert, 119
Newby, Samuel, 78, 83
Newby, Thomas (of Pasquotank), 103, 104
Newby, Thomas (of Perquimans): advised by George Walton, 37–40, 40–45; attends re-enslavement trial, 59, 60–61; frees slaves, 54, 87–88, 89, 90, 103, 118, 128, 204n13; petitions against importation of slaves, 78; as member of committee to aid manumissions, 93, 97; petitions for permission to free slave, 89–90, 111; to present petition to General Assembly, 130; promotes manumissions, 58–59; as slaveholder, 89, 204n13; seeks guidance on manumission, 37, 82; signs petition defending manumissions, 67, 130; writes David Ferris, 45, 199n41
Newby, Zachariah, 103
Newby family, 27
New England, 27, 130; Quakers in, 4
New Garden, N.C., 70, 188, 189
New Garden Boarding School, 190
New Jersey, 4, 5, 13, 22, 51, 130
Newland, James, 83
Newport, Ind., 189
New York City, 145, 171
New York State, 130
Nicholas, John, 171–72, 178
Nicholson, Christopher, 104
Nicholson, Jacob: biography, 3, 144; petitions Congress, 3, 143–48
Nicholson, Joseph, 144
Nicholson, Jupiter: biography, 3, 144; petitions Congress, 3, 143–48
Nicholson, Nicholas, 104, 118
Nicholson, Thomas: advocates gradual emancipation, 84; advocates immediate emancipation, 84–86; antislavery views of, 70, 191; biography, 11; circulates "Liberty and Property," 84; dream of, 35; frees slaves, 11, 104, 118, 131–32, 144; and John Woolman, 70; as leader of manu-

Nicholson, Thomas—*continued*
mission movement, 91; letter on gradual emancipation, 73–75; letter to B.H., 131–32, 206n15; as member of committee to aid manumissions, 93; as moral reformer, 11; to present petition to General Assembly, 130; publishes antislavery tract, 11; serves on Friends' committee on query on slavery, 83; signs petition defending manumissions, 130; signs Standing Committee sentiments on slave trade, 78–79; upbraids informer, 131–32; writes "Considerations on Slavery," 84–86; writings of, 67, 203n7
Nickson, Phineas, 145
Nickson, Zachary, 144
Night patrols. *See* Slave patrols
Nixon, Kezia, 103
Nixon, Mary, 104
Nixon, Zachariah, 79, 83, 93, 97, 104, 130
Norfolk, Va., 109, 145
North Carolina: American Revolution in, 107–9; antislavery in, 9, 11–12, 17, 69–70, 140; Bill of Rights, 115, 124–25, 129; Committee of Safety, 108; Constitution, 63–64, 113–14, 114–15, 116, 122, 123, 124, 125, 129, 131, 133–34, 202n83, 205n8; Continental Line regiment, 108; disenfranchises blacks, 190; emigration from, 184–85; fear of slave rebellions in, 19, 108–9; George Walton travels from, 40; John Woolman visits, 23; laws restrict manumission, 21, 24, 36, 71, 73, 74, 80, 151, 152, 155, 156, 172–73; Loyalists in, 108; manumission in, 2–3; manumission societies in, 189; manumitted slaves from, 143; manumitted slaves leave, 3; Nantucket Quakers immigrate to, 188, 189; number of Quakers in, 185; Philadelphia Friends visit, 200n53; post–Civil War emigration from, 190–91; Quaker emigration from, 190; Quaker governor of, 5; Quakers in, 4–5, 69; Quakers lose dominance in, 11–12; re-enslavements in, 2–3, 100–105, 146, 159, 164, 166, 167, 171, 175, 182, 199n41; and relations with Pennsylvania, 70; sentiment against blacks in, 167; slave laws, 150; slave patrols in, 49, 51, 109; slavery in, 9–10
North Carolina General Assembly: act of, regarding manumission, 113–14, 114–16; Act to Prevent Domestic Insurrections, 111–12; adopts general emancipation law, 183; allows religious societies to accept gifts of property, 184; amends Act to Prevent Domestic Insurrections, 135–36; authorizes re-enslavements, 2, 59, 60, 64, 66–67, 94, 102, 111–12, 120, 126–27, 129, 135–36, 150, 154, 173; committee of correspondence, 108; confirms past sales of re-enslaved blacks, 126–27; and delegates to Continental Congress, 108; denounces Quaker manumissions, 19, 24, 66–67, 126–27, 128, 143; disallows Mark Newby's posthumous freeing of slaves, 204n25; and importation of slaves, 78; jurisdiction of, 152; and Governor Josiah Martin, 108; members of, 113; petitioned, 67, 70, 102, 111, 128–30, 133–34, 183, 197n4; proposed bill to restrict manumissions, 137–38; restricts manumissions, 80–81, 133–34, 183; subject to constitution, 115–16
North Carolina General Court, 144
North Carolina militia, 57, 108, 109
North Carolina Provincial Congress, 108, 113
North Carolina Superior Court: hears grand jury presentments on manumissions, 137; reverses re-enslavement decisions, 66, 102, 122–25, 129–30, 143
Northwest Ordinance, 184
Nullification Crisis, 190

Oaths, swearing of, 3, 5, 10, 95, 177, 210n68
Ocracoke Bar, N.C., 46
Ohio, 184, 185, 186, 190, 191
Ohio River, 184, 189
Old Neck, N.C., 128; Friends' quarterly meeting at, 56–57, 60; Meetinghouse, 38, 69
Oregon, 190
Osborne, Charles, 187–88
Overman, Charles, 104
Overman, Ephraim, 97
Overman, John, 83
Oxley, Joseph, 200n54, 201n67

Pailin, John, 205n10
Palin, Henry, 104
Park/Parke, Humphrey, 83, 97, 98, 99
Parker, Isaac, 169–70

Parker, Job, 83, 98, 99
Parker, Josiah, 171
Pasquotank, N.C.: monthly meeting, 38, 92; quarterly meeting at, 54
Pasquotank County, N.C., 38, 101, 103, 104, 185, 200n65; Court of Pleas and Quarter Sessions, 102, 122–25, 127, 205n10
Pasquotank River, 38
Patagonia, 12
Patience (John Sanders's manumitted slave), 104
Patience (Thomas Newby's [of Perquimans] manumitted slave), 88, 103, 118, 123
Patience (William White's manumitted slave), 105
Peggy (Robert Newby's manumitted slave), 103, 119
Pemberton, John, 60, 201–2n75
Penn, William, 4
Pennsylvania: antislavery in, 5–12, 11; authorizes playhouses, 167–68; congressmen from, 149; emancipation in, 13, 17, 140, 165, 167, 177; General Assembly, 6; immigration to, 6, 8; manumission in, 130; politicians of, 162; as Quaker haven, 4; Quaker immigration to, 5, 6; Quaker reform movement in, 22; Quakers lose dominance in, 11–12, 16; and relations with North Carolina, 70; slavery in, 8, 9, 194n20; traveling Friends from, 56
Pennsylvania Society for Promoting the Abolition of Slavery, 209n56
Penny (Aaron Morris Jr.'s manumitted slave), 103
Perquimans, N.C., 58, 88
Perquimans, N.C., monthly meeting: admits George Walton, 27; appoints committee to promote manumissions, 57, 58, 98, 99; appoints George Walton to committees, 67; center of antislavery agitation, 36; committee draws up manumission papers, 87–88; delays acting on manumission question, 37; and discipline of slaveholding members, 12; enforces marriage discipline, 12; expels George and Mary Walton for alcoholism, 183; extracts of minutes of, 97–99; and manumission, 91; membership in, 37, 197n4; produces manumission papers for Thomas Newby, 54; progress of manumission in, 98, 99; recommends George Walton as a public Friend, 67; recommends public Friends, 198n15; refers concern on slaveholding to yearly meeting, 37, 82; and slave trading, 99
Perquimans County, N.C.: antislavery in, 70; clerk of, 101; economy, 27; Friends' meetings in, merge, 185; Friends Yearly meeting in, 133; manumissions in, 103, 144, 200n65; meetinghouses in, 69; Quaker meetinghouses in, 38; Quakers in, 11, 73; residents of, 1; slaveholders in, 87; slavery in, 9–10, 202n84; tax lists, 89, 204n13
Perquimans County, N.C., Court of Pleas and Quarter Sessions: decision reversed on appeal, 66, 102, 122–25; denies petition to free slave, 111; manumission petition sent to, 89–90; orders blacks sold, 102, 117–18; tries manumitted slaves, 63–63, 113–16, 120, 127
Perquimans River, 38
Perrishoe, Joshua, 97
Perry, Jesse, 64, 114, 116
Peter (Benjamin White's manumitted slave), 118, 123, 131
Peter (William White's manumitted slave), 105
Pharaoh, 41
Phebe/Phoebe (Mark Newby's manumitted slave), 103, 118, 123
Phelps, Benjamin, 119
Philadelphia, Pa.: blacks in, 2, 139; Continental Congress meets in, 108; Friends in, 200n53, 201n66, 201n75; Friends' yearly meeting in, 3, 5–6, 159, 178; George Walton travels to, 45; humanitarian associations of, 149; manumitted North Carolina slaves in, 2, 143, 145, 146; mercantile firms of, 149; new jail in, 168; residents of, 199n41; slavery in, 5, 8, 194n20; traveling Friends from, 51, 57, 60; yellow fever in, 159–60, 208n32
The Philanthropist, 187
Piney Woods, N.C., 38, 58, 59
Pitt County, N.C., 109
Plato, 12
Playhouses, 158, 164, 166, 167–68, 169, 171, 178
Pleasant (James Elliot's manumitted slave), 103

Pleasants, Robert, 199n41
Pompey (Thomas Nicholson's manumitted slave), 104, 118, 123
Portsmouth, Va., 2, 62, 144, 145
Portugal, 13
Precilla (manumitted slave), 124
Predestination, 4
Presbyterians, 7
Primitivism, 15
Priscilla (Caleb White's manumitted slave), 105
Priscilla (Robert Newby's manumitted slave), 103
Priscilla/Silla (Thomas Newby's [of Perquimans] manumitted slave), 103, 118, 123
Pritchard, Matthew, 104, 124
Pritchard (Pritchet), Thomas, 145
Pritchet, Thomas: biography, 3, 145–46; petitions Congress, 3, 143–48
Providence, R.I., 22
Public Friends, 23, 25, 55, 67, 198n15, 201n66; defined, 196n64

Quakers. *See* Society of Friends
Quea (Josiah White's manumitted slave), 105

Ralph, Enoch, 145
Ramsay, James, 17
Rebekah (Aaron Morris Jr.'s manumitted slave), 103
Rebekah (Benjamin Winslow's manumitted slave), 105
Reding, Joseph, 205n10
Reding, Thomas, 205n10
Reese, Thomas, 205n10
Reeves, Hannah, 51
Reeves, Mark, 57, 201n67
Reformation, Protestant, 3
Religion: and antislavery in England, 17–18
Religious Society of Friends. *See* Society of Friends
Republican Party, 162
Restoration, Stuart, 4
Rhode Island, 13, 21, 130
Rhode Island General Assembly, 21
Richard (Thomas Nicholson's manumitted slave), 104, 118, 123
Richard/Dick (Samuel Smith's manumitted slave), 104, 119

Richardson, Joseph, 118
Riddick, Dr., 119
Robertson, William, 144
Robin (Jacob Wilson's manumitted slave), 105, 124
Robin (William White's manumitted slave), 105
Robinson, William, 104, 119
Rose (Joseph Jones's manumitted slave), 103
Rose (Joshua White's manumitted slave), 105
Rose (manumitted slave), 123, 12
Rose (Matthew White's manumitted slave), 105, 118
Rose (Thomas Newby's (of Pasquotank) manumitted slave), 104
Rose (1) (Thomas White's manumitted slave), 105, 118, 123
Rose (2) (Thomas White's manumitted slave), 118, 123
Russia, 12, 13
Ruth (John Smith's manumitted slave), 104
Ruth (Thomas White's manumitted slave), 105
Rutherford, Robert, 152–53
Rutledge, John, Jr.: on committing Friends' memorial to select committee, 178; debates Friends' memorial, 163–64, 174; moves postponement of debate, 179; offers amendment to House report on Friends' memorial, 180–81; referenced in debate, 165, 176

Saint, Thomas, 58
Salazar, António de Oliviera, 13
Salem, N.J., 57, 200n54, 201n67
Salter, Robert, 118
Sam (Thomas Newby's [of Pasquotank] manumitted slave), 103
Samson (Josiah Trueblood's manumitted slave), 104
Samuel (Mary Nixon's manumitted slave), 104, 123, 124
Sanders, John, 78, 104
Sarah (Josiah Jordan's manumitted slave), 103
Sarah (manumitted slave), 123, 124
Sarah (Thomas Nicholson's manumitted slave), 104

Sarem, N.C., 65, 202n85
Satan (the Devil), 1–2, 19, 32, 33, 34, 35
Sawney (Aaron Trueblood's manumitted slave), 105
Schureman, James, 178
Scots-Irish, 6
Sectarianism, 6, 7, 11, 12
Serfdom, 13
Service, John, 98
Sewall, Samuel, 166–67
Sharp, Granville, 17
Sharper, Benjamin, 51
Shay, Michael, 140
Shepherd, John, 60, 65
Shepherd, Mrs. John, 65–66
Shepherd, Stephen, 65
Shrewsbury, N.J.: monthly meeting, 201n67; quarterly meeting, 10
Sibba (Benjamin White's manumitted slave), 105, 118, 123, 131
Silla/Priscilla (Thomas Newby's [of Perquimans] manumitted slave), 103, 118, 123
Sitgreaves, Samuel: 151, 152, 178, 179
Skinner, Joshua, 83
Skinner, W., 117
Skinner, William, 64, 202n84
Slave patrols: George Walton discourages Quaker participation in, 51–54; in North Carolina, 49–50, 51, 109
Slave rebellions: during War of Independence, 20; fear of, in North Carolina, 19, 49, 51, 66–67, 108–9, 126, 127, 129; fear of in United States, 140–41; goals of, 12; inciting of, 164, 167, 168; Nat Turner's, 190; North Carolina act to prevent, 111–12; and Quakers, 52; in West Indies, 19
Slavery: abolished in Brazil, 13; abolished in parts of the United States, 13, 21; abolished in Spain's colonies, 13; banned in Northwest Territory, 184; British policy on, during War of Independence, 20–21; ended in England, 19, 21; ended in United States, 192; and federal authority, 141–42, 149, 154, 171; Friends seek to end, in United States, 142; in Friends' Western Quarter, North Carolina, 100; in Georgia, 20; harms slave owners, 73–74, 78; laws supporting, 12; and marriage, 51; in North Carolina, 9–10;

North Carolina Friends' policy on, 82–83; in Pennsylvania, 8, 194n20; in Perquimans County, N.C., 89, 202n84; in Philadelphia, 8, 194n20; politicization of, 17, 18; positive good theory, 190; Quaker queries on, 77, 79, 83; and Quakers, 5–12; as sectional issue, 162, 176, 190; and Thirteenth Amendment, 191; as unchristian, 85; in world history, 12
Slaves: education of, 97, 99; flee to British armed forces, 20; hiring of, 94; petition for freedom in Massachusetts, 21; re-enslavement of, 2–3; treatment of, 73–75, 77, 79, 93, 94. *See also* Blacks; Manumission
Slave trade: abolition of, in the United States, 17; to the Americas, 12–13; British Parliament outlaws, 13; and Brown family of Providence, R.I., 22; campaign in England to end, 196n51; Congress outlaws, 13; English Friends banned from participation in, 18; Friends petition Confederation Congress to end, 142; Friends petition Congress to end, 142, 149, 158, 170, 171; Friends renounce, 7, 130; Friends' yearly meeting in North Carolina restricts, 36; in Georgia, 171; morality of, 121; in North Carolina, 17; North Carolina Friends petition against, 70, 78; North Carolina Friends renounce, 92–93; among North Carolina Quakers, 92; North Carolina Standing Committee's sentiments on, 78; North Carolina yearly meeting's policy on, 70, 76–79; in Perquimans monthly meeting, 99; powers of Congress over, 141–42; Quaker involvement in, 93; renounced by Continental Association, 160; taxes on, 171; in Rhode Island, 21; Thomas Nicholson on, 73–75; treaties to end, 13; Virginia Quakers petition against, 70
Smith, John, 104
Smith, Samuel (Maryland congressman), 177, 178
Smith, Samuel (North Carolina Quaker), 104, 119
Smith, Thomas, 118
Smith, William, 153, 154, 155
Smithwick, Joseph, 118
Sobel, Michel, 35

Society of Friends: and allies in antislavery, 15; and American Revolution, 54; and antislavery, 2, 3, 5–12, 14, 17–18, 139, 206n1; beliefs and practices, 3–4; and benevolence, 5; character of, 163–64, 164–65, 165–66, 167, 168, 170, 173, 174, 176, 177, 179; converts to, 22; and dreams, 29, 34, 35; and immigration to Pennsylvania, 6; leadership of antislavery movement by, 18; marriage regulations, 27; members as leaders of emancipation societies, 140; members as slave owners, 5, 14; missionary work, 4; organizational structure, 193n2; pacifism, 19, 50, 52, 74; persecuted, 44, 47; and swearing of oaths, 210n68
—in America: adopts antislavery discipline, 8–9; benevolent reform in, 10–12; consults Friends' Meeting for Sufferings in London, 80; history of, 4–5; in Indiana, 185, 188; moral reform in, 10–12; neutrality of, in War of Independence, 142; in New Jersey, 23; in Ohio, 185, 188; in Virginia, 23, 62, 91, 185
—in England: and antislavery, 17–18; and civil liberties, 7; history of, 3–4
—in North Carolina: and American Colonization Society, 187; and antislavery, 17, 24, 140, 191, 192; as suspected Loyalists, 111, 167; assists blacks, 188–89; Congress debates manumissions by, 142; David Ferris on, 199n41; decline of, 185; disguise manumissions, 138; early history and growth, 69; and Friends' communications network, 22–23; and George Walton, 1; John Woolman visits, 23; and manumission movement, 2, 93; meeting for blacks, 59; meetings merge, 185; members as slaveholders, 2, 95–96; members emigrate to free states, 184–86; members free slaves, 2–3, 57, 67–68, 113–14, 117, 120–21, 124, 128, 135, 138, 143, 159, 167, 183, 188–89, 189, 190, 197n4, 200–201n65; motivations for emigrating, 185–86, 190; number of members, 185; organized, 4–5; progress of manumission in, 91–99; reform movement in, 22–23; and reluctance of members to free slaves, 91; and slave patrols, 49–50, 51–54; and slave trading, 93; and slavery, 69. See also Friends' yearly meeting in North Carolina

—in Pennsylvania: and antislavery, 5–12, 16, 22; and communications from North Carolina Friends, 137; declines in dominance, 10; manumission by members, 8; meetings vary on slavery, 8; members, 199n41; petitions Congress on North Carolina reenslavements, 100, 172; petitions Congress on slavery, 149, 171, 208n22; political and moral influence of, 16; quality of piety of, 34; reform movement in, 6–8, 22, 201–2n75; and religious visits, 23; religious zeal of, 7; seeks legislation to end slave trade in United States, 17; seeks to end slavery in United States, 142; and slavery, 5–8; visitors from, to North Carolina, 69; and withdrawal from political office, 6

Some Considerations on the Keeping of Negroes (John Woolman), 7, 16
Somerset decision, 19–20, 21
South America, 13
Southampton County, Va., 63
South Carolina, 20, 102, 104, 108
Spain, 13
Spence, Samuel, 123
Stabler, Edward, 57, 60, 201n69
Stafford, Alexander, 145
Stafford, William, 145
Stamp Tax, 107
Stanton, Borden, 186
St. Kitts (St. Christopher), 19
Stowe, Harriet Beecher, 189
St. Paul's Church, Edenton, N.C., 202n76
Sue/Susanna (Thomas Newby's [of Perquimans] manumitted slave), 88, 103, 118, 123
Summerton, Va., 56, 62, 65; monthly meeting, 202n82
Susanna/Sue (Thomas Newby's [of Perquimans] manumitted slave), 88, 103, 118, 123
Swanwick, John: biography, 149; debates freemen's petition, 150–51; debates Friends' memorial, 164–65; introduces freemen's petition into House of Representatives, 149–50, 154
Switzerland, 162
Symons, Elizabeth, 104
Symons, Jesse, 104
Symons, John, 78

Symons Creek, N.C., 64; monthly meeting, 11, 38, 69–70

Talbot, John, 83
Tamar (Henry Palin's manumitted slave), 104
Taylor, William, 61
Tennessee, 184–85, 187
Texas, 188
Thatcher, George: debates freemen's petition, 150, 153–54; debates Friends' memorial, 163, 176; moves House committee report be committed, 178–79; moves to amend House report on Friends' memorial, 180; referenced in debate, 155, 177
Thirteenth Amendment, 13, 191
Thomas, Able, 56
Thompson, Joshua, 51, 200n54
Thornbrugh, Thomas, 83
Thornton, Joseph, 104, 119
Thoughts upon Slavery (John Wesley), 22
Tobago, 19
Tobey/Toby (Matthew Pritchard's manumitted slave), 104, 124
Toleration, Act of, 4
Tom (John Anderson's manumitted slave), 102
Tom (Thomas Newby's [of Perquimans] manumitted slave), 88, 103, 118, 123
Tom (William Griffin's manumitted slave), 103
Toms, Zachariah, 78
Townshend, William, 104, 119
Townshend Duties, 107
Treaty of Paris (1783), 18, 142
Trueblood, Aaron, 105
Trueblood, Abel, 78
Trueblood, Caleb, 78, 105
Trueblood, John, 104, 145
Trueblood, Josiah, 104
Trueblood's, N.C., 38, 57
Turner, Nat, 190

Uncle Tom's Cabin (Harriet Beecher Stowe), 189
Underground Railroad, 2, 186, 188, 189–90, 190
United Kingdom, 13
United States Congress: debates manumissions by North Carolina Friends, 3, 142; outlaws international slave trade, 13; petitions to, 2–3, 158–61, 171, 188; and powers over slave trade, 141–42; slaves of members of, 165
United States Constitution: allows oaths or affirmations, 210n68; and ex post facto laws, 170–71, 177; and fugitive slaves, 2, 24; and jurisdiction of federal courts, 173, 177; and slavery, 141–42, 146, 147, 152, 164, 166–67, 167, 171, 174, 175; Thirteenth Amendment, 13, 191
United States House of Representatives: antislavery petitions in, 143, 208n22; committee of the whole, 178, 179–81; committee of ways and means, 167; committee on Fugitive Slave Law, 150; debates ending slave importations, 149; debates freemen's petition, 149–57; debates kidnapping of blacks, 175, 178; debates manumissions by North Carolina Friends, 143; freemen's petition to, 143–48; petitioned to end slave trade, 209n57; petitioned to stop kidnappings of blacks, 208n45; slavery and representation in, 141
—debates Friends' memorial, 162–81; approves second reading, 178; commits committee report, 179; commits to select committee, 178, 210n75; committee reports on, 179–80
United States of America: and relations with Algiers, 207n14; slavery abolished in northern states of, 13; on slavery in Mauritania, 13–14
United States President, 167
United States Senate, 162
United States Supreme Court, 113, 209n63
Unthank, John, 83

Varnum, Joseph Bradley, 155–56, 156
Venable, Abraham Bedford, 177
Vestal, David, 93
Violet (Josiah White's manumitted slave), 105, 119, 123
Virginia: Baptists in, 91; black code, 21; British invasion of, 21; emigration from, 186; escaped slaves in, 2; George Walton visits, 61–62; House of Burgesses, 78; jails manumitted blacks from North Carolina,

Virginia—*continued*
67; Loyalist Friends exiled to, 202n75; manumission in, 130, 140; Methodists in, 91; militia, 109; and Nat Turner's Rebellion, 190; North Carolina blacks move to, 144, 145–46; Philadelphia public Friends visit, 202n75; post–Civil War emigration from, 191; Quaker marriage in, 56; Quakers in, 91, 185, 199n41; restricts manumission, 71; royal governor offers freedom to slaves, 109; royal governor rallies slaves to his banner in, 20; traveling Friends from, 57, 60
Vix, Va., 63

Walton, Elizabeth, 27
Walton, George: advises Thomas Newby, 37–40, 40–45; begins public ministry, 48; as benevolent reformer, 11; biographical parallels with Moses Brown, 22; biography, 27–28; and black activism, 19; as clerk of Standing Committee, 67; and confrontation with North Carolina government over manumission, 49; death, 183; delivers letter to Thomas Newby, 45; discourses on religion with Baptist couple, 63; dreams of, 19, 29–32, 33, 54, 67–68, 191–92; elected clerk of Standing Committee, 128; expelled from Society of Friends for alcoholism, 183; and Francis Jones, 40, 198n15; frees slave, 57, 67, 101, 105, 128; identified, 1; interprets his dreams, 29, 32–33, 34, 36; and John Woolman's influence, 23–24; joins Quakers, 12, 22, 24, 27, 34, 36; as leader of manumission movement, 2, 12, 28, 35, 37, 45–46, 68, 91; and motivations for antislavery, 23–24; to present petition to General Assembly, 130; as public Friend, 25, 55, 67; records dreams, 1–2, 29, 40, 47; refuses to serve as slave patroller, 49–50, 51, 53; on religious visits between Friends' meetings, 23; reports on trial of manumitted slaves, 63–64; represents Perquimans in quarterly meetings, 67; serves on Friends' committees, 54, 57, 58, 67, 83, 97, 98, 197n4; signs petition, 67, 130; in thunderstorm, 62; writes to William Taylor, 62
—attends: burials, 56, 60, 61, 65, 198n15; marriage, 56; meeting for blacks, 59; trial of manumitted slaves, 59, 60–61; yearly meetings in Virginia, 50–51, 198n15
—attends Friends' meetings: at Chuckatuck, Va., 62; at Little River, N.C., 56; at Newbegun Creek, N.C., 58; at Sarem, N.C., 65; at Summerton, Va., 62; at Trueblood's, N.C., 58; at Vix, Va., 63; at Western Branch, Va., 62
—attends quarterly meetings: at Little River, N.C., 58; at Old Neck, N.C., 57–58, 60; at Symons Creek, 64; at Wells, N.C., 56
—opinions: on blacks, 40; on participation in slave patrols, 50, 51–54; on slavery, 22, 24, 28, 34, 36, 191
—travels: from North Carolina, 40; to Philadelphia, 45; to Virginia, 61–62; to West Indies, 45
—visits: John Denson, 62; John Whitehead, 63; Quakers to encourage manumissions, 57, 58–59; Robert Jordan, 62; the Widow Baker, 65–66
—writings: journal, 49–66; letter to Francis Jones, 45–46, 46–48; letter to Friends, on slave patrols, 51–54; letter to Thomas Newby, 40–45
Walton, Mary Newby Winslow, 27–28, 33, 34, 183
Walton, Sarah Earls, 27, 31
War of 1812, 50
War of Independence: and antislavery movement, 17, 18, 139; battles of, 54; and the end of slavery, 21; mentioned, 187, 188; as opportunity for black resistance to slavery, 19–20; Quakers in, 142
Washington, D.C., 187, 191
Washington, George, 108
Wells, N.C.: Quaker meetinghouse at, 38; quarterly meeting at, 56; yearly meeting at, 133
Wesley, John, 21–22
West Africa, 187
Western Branch, Va.: Friends' meeting at, 62; Friends' monthly meeting at, 55; Friends' quarterly meeting at, 55
Western Freedmen's Aid Commission, 191
West Indies, 19, 27, 45, 145, 174
Wheatley, Phillis, 139
Whedbee/Whidbee, George, 64, 114, 116

White, Benjamin, 79, 105, 118, 131
White, Caleb, 58, 88, 93, 97, 99, 105, 118, 130
White, Catherine, 189
White, John, 79
White, Joseph, 79
White, Joshua, 105
White, Josiah, 32, 58, 83, 99, 105, 119, 130, 197n4
White, Lydia, 105, 118
White, Margaret, 105
White, Matthew, 78, 97, 99, 105, 118, 130
White, Rachel, 61
White, Thomas, 83, 98, 105, 118, 130
White, Thomas, Jr., 83
White, William, 58, 98, 99, 105, 130
Whitehead, John, 63
Whitney, Eli, 141
Wilberforce, William, 17
Will/William (Benjamin White's manumitted slave), 105, 118, 123
Willing, Morris, and Swanwick Co., 149
Wilson, Abraham, 119
Wilson, Jacob, 79, 88, 93, 99, 105
Wilson, Reubin, 98

Winslow, Benjamin, 105
Winslow, Caleb, 98, 99, 105, 130
Winslow, Jacob, 105
Winslow, Mary. *See* Walton, Mary Newby Winslow
Winslow, Thomas, 56
Winslow, Timothy, 27
Wolf, Eva Sheppard, 91, 140
Women, Quaker, 4
Woolman, John: abstains from use of products of slave labor, 187–88; as antislavery activist, 16; dies, 21; publishes antislavery tract, 7, 8, 16; as Quaker reformer, 22, 23–24; and Thomas Nicholson, 70; visits North Carolina, 23, 69–70
Wright, Christopher, 64, 114, 115, 116

Yale College, 113
Yellow fever, 159, 208n32

Zango/Langa (Mark Newby's manumitted slave), 103, 118, 123
Zelpha/Zilpha (Caleb White's manumitted slave), 105, 118, 123

Michael J. Crawford is senior historian of the Naval History and Heritage Command. He is the author of thirteen books, including *Seasons of Grace: Colonial New England's Revival Tradition in Its British Context*.

www.ingramcontent.com/pod-product-compliance
Lightning Source LLC
Chambersburg PA
CBHW020050170426
43199CB00009B/232